Church and Ethical Responsibility
in the Midst of World Economy

Church and Ethical Responsibility in the Midst of World Economy

Greed, Dominion, and Justice

PAUL S. CHUNG

With a Foreword by Ulrich Duchrow

CASCADE *Books* • Eugene, Oregon

CHURCH AND ETHICAL RESPONSIBILITY IN THE MIDST
OF WORLD ECONOMY
Greed, Dominion, and Justice

Cascade Books
An Imprint of Wipf and Stock Publishers
199 W. 8th Ave., Suite 3
Eugene, OR 97401

www.wipfandstock.com

ISBN 13: 978-1-60899-972-9

Cataloguing-in-Publication data:

Chung, Paul S.

    Church and ethical responsibility in the midst of world economy : greed, dominion, and justice / Paul S. Chung ; with a foreword by Ulrich Duchrow.

    xxvi + 294 pp. ; 23 cm. Includes bibliographical references and index.

    ISBN 13: 978-1-60899-972-9

    1. Economics—Religious aspects—Christianity. 2. Capitalism—Religious aspects—Christianity. 3. Church and social problems. 4. Theology. I. Duchrow, Ulrich. II. Title.

BR115.E3 C541 2013

Manufactured in the U.S.A.

Dedicated to Ulrich Duchrow, a representative of prophetic theology in the ecumenical globe, with appreciation of his lifelong commitment to economic justice and peace and in his solidarity with Asian minjung theology

Contents

Foreword

WHO CAN WRITE A book like this one? I guess only someone who has worked for a long time in interdisciplinary, intercultural, and interreligious ways. Paul Chung has already brought into dialogue Martin Luther with Buddhism, Karl Barth with religious pluralism, as well as Asian *minjung* theology with Buddhism, Daoism, and Confucianism—in order to construct an "Irregular Theology." Now he masters the social, economic, historical, and cultural complexities of capitalism in the context of today's crises. What is his special contribution to the broad debate on this subject spurred by the nearly complete collapse of the financial system in the years since 2007?

Most of the authors writing on the crisis limit themselves to its economic and political dimensions. Some look only at the subprime credit crisis, which triggered the larger financial crisis, and ask how mistakes like this can be avoided. Others, like the Stiglitz Commission of Experts of the President of the UN General Assembly, go a step further, developing "Reforms of the International Monetary and Financial System" on the basis of "Principles for a New Financial Architecture." Still others add the political dimension, including the analysis of institutions like the International Monetary Fund, the World Bank, or the WTO. Some even look at the issue of empire or at the social and ecological implications of the crisis.

Very few scholars see that all of Western civilization faces a deep crisis, or rather a host of crises. What is the reason for the crises confronting us—not only regarding finance and economy, but food shortage for nearly one billion inhabitants of the earth in spite of adequate production; the death of more than thirty million people annually from hunger; depletion of fossil fuels; climate change and its devastating consequences; the dramatic dying off of species, etc.? Obviously these crises are interconnected at a deep structural and cultural level. And this level is deeply rooted in history. Therefore, it is a special value of this book that it reveals the roots of the present situation, tracing it back to the origins of capitalism—not only as an economic-political system, but also as a culture. Economically and politically, Professor Chung unfolds precisely the different phases of capitalism—mercantile, industrial, and financial capitalism, linked each time to hegemonic powers (Spain, The Netherlands, Britain, and the United States) and to ideological justifications (mercantilism, liberalism, neoliberalism). Culturally he analyzes the philosophers who have developed the concepts and categories to grasp what was happening in economy, politics, science, and technology, with a feedback effect on real history by forging attitudes, behaviors, and strategies. To mention just a few names of special importance, he considers Thomas Hobbes, John Locke, G. W. F. Hegel, Karl Marx, Max Weber, and Jürgen Habermas.

It is already a sign of courage to discuss the problems we are facing under the name of capitalism. When I was looking for a publisher for my book *Alternatives to Global Capitalism—Drawn from Biblical History, Designed for Political Action* in the mid-1990s, I did not find one in the United States. Orbis Books, for example, answered: "There is no market for this in the US." By the way, this is true for the official church structures in Germany up to this day. What does this mean? We are facing a taboo here against pointing at the religious character of capitalism. Already Walter Benjamin pointed out that capitalism is a religion. He did this on the basis of Karl Marx's analysis of the fetishism of the commodity, money, and capital. As a matter of fact, Marx wrote his main work, *Capital*, as a critique of the "earthly gods" governing the lives of humans and the earth, guiding them towards their destruction. This takes up the biblical insight that idols request human sacrifices. So also Jesus stopped the sacrifice business in the temple, the central bank of the province of Judea at the time (cf. Mark 11:15–19).

It is not overstepping the mandate of theology when Paul Chung critically reviews the political economy from the perspective of religion. On the contrary, it is part of the reductionist thinking of modernity to suppress the spiritual aspect of reality by splitting it off into a private sphere of arbitrary decision. There is always some faith governing the perception of reality and social structures and praxis. Therefore, we must always ask, who or what functions as god in a given society? And in whose interest? Neglecting this question, the whole rationality of modernity until today shows its ugly face of utter irrationality. Franz Hinkelammert, the Latin American liberation theologian and economist, puts this into an image: we compete among each other to be the one who can best sharpen the saw with which we cut the branch on which we are sitting. The destructive character of modernity is at the same time suicidal. We hail maximum economic growth, measured in monetary terms, although we know that in doing so we are depleting the earth's resources, suffocating in waste, and heating up the climate to the extent that islands and whole regions are drowned, the weather produces disasters, deserts expand (with all the consequences of forced migration), etc. And why must the economy grow? It must grow exclusively because capital must be accumulated. Capital by definition is an asset that must be invested for maximum profit, and this must be reinvested for the same abstract purpose, reinvested again and again and again—endlessly and limitlessly.

Breaking this vicious cycle requires that the religious, absolutist, legalistic character of capitalism be challenged on its own ground. It is the law that kills, as the Apostle Paul summarizes his critical theological analysis in the context of the Roman Empire. Jesus had already addressed this issue by pointing out that our relation to God implies breaking the law of absolute debt repayment because it kills. "And forgive us our debts [beyond our capacity to pay back] as we also have forgiven our debtors [the debts beyond their capacity to repay]" (Matt 6:12). Repayment of debt is the absolute law of the property-money economy. It enslaves and ultimately kills when a person or a family cannot repay a debt—for example, because of a poor harvest. In the Roman Empire this law is linked to the divinization of the emperor. This god was most totally worshiped in the form of money, which bore the image of the emperor, as the book of Revelation points out (13:17). It was not as late as Adam Smith that the market, in theistic terms, was regarded as the "invisible hand" of the system. Making the capitalist market the god of today kills visibly. The deaths are called "collateral damage."

Therefore, theology has to deal with this life-and-death issue. Paul Chung does it by choosing the biblical perspective "from below." God Yahweh reveals God's self as the liberator of slaves (Exodus 3ff.). The prophets take the same approach by fundamentally challenging political and economic powers. Jesus proclaims good news for the poor by putting the domination-free, humane and just reign of God against the imperial system at all levels—putting his life on the line. The Apostle Paul summarizes this perspective by writing in his first letter to the Corinthians:

> Has not God made mad the wisdom of this world system? . . .
> Consider your own call, brothers and sisters: not many of you
> were wise by human standards, not many were powerful, not
> many were of noble birth. But God chose what is mad according
> to the categories of the world system to shame the wise; God
> chose what is weak according to the categories of the world

system to shame the strong; God chose the plebeians and the despised according to the categories of the world system, things that are not, to reduce to nothing things that are . . ."

This passage is of great significance for the understanding of the present situation and for the method to critically approach it. Paul is probably the first one to analyze that wisdom can be madness. No one doubts that Greece and Rome belonged to the "developed countries" of that historical period. Up to this day, Greek philosophy and Roman law are referred to as the roots of Western civilization. But today we see clearly that this civilization has become systemically destructive and suicidal. Why? It stands for the compulsory law that the rich must become richer and the powerful more powerful despite the costs to the whole community of humanity and to the earth. This kind of rationality is turning out to be madness, absurd irrationality.

So it is reasonable to look for a god other than the capitalist market with its utilitarian rationality and imperial power. What is commonly regarded as irrational—faith in the God of love and relationality—turns out to be the most rational behavior—if life in the double sense of survival and fulfillment is to be taken as the final criterion. All kinds of faith? No, "faith" also can be kidnapped by madness, as all kinds of fundamentalisms demonstrate these days—spearheaded by the religious right in the United States and everywhere nurturing imperialism (and consequently producing its mirror image in the form of murder-suicide terrorism). Therefore, we need the critique of religion as the basis for bringing the saving power of faith to bear upon politics, economics, and culture. This saving power can only blossom when we realize that in a global society, we can only survive together. The "other" becomes the criterion for my own survival. This is beautifully reflected in Levinas's translation of Jesus' summary of faith, in the tradition of Martin Buber: "Love God [the God of love and relationality] with all your heart, and with all your soul, and with all your strength, and with all your mind; and your neighbor—he/she *is yourself*" (Luke 10:27). This means that, because you can only survive together with your neighbor in a global world, you have to realize this personally and to struggle for a culture and for political and economic structures that foster this living together with each other and the earth. The criterion for this is, of course, that the poorest and weakest may live. So the hermeneutics from below is the only reasonable rationality, called divine wisdom.

It is here where Paul Chung's wealth of knowledge concerning religions comes in: the empathy of Buddhism, the life-honoring dialectics of Daoism, the community perspective of Confucianism. Yet he does not engage in abstract, neutral interreligious "dialogue" here. The criterion is again life-enhancing praxis—that is, all religions are looked at from the perspective of the underside of history, as Dietrich Bonhoeffer, one of his main theological teachers, formulated it. In this way his *minjung* theology is truly liberation theology, geared at emancipation from the captivity of Western imperial theology and mission, mirroring a life-killing civilization. The totalizing of the laws of the capitalist market, penetrating all spheres of life, made modernity deeply ambiguous. Even its emancipative traditions must be liberated by critically exposing it to more holistic worldviews. This book brings us nearer to a new interreligious culture of life, so badly needed by us endangered humans and by the earth.

Ulrich Duchrow
Professor of Systematic Theology
University of Heidelberg

Preface

IN THE POST-SOCIALIST ERA, neoliberal economic globalization has appeared as the meta-ideology. A metaphor of "disenchantment of the world" (Max Weber) is replaced by "colonization of the lifeworld" (Jürgen Habermas). This theory of late-capitalist reification comes to terms with state-controlled organizational structures of mass-media agencies, underlying cultural impoverishment and fragmentation of everyday consciousness.[1]

Since 1970, many experts have observed functional changes (locally and globally) to the world-economy. Fordist mass production was based on systems of specialized machines for higher production and rationalization of the production line with relatively high wages for the workforce. Such a Fordist system operates within the organizational domains of giant corporations. It is vertically integrated and bureaucratically managed. The central feature of organized capitalism in the sense of Fordism-Keynesianism is the administration and conscious regulation of national economies by managerial hierarchies and government officials. However, organized capitalism is jeopardized by an increasing spatial and functional deconstruction and decentralization of corporate powers.

Capitalism is considered to be in the midst of a historical transition from Fordism-Keynesianism to a new regime of accumulation, called flexible accumulation. The breakdown of Fordism-Keynesianism implies a move toward the empowerment of finance capital on the basis of the nation-state. This is the end of organized capitalism and the beginning of a discourse of disorganized capitalism.

Economic globalization has surfaced as the only viable option in the world economic system. The capitalist economy is driven by the need for more growth and more profit. Driven in this economic surplus, capitalism is inclined to destroy the fountains of wealth and embody the alienation

1. Habermas, *Theory of Action*, 2:332–45.

and reification in the expression of people's lives by misusing natural resources (ecological crisis) and colonizing the lives of working people. In the 1990s talks began in the United Nations, Bretton Woods institutions, and the WTO, resulting in a facilitation of globalization. The world market should work as efficiently as possible so that the market provides guidance and facilitates the working of the market mechanism.[2]

Recently, global capitalism associated with disorganized capitalism has undergone a profound crisis. Its very legitimacy and rationality as a world system have been shaken to the core. Against the trend of neocolonialism, postcolonial or liberative struggle in people's social movements aims at promoting global solidarity in terms of critique and resistance to neoliberal economic globalization. In fact, the capitalist relationship as a whole is dynamic and contradictory in terms of accumulation, competition, and monopoly. The socialization of labor by capital makes social-cultural formation confront people in the form of capital and "reification." Hence, human labor is subsumed under the dominion of capital as a whole, that is, global dominion of the capitalist mode of production.[3]

In the phase of the empire of economic globalization, the owners of capital have created a bubble in the financial markets by various kinds of speculation in order to drive up the desire for profit through so-called casino capitalism. In light of this dangerous direction, it behooves us to reject TINA ("There Is No Alternative") syndrome.[4] According to TINA, the nation-states have retreated, and in their place the international economic system (codified by the IMF and the World Bank, which are associated with institutions such as the Trilateral Commission and the G-7/8 countries, or G-20, and financial markets) appears to be in command and control.

Along with the ideology of economic globalization, "the end of ideologies" has changed into "the end of history,"[5] underscoring the resurgence of pessimism, exclusion, and deconstructive relativism in personal and social values. According to Fukuyama, liberal democracy has constituted the end point of humankind's ideological evolution and the final form of human government; in effect, liberal democracy created the end of history. Fukuyama's troubled sense of pessimism is born of two destructive world wars, totalitarian ideologies, and threatened annihilation in the

2. Brubaker and Mshana, *Justice Not Greed,* 22.

3. Mandel, *Late Capitalism,* 571.

4. Amin, *Capitalism,* 151.

5. Fukuyama, *End of History and Last Man.*

form of nuclear weapons and the environmental crisis. This pessimism led Fukuyama to praise liberal democracies and liberal principles of the free market as the only coherent political aspiration around the globe. The principle of the free market has brought unprecedented levels of material prosperity both in the developed countries and the Third World.[6]

In the theory of the end of history, however, there is vulnerability to unprecedented levels of injustice, inequality, and violence generated by the free market principle. Such an irrationality led to war at the international level, and regression to superstition, spiritual occultism, and misanthropy in domestic society. In the Latin American context, the sweeping effect of globalization submits the dualistic concept of dependency/independency to the logic of the world market. However, in the process of globalization tied to jobless growth, dependency theory has again acquired significance.[7]

An ideology of technological rationalism in the globalization of late capitalism appears to be a specific example of reification; it has the function of the mystifying concealment of social conflict, contradiction, and war. In Habermas' fashion, a lifeworld is violated, reified, and colonized by political power, capital dominion, and mass media.[8] For Habermas the term *late capitalism* implies that social development involves contradictions or crises. He thematizes social integration in relation to the systems of institutions that integrate individuals socially. Here social systems are viewed as lifeworld symbolically, culturally, and linguistically structured and framed. Crises occur as disturbances of lifeworld and social integration.[9]

From an ecological perspective, the growth of the economy has meant the exponential increase of raw material inputs from, and waste outputs into, the environment. The exhaustion of resources or pollution is worsening the reification of our lifeworld. For the common good, scholars such as Daly and Cobb claim that the economy should be redirected toward community, the environment, and a sustainable future. Economics can be approached and undertaken for the common good of community. Such a proposal challenges the absolutizing side of individualism tied to the market economy.[10]

---

6. Ibid., xiii.

7. Duchrow and Hinkelammert, *Property*, 142–43.

8. Habermas, *Theory of Action*, 2:332–45.

9. Habermas, *Legitimation*, 4–5.

10. Daly and Cobb, *For the Common Good*, 18.

In the study of capitalism, the capitalist mode of production tends to be narrowed down to an economic system in which labor power becomes a commodity sold to the buyer. However, the study of capitalism must take into account social relations of production in dealing with productive forces and economic expansion to the foreign market. Capitalism is conditioned upon a certain stage of social productivity and upon the historically developed form of the productive forces. From this historical prerequisite a new mode of production takes its departure. An integration of social relations of production (rationalization for profit and surplus value) with productive forces (organization of labor power) is also to be seen in connection with the intellectual, political, legal, and cultural spheres. In the historical genesis and development of capitalism, it is important to take into account extra-economic (especially colonial) elements. The external factor of colonialism must be analyzed in the historical development of capitalism. A definition of capitalism built on the global analysis of a world-economy system distinguishes diverse forms of capitalism in terms of mercantile, industrial, and late capitalism (including monopoly-imperialistic and neoliberal capitalism in a neocolonial phase). Early capitalism generally refers to the mercantile and industrial eras of colonialism, while late capitalism denotes the monopoly-imperialistic phase of capitalism (including the global capitalism of empire in the neoliberal fashion).

In examination of the economic world-system in social and historical development, it is decisive to analyze a long century of capitalist development in the dialectical interaction between economic reality and political, rational, and civilizational factors. These interactions have guided and strengthened economic expansion. For instance, in the formation of the capitalist mode of production, the world-economy system assumed a colonial form: conquest, enslavement, robbery, murder—in short, political and military forces—played the greatest part. The first sporadic traces of capitalist production can be found in the early fourteenth or fifteenth centuries in certain towns of the Mediterranean. The capitalist era dates from the sixteenth century, and England is a classic form.

In the capitalist expansion of the West we pay attention to the "Christian character" of capitalist development and civilization in the international trade and exchange with colonized countries. Political, philosophical, legal, and ideological systems and infrastructure were involved in justifying and promoting European colonialism in the New World by sanctioning it in a religious garment. In the study of historical capitalism, it is important to include a history of the church's mission and its ethical responsibility in regard to greed, poverty, dominion, and justice.

Organizational Themes

In discussion of diverse approaches to and interpretations of capitalism, colonialism, and their attending civilization, our interest lies in understanding the interplay between capitalist development and its rationale that is based on religious discourse, disciplinary power, self-regulating markets, and metropolis-peripheral relations in social, economic, historical, and cultural complexities. This dialectical interplay occupies the sought-after and privileged locus in the study of capitalism as an integrated political economic culture. In the introduction we will deal with the church's endeavor to promote human rights and ecological sustainability in the midst of economic globalization. A theory of interpretation in historical and sociocritical framework is to be re-envisioned in the study of capitalism and its civilization.

World capital accumulation, capitalist development, and underdevelopment were dominated by a marked increase of European commercial or mercantilist activity and the growth of colonial production for export. This colonial expansion remarkably shapes and promotes an economic attitude toward accumulation of capital and pursuit for profit in the colonizing countries. Therefore, chapter 1 begins by analyzing an era of European colonialism—tied to Christian mission and its ethical failure—as the point of departure of industrial capitalism. The technological advantages of sixteenth-century Europeans were combined with their adventurous outlook. External appropriation of surplus value was, in turn, stimulated, controlled, and exploited by European metropolitan commerce. Military force is the midwife of all important changes at the stage of capital accumulation. Christianity sanctioned this in the name of God. This phase of the history of capitalism belongs to the first (Genoese) systemic cycle of accumulation. Analyzing capitalist development in its initiating state, we shall deal with Bartolomé de Las Casas' legacy of ethical critique as prophetic mission.

Chapter 2 reviews Weber's thesis of Calvinism and capitalist spirit regarding the ethics of the reformers, Martin Luther and John Calvin, contemporaries of Las Casas. It is essential to examine Weber's sociological perspective on Western civilization in terms of disenchantment of the world and its final consequence ending with an "iron cage." Economic ideas evolved in correlation with institutional development and advanced structures of culture. In dialogue with Weber's sociology, we are interested in emphasizing economic justice in the analysis of the legacy of the Reformation.

Chapter 3 deals with the political ideas of social contract and civil society (Hobbes, Locke, Rousseau, and Hegel), relating them to the economic theory of capitalism. The theory of social contract associated with civil society is closely connected with possessive individualism. A notion of possessive individualism tied with Hobbes and Locke comes into dialogue with Rousseau and Hegel, whose views articulate a civil society in connection with economic democracy and moral responsibility.

In chapter 4 industrial capitalism and the self-regulating market is examined in regard to enclosure and the milling machine in its historical connection with the industrial revolution. Colonial trade and military force is reiterated in British mission and the Opium Wars. Like the previous Spanish colonial mission in the New World, Christian mission in nineteenth-century India and China constitutes an unfortunate chapter of imperial mission. Marx's idea of the Asiatic mode of production is relevant within the framework of the capitalist world-economy and colonialism. As for the representative of the self-regulating market, the economic theories of Adam Smith and David Ricardo should be examined to relate free competition and foreign trade to the economy of the British colonies.

Chapter 5 is an attempt to deal with Hegel's idea of alienation and labor and Marx's critical method of capitalism in social-historical perspective. Human action or praxis is influenced and shaped by circumstances transmitted from the tradition as well as social location of human life. As humans make their own history, they do not make it under these circumstances. This perspective overcomes the limitations of Marx's materialist inquiry of social history. For Marx, commodity production is a historically conditioned form, becoming the valid subject of sociohistorical investigation. Nonetheless, Marx's optimism does not adequately consider the influence of historical, sociocultural knowledge systems on human critical reason.

Marx's concept of labor and alienation needs to be discussed in Hegel's logic of the master and the slave focusing on the struggle for recognition, freedom, interaction, and language—Marx sidestepped these. This view complements Marx's notion of human praxis over against human interpretation and recognition. Hegel's concept of the struggle for recognition is to be viewed in two contradictory perspectives: for the sake of neoliberal market democracy or for the sake of emancipation in anti-colonial context.

Chapter 6 presents a study of the dynamics and limitations of Marx's economic thought in view of capitalist development in colonies and the world-economy. Marx as an economic thinker is called one of the masters of suspicion (Paul Ricoeur); his theory retains an explanatory power in the analysis of civil society and capitalist civilization. Society is changing and can be changed in accordance with human critical acceptance of history's influence. The logic of capital and the accumulation process brings human society to crises. Human life and consciousness in social location stand under historically mediated circumstances. Critical-dialectical method accounts for how to interpret human life in both intellectual and material events in regard to sociohistorical context and world-historical connection. However, the economic interpretation of capitalist history remains incomplete, because the human being is not simply an economic animal. Human beings as critical-dialectical beings are on the way to overcoming the crises of capitalist society. This hermeneutical-eschatological reframing of civil society corrects Marx's optimism about the transition from the realm of necessity toward the realm of freedom.

Chapter 7 investigates the political and economic reality of late capitalism. Monopoly capitalism marks a new and different phase of industrial capitalism and challenges the limitations of Marx's own idea about the world market. A political form of imperialism can be defined as a stage of finance capital in the development of the world-economy. As "monopoly capital" became the major form of wealth, capital export became the outstanding feature in economic relations at the international level. The rival superpowers collaborated for their economic interests through multinational economic corporations and international systems. In that context, the centralized country monopolized the peripheral country by controlling capital investment and also by dividing unoccupied territories of the world into their satellites. The focus is on the relation between monopoly and competition in the context of monopoly capitalism.

Ernest Mandel continues to incorporate this model into his analysis of late capitalism. Habermas, however, attempts to renew the theory of late capitalism by analyzing colonization of lifeworld and projecting a civil society built on deliberate democracy and social justice. For explanation of the long wave of the capitalist system and its legitimacy, Kondratieff cycles come into focus. This model of the long wave of capitalism makes the breakdown theory of capitalism obsolete and bridges with the theory of world-system perspective on capitalism as world-economy.

Chapter 8 introduces a relation between capitalism and the world-system. It includes a discussion of perspectives from the peripheral world-system by way of correcting a metropolis-centered idea of imperialism. A Eurocentric theory of imperialism is modified and corrected by scholars who are more interested in analyzing the phenomenon of the creation of underdevelopment in Latin America. A shift is made from Marx's notion of the rate of profit on the domestic level to the international transfer of surplus value which can be seen in relation between the peripheral countries and the metropolis. This is what is represented by Baran and Sweezy's theory of international transfer of surplus value, Frank's dependency theory of underdevelopment, and Wallerstein's world-systems analysis. Within the framework of world-economy system, unequal exchange marks a field of debate and interest.

Chapter 9 engages with neoliberalism and empire in economic globalization. Neoliberalism expresses its faith in the self-regulating market and free and unlimited flow of capital transcending geographical barriers. According to the principles of neoliberal globalization, the economy should dictate its rules to society, not the other way around. Foreign investors in central countries are snapping up companies and banks in peripheral countries. These purchases are expected to result in heavy layoffs. The results of years of work by thousands of people in peripheral countries are transferred into foreign corporate hands, leaving laborers on the streets. This economic inequality stands under the principles of competition and maximization of shareholder value. The fetishism of economic growth and profit prevails. Global capitalism appears to be the guarantor of individual freedom for central countries at the expense of people in peripheral countries. A theory of neoliberalism represented by Hayek and Friedman comes into critical focus. This chapter further examines a theory of Empire in regard to globalization. Against neoliberal globalization and imperialism, proponents of the theory of Empire insist on a postmodern paradigm from imperialism to empire. A bio-political approach (*a la* Foucault) to the reality of Empire articulates the interplay of cultural knowledge and political-economic power at the world scale. This theory of Empire finds its echo in postcolonial theologians. We shall review postcolonial critique of economic globalization according to this theory of Empire.

Finally, Chapter 10 presents the theological-ethical response to the economic reality of globalization. For alternatives to global capitalism in ecumenical debate, a theology of economic justice and ethical responsibility (proposed by Helmut Gollwitzer and Ulrich Duchrow) deserves special attention. The ecumenical study of economic justice and ethical responsibility broadens our theological construction of a prophetic theology of life. It is decisive to incorporate the WCC and LWF studies of economic justice in the context of globalization for our project of the church's prophetic commitment to justice and emancipation in confrontation with greed and dominion. In the epilogue we shall outline our interpretation of historical capitalism from the sixteenth century to the twenty-first century of neoliberal capitalism, including its crisis and future prospects. The church's responsibility in the field of world-economy will be emphasized.

Acknowledgments

THIS STUDY OF CHURCH and its ethical responsibility in the midst of world economy is motivated by the impact of the 2008 global crisis of the world-economy system. The reality of an economic downturn is imbued with an optimism of market logic that advocates for restoration of normality. It is difficult to understand the contemporary phase of economic globalization unless analysis is undertaken on the profound upheavals capitalism has caused throughout the world.

Religion and economics was a classic example for Max Weber, who gave an account of religious ethos and its role in economic life. His ethic of responsibility, however, does not account for those underprivileged in the economic sphere. In the current cultural trend economics functions as a form of religion, calling for acceptance of the self-regulating market on blind faith. We observe that there is a parallel between economic principles based on blind faith and religious principles based on blind faith. In the Church we hear that God seems to sanction the current reality of the self-regulating free market in economic globalization. However, in the Judeo-Christian perspective we are aware that "the stone that the builders rejected has become the cornerstone" (Ps 118:22; Mark 12:10–11). Conformity to the gospel of Jesus Christ is not identified with conformity to the status quo, the dominant principle of economic globalization.

I have undertaken the study of church and world-economy to promote a prophetic theological ethic in an age of economic globalization and empire. My interest in the field of the economic history of capitalism is shaped in a sociohistorical and interpretive manner. Historically, I attempt to trace the genesis, development, crisis, and revival of capitalism by attending to its ideological, social, and political structures and events. Interpretively, I am committed to analyzing and interpreting the reality of global capitalism as a world-system in connection with the perspective of those on the underside of the universal capitalistic history. The reality of victims of the world economic reality, today's Lazarus (*minjung* in Korean parlance), shapes a lively principle of interpretation in the investigation of the "Christian character" of capital accumulation and colonialism. A theology of God's life undergirds a prophetic theology of life and life-enhancing culture, and it can be adequately implemented when it is associated with a critical analysis of economic reality and structure at a global scale. It calls for *metanoia* from previous wrongdoing of greed, privilege, and power toward justice and emancipation coming from God's reign.

Special thanks must be given to Prof. Dr. Ulrich Duchrow at Heidelberg for the foreword. For the current book I am indebted to his guidance and comments in improving knowledge in the field of church and world-economy. I was privileged to join the LWF and WCC conference on Buddhists and Christians engaging structural greed today held at the Institute of Religion, Culture and Peace, Payap University, Chiang Mai, Thailand (August 22–27, 2010).

I appreciate Andreas Pangritz at the University of Bonn, Germany, who offered valuable comments on Helmut Gollwitzer's prophetic theology and world-economy. Guillermo Hansen at Luther Seminary offered important comments on my understanding of liberation theology and economic justice. Gary Simpson must be thanked for his public theological insight into my perspective on the public sphere of late capitalism. I appreciate Dana Scopatz and Peter Watters, my assistants, for their work on proofreading.

Easter 2012
St Paul, MN

Church and Economic Justice

A THEOLOGICAL CONCEPT OF the church's mission and its ethical responsibility cannot be properly understood and practiced apart from God's justice for those who suffer in the world. The God who forgives is the One who demands justice. The church is a community of witness to the universality of the gospel, especially in regard to the fragile, the voiceless, and the vulnerable. Economic justice is an indispensable part of the church's responsibility for society. An integration of theology with the study of economics takes on a new and major significance given the reality of devastation that economic globalization has brought.

In the American context, Herman Daly and John Cobb have emphasized the communitarian concerns of Thomas Jefferson, Alexis de Tocqueville, and early Americans in general. This is in contrast to the idea of America as built on individualism and entrepreneurialism. Emphasizing the importance of community in American life, Daly and Cobb take issue with the chief feature of *homo economicus* built on extreme individualism and the divinely implanted force of egoism; in this tradition, God is portrayed as the one who implanted self-interest in the human being as the motive force of progress.[1]

For their communal ethic of economic justice, Daly and Cobb are convinced of the importance of Aristotle's distinction between *oikonomia* and *chrematistics*. The former (from which our word economics derives) is the management of the household; its purpose is to increase the use-value to all members of the household over the long run (including the

---

1. Daly and Cobb, *For Common Good*, 89.

larger community of the land, of shared values, resources, institutions, language, and history). Aristotle views the market from the perspective of the community; it utilizes the market as an excellent instrument for the management of the community in terms of increasing use-value while minimizing its harmful effects. However, the latter term, *chrematistics*, is defined as the branch of political economy related to the manipulation of property and wealth; its purpose is to maximize short-term monetary exchange-value to the owner. It seeks unlimited growth, and continues to work for the growth of the market measured by exchange-value.[2]

Daly and Cobb take over Aristotle's concept of *oikonomia* to develop their definition of economics for community in connection to ecology. Economics is directed to the promotion of the life of community and ecological sustainability.[3]

In the Catholic framework, scholars attend to socially concerned, community-building aspects of human activity. The work of Heinrich Pesch, a Roman Catholic economist, was informed by papal encyclicals. He understood economics as the study of the process of providing the material goods of a people, which is bound to the political and social life of the community.[4] Pesch's solidarity model of economics incorporated the idea of community and proposed an economic order and a moral-organic unity that embrace many independent private economic units.

An economic view of the person in community was sharpened in Latin American contexts. Liberation theologians articulated the significance of the poor for Christian theology and its practical mission. They contributed to the field of socio-political liberation, pedagogical liberation (e.g., Paulo Freire's *Pedagogy of the Oppressed*), and the biblical praxis of the base Christian communities. Gutiérrez in his groundbreaking work *A Theology of Liberation* (1971)[5] aptly defined his theology as a critical reflection on Christian praxis in light of God's Word. At Puebla, the phrase "preferential option for the poor" was coined in dealing with God's concern about the poor.[6] In this light the poor are not merely the object of the church's mission, but bearers of God's mission. They are interlocutors of theology, its ethical criteria, and mission. Liberation theology takes seriously the human rights of the poor in stating that "to know God is to do

---

2. Ibid., 138–58.

3. Ibid., 190–206.

4. Mulcahey, *Economics*, 13–14.

5. Gutiérrez, *Theology of Liberation*.

6. Ibid., xxv–xxvi.

justice."[7] The mission of the church involves self-repentance by criticizing the prevailing system, which sacralizes the oppressive structures to which the church is tied. Prophetic denunciation is directed against "every dehumanizing situation that is contrary to fellowship, justice, and liberty."[8]

Against the Western model of colonialism, postcolonial theologians share the concern for liberation. They endeavor to write and work against colonial assumptions, representations, and ideologies in the practice of a resistant discourse.[9] In light of the colonized other, postcolonial theology retrieves the place of victims of the old imperialism and victims of globalization with emphasis on resistance, hybridized identity, and discursive practice. Accordingly, scholars discuss and explore the complex relations between Christian theology, church, and Empire. Insofar as Empire as massive concentrations of power permeates and influences all aspects of life, Christianity cannot avoid the reality of Empire any longer. As Rieger asserts, "Empire seeks to extend its control as far as possible, beyond the commonly recognized geographical, political, and economic spheres, to include the intellectual, emotional, psychological, spiritual, cultural, and religious arenas."[10]

A study of Europe in the World System of 1492–1992 was undertaken in the "Conciliar Process for Justice, Peace and the Integrity of Creation" (launched in Basel in 1989). This study demonstrates the changing shape of the capitalist world system from the Spanish epoch of the sixteenth century to capitalism in history and the present. It is one of the major guidebooks for us in understanding the contemporary upheavals and crises brought by the economic globalization.[11]

Ulrich Duchrow maintains that meeting the basic needs of concrete human beings and ecological sustainability must become the point of departure for a new economic approach and system.[12] Sharing Duchrow's concern, Daly and Cobb also attempt to redefine *homo economicus* in terms of person-in-community, moving toward a paradigm shift in economics. Rethinking economics from the view point of person-in-community,

---

7. Ibid., 110.

8. Ibid., 152.

9. Sugirtharajah, *Asian Hermeneutics*, ix–x.

10. Kwok Pui-lan et al., eds., *Empire*, 3.

11. Duchrow, *Europe*.

12. Duchrow, *Global Economy*, 158–62.

they are convinced that economy should be embedded in social relations, rather than social relations being embedded in the economic system.[13]

In the recent ecumenical context, we observe serious attempts to improve the church's commitment to economic justice. The WCC document of the 9th Assembly of the World Council of Churches (held in Porto Alegre, Brazil, 2006)—"God, in your grace, transform the world"–discerned the sign of the times tied to the civilization of globalization. It emphasized that human dignity, human rights, and social justice are basic values and the yardstick by which to measure economic activity on a global scale. The economic reality of globalization should be shaped in accordance with promotion of dignity of life, service to human freedom, enabling the expression of cultural diversity. Every Christian must be part of a globalization of justice and solidarity, and appropriate political conditions must create social equality and promote social cohesion.

In the WCC documents we read that global inequality is denounced and a worry is expressed about ecological devastation tied to the process of globalization. An ideology of neo-liberalism is critiqued as a myth—in analogy to Procrustes who waylaid travelers and chopped short their legs to fit into "one size fits all." In this context the neo-liberal economists are called the Procrustean economists of our time, chopping the legs of poor nations to conform them to the economic program of rich countries.[14]

THEORETICAL FRAMEWORK: ECONOMIC SYSTEM AND INTELLECTUAL SPHERE

Clodovis Boff develops a liberative–ethical epistemology. According to him, the concepts, notions and facts which are given historically are raw materials to be transformed in accordance with theoretical models. However, the theoretical practice in Boff's sense tends to be disconnected from the social and cultural reality of the "raw materials." Boff does not acknowledge that human intellectual practice is conditioned by society and history, not independent of them.

According to Boff, a science of interpretation works on existing, given concepts. The theoretical practice or interpretation transforms the raw materials into another concrete knowledge system and the result is knowledge achieved, mediated, and mutated through interpretation of theoretical practice. Because there is no direct identity between the initial

13. Polanyi, *Transformation*, 57; cf. Daly and Cobb, *For Common Good*, 8.

14. *God, in Your Grace...*, 214.

state and the final state, a real transformation, or paradigm shift takes place through the mediation of theoretical practice. Boff calls such reconstruction an epistemological break. Although Boff considers the final state to have been arrived at through the theoretical process, actually it is an abstract principle (dialectic materialism) that drives the interpretive process, including the understanding of social material life that he takes as "raw material." The whole process, social givens →transformation (analysis, understanding, and interpretation;)→theory (reconstruction) makes a reference to an external, independent reality (the concrete-real). Therefore, it should be noted that this epistemological process is undertaken without experiencing the independent social reality outside of human cognition.

In contrast to Boff, I contend that in the scientific theory of interpretation, it is important to distinguish the concrete-in-thought from the concrete in social reality. The concrete-in-thought provides analogical knowledge of the concrete-real in the social location. As such it is directly driven by the concrete-real, with no epistemological break.

This perspective prevents a literal application of a ready-made knowledge to the society. Without mediation with social concreteness, theoretical practices remain abstract, because they would take place in a vacuum. A hermeneutical engagement with social life connection and theoretical practice challenges any abstract notion of the results of theoretical practice, because hermeneutical logic is undertaken in an open-ended manner in terms of appreciation, critical distance, and reconstruction.

According to Boff the relationship between socio-critical analysis and interpretation of praxis is grounded in correspondence of relations:

> Jesus of Nazareth is to his context
>> as
> Christ and the church is to the context of the church
>> as
> Church tradition is to historical context
>> as
> Our theology is to our context.

Boff's model of correspondence of relations takes into account a dialectical encounter between the text and context in regard to the scripture and our horizon.[15]

Nevertheless, social scientific research and method does not take place in a vacuum, but within life relations between interpreter and empirical data (object of social givenness). A scientific process (raw materials →

---

15. Boff, *Theology and Praxis*, 147.

transformation by human labor → product) must not be disengaged from the structure of social relations, in which the scientific process of production takes place. This perspective implies that knowledge is a historically constituted system. Thus socio-historical relations must be included in the production of knowledge systems to sharpen epistemological dynamism in interaction with the social life context.

Furthermore, such a perspective considers historical mediation in regard to the biblical text via Jesus' context to our church and contemporary context; it denotes hermeneutical mediation of the historical influence of Jesus' praxis of the gospel with our church. It integrates our socio-critical knowledge with social reality, and undertakes critical analysis of the interpreter's social existential life connection. It acknowledges the fraction of human imagination, socio-cultural infrastructure concerned, and human awareness and expression of life reality. The theory incorporates a critique of ideology into itself, and in this regard history of effect influencing human understanding becomes efficacy only at a moment of critical distance and also in recognition of the place of human interest in emancipation. The historically conditioned documentations and social connections influence and shape the interpretation of economic reality and cultural forms of rationality in the history and development of capitalism.

One has critical distance from the limitations of capitalism, but we live in the cultural heritage and economic relations of capitalism. We are free to reinterpret values and limitations from the past and engage in transformation of the historically and socially given capitalism in a projection of our future autonomy, freedom, and emancipation. Analyzing the value of the past and the social reality as historically and socially given, we reinvision and reevaluate the socio-historical giveness and reconstruct our interpretative practice for a better future. The continuous effort for recognition of cultural value and heritage, discovery of such for our present reality, and their reevaluation in encounter with social location characterize our interest in freedom, justice, and solidarity with those voiceless and vulnerable. This perspective becomes significant in our discussion of a transition from the bondage of capital fetishism toward exodus in real freedom and justice.

Theory of freedom and emancipation is to be approached with eschatological reservation. It remains fragmentary and open-ended, calling for further clarification and renewal in interaction with empirical reality in different situations. Socio-historical and cultural complexities and differences guide interpretative mediation and theoretical practices anew in the direction of self-renewal and approximation to the empirical reality in social cultural location. The critical–dialectical science uncovers the economic foundation of modern society in a step by step fashion and open-ended manner.[16]

Socio-economic life cannot be understood properly without considering its connection with institutional, religious, and cultural discourse. The capitalist mode of production has developed within a specific socio-economic framework in different times and places, fully connected with an institutional, cultural, and intellectual sphere. In the analysis of empirically given circumstances, we must consider natural environment, racial relations, and external, historical influences. Colonial and semi-colonial countries which are "backwards" countries have become an integral part of a world dominated by imperialism. Here, an analysis of international relationships of exchange between metropolis and colonial country becomes an indispensable part in the discussion of the reality of the world-economy.

Such a perspective can correct a tendency of economic reductionism and also uphold renewal of an interpretive, non-participatory attitude toward the political-economic sphere. An interpretation of economic reality becomes meaningful when it clarifies the crisis of world-economy. It holds truth when it is grounded in the concrete life and in solidarity with those who are "the outcast, the suspects, the maltreated, the powerless, the oppressed, the reviled, in short . . . those who suffer."[17]

CAPITALISM AND CIVILIZATION: DIVERSE DEFINITIONS AND APPROACHES

Capitalism and Cultural-Economic Ethos

In exploring the origin of capitalism, human ethical and cultural behavior comes into relationship with the existence of economic forms and the modern world. The capitalist amasses capital as the dominant motive of economic activity and adopts an attitude of sober rationality and precise calculation to which the capitalist subordinates everything in life.

Accordingly, Weber states that the spirit of capitalism seeks profit in terms of rational and systematic enterprise. Capitalism is identified by Weber as "the pursuit of profit, and forever renewed profit, by means of

16. Sweezy, *Theory of Development*, 11.

17. Bonhoeffer, *Letters & Papers*, 17.

continuous, rational, capitalistic enterprise," in the "expectation of profit by the utilization of opportunities for exchange."[18] Weber's concept of capitalism in general implies rationally conducted exchange for profit. The competitive struggle under the power of competing national states in peace or war produced the opportunities for modern Western capitalism. Through commercialization of economic life, capitalistic methods were pursued, using economic means such as bonds, shares, finance, banking, and stock markets. These developments enabled capital to be more mobile and allowed owners of capital to pursue maximum profits in any commercialized area. The competition for mobile capital amounted to an alliance between the rising states and the sought-after and privileged capitalist powers. This alliance was a major factor in creating modern capitalism.

The concentration of political power in the hands of governmental and business agencies has also been essential to the recurrent material expansions of the capitalist world-economy. In the prodigious expansion of the capitalist world-economy over the last five hundred years, inner state competition was in association with an ever-increasing concentration of capitalist power; this perspective had been central in the world-system at large.[19]

Differing from Weber's perspective, Karl Marx sought a definition of capitalism in terms of a particular mode of production. His theory of the capitalist mode of production emphasizes the interaction between productive forces and production relations in critical view of the superstructure of a spirit of enterprise. Capitalism is a system under which labor-power becomes a commodity. The labor-power as commodity is bought and sold on the market like any other object of exchange. Marx emphasizes the emergence of class differentiation between the capitalist and the worker which undergirds the capitalist's endless profit as the motive of economic activity.[20] However, today the term capitalist is often used to refer to an ideological supporter of the capitalist system, leading to workers considering themselves capitalists, which would be incoherent under Marx's use of the terms.

---

18. Weber, *Protestant Ethic*, 17.

19. Arrighi, *Twentieth Century*, 12–13.

20. Dobb, *Studies*, 7, 10, 17.

Capitalism and the System of Capital Accumulation

In light of systemic capital accumulation Arrighi utilizes Fernand Braudel's notion of the *longue durée* of historical capitalism in the study of the general history of capitalism. The *longue durée* refers to the cycle of ups and downs occurring within the framework of a given structural time. In contrast to Marx's priority on the dominant role of the economic sphere, a model of *longue durée* emphasizes the dominant role of political sovereignty in the global scale of world-economy. This logic of the top layer (government) remains relatively autonomous from the logic of the lower layers (economics).[21]

For the reconstruction of capitalist history, Arrighi's focus is on that top layer while offering an integrative view of the middle layer of market economy and the bottom layer of material life.[22] In this top domain the possessor of money meets the possessor of political power rather than the possessor of labor-power. Here we decipher the secret of making the large and regular profits enabling capitalism to prosper and expand over the last five to six hundred years.

For the framework of financial expansion, Arrighi incorporates Marx's general theory of capital: M (money capital: liquidity, flexibility, freedom of choice) → C (commodity capital) → M'(expanded liquidity, flexibility, and freedom of choice) gives Arrighi an historical account of a recurrent pattern of historical capitalism as a world system. A full systematic cycle of accumulation (MCM') is identified by a fundamental unity of the primary agency and structure of world-scale processes of capital accumulation in the fourfold sense. This cycle is divided by 1) a Genoese cycle (from the fifteenth to the early seventeenth centuries), 2) a Dutch cycle (from the late sixteenth century through most of the eighteenth century, 3) a British cycle (from the latter half of the eighteenth century through the early twentieth century), and 4) a U.S. cycle (beginning in the late nineteenth century continuing into the current phase of financial expansion). Arrighi, in the analysis of world-scale processes of capital accumulation, uses a notion of "long century" as the basic temporal unit,[23] accounting for the development of the modern world-system through long cycles of accumulation from the thirteenth century to today.

21. Arrighi, *Twentieth Century*, 25–26.

22. Ibid., 24.

23. Ibid., 6.

Bio-politics and Capitalism

Foucault remains one of the major figures influencing the model of Empire (Hardt and Negri) and postcolonial theology. At issue for Foucault is an emphasis on the technological rationality of disciplining the human body as the prerequisite for the rise of capitalism. Foucault argues that insofar as the capitalist mode of production alienates human labor in the system of commodity production, it is necessary to reexamine the capitalist mode of production in light of the discipline of docile bodies. In the seventeenth and eighteenth centuries the technique of discipline on human bodies made possible "the meticulous control of the operations of the body" imposing upon a relation of docility-utility in which the disciplines became general formulas of domination.[24] Thus discipline increases the forces of the body in terms of economic utility. To the extent that economic exploitation separates the productive force and the product of labor, disciplinary coercion invents a new political anatomy. It establishes in the body a linkage of an increased aptitude of the forces of the body to an increased obedience of the body under political domination. Such new micro-physics of power constantly penetrated to ever broader spheres, as if covering the entire body of society.[25]

Accordingly, labor is under the control of capital, and one of the functions of capital is directing, superintending, and adjusting the labor. It requires special characteristics of controlling the human body.[26] Foucault reinterprets Marx in terms of an integrative system of surveillance and disciplinary power. The accumulation of people cannot be separated from the accumulation of capital. In this connection the growth of a capitalist economy engenders the specific modality of disciplinary power.[27] This perspective offers a counter-weight to Marx's tendency toward economic reductionism.

The disciplinary power of human life centers on the body, disciplining and optimizing its capabilities, and consequently extorting its force. It increases its usefulness and docility, integrating it into systems of efficient and economic controls. Foucault characterizes the disciplines in terms of an anato-politics of the human body, or bio-power.[28] The organization of

24. Foucault, *Discipline and Punish*, 137.
25. Ibid., 139.
26. Ibid., 175; cf. Marx, *Capital, I.* 313.
27. Ibid., 221.
28. Foucault, *History of Sexuality* 1, 139.

power over life was deployed around the disciplines of the body and the regulations of the population. The subjugation of bodies and the control of population marked the beginning of bio-power that was an indispensable element in the historical development of capitalism.

The implementation of bio-power results in the codification of structures of domination. The development of capitalism becomes possible through the controlled insertion of bodies into the machinery of production and the adjustment of the phenomena of population to economic processes. The exercise of bio-power partly adjusts the accumulation of people to that of capital, joins the growth of human groups to the expansion of productive forces and the differential allocation of profit. There is an intimate connection between bio-power and the development of capitalism.[29] Thus, Foucault's view finds its influence in the circle of theoreticians of empire and post-colonial theology.

Capitalism and World-System

Within the Third World perspective on world-economy there are scholars who attempt to see the reality of global capitalism from the perspective of those colonized in the Third World. Karl Polanyi remains influential in the world-system analysis, especially in the work of Immanuel Wallerstein. Polanyi takes a critical stance toward the view that the market society is a natural phenomenon.

Polanyi focused on the institution of the market and its change in historical development. The market is not a universal social phenomenon. This perspective contradicts the liberal and neo-classical economic theories, according to which the self-regulating market emerged by making all production for sale on the market. Polanyi critiques the liberal and neo-classical theory as a commodity fiction.[30]

There were no market relations,—not to mention trade and a division of labor over long distances—before the "Great Transformation" took place in Europe during the nineteenth century. In this light, Polanyi states that people in different cultures could organize and coordinate their economies and economic relations in terms of non-economic social relations of reciprocity and redistribution with the help of symmetry and centricity. Even when the capitalist nation developed uniform domestic markets,

29. Ibid., 141.
30. Polanyi, *Transformation*, 73.

local markets and long-distance trade markets were not integrated into a capitalist world market over a long period.[31]

Influenced by Polanyi, Wallerstein develops three forms of world economy: mini-system (reciprocity), world-empire redistribution, and world-economies market exchanges.[32] Proposing the Third World perspective, Wallerstein asserts that the correct unit of social economic analysis is the world-system, within which sovereign states are to be seen as one kind of organizational structure. For his social scientific method, this emphasis on a global framework is of special significance.[33] For the sake of the world-system Wallerstein develops a socio-critical method of totality which says that the isolated facts of social life are to be seen as aspects of the historical process. In this connection aspects of the historical process can be integrated in a totality of the world-system.

In Wallerstein's view, a European world-economy came into existence in the sixteenth century on the basis of the capitalist mode of production. For the European world-economy as a whole he considers 1450–1640 the most important time period. In this period a capitalist world-economy was created in a vast but weak sense.[34] The world-system was consolidated between 1640 and 1815. Between 1815 and 1917 world-economy was conducted into a global enterprise, enabled by the technological transformation of modern industrialism. The final analysis is the period from 1917 to the present in which he deals with the consolidation of the capitalist world-economy.[35]

Historical capitalism has operated within the framework of a world-economy. The state power as the second element in the operation of historical capitalism established the legal right to determine the rules which govern the social relations of production within the nation-state. Within the framework of the capitalist world-economy, the struggle for benefits and the imperative of accumulation have operated throughout the system. The state decision was taken in direct reference to the economic implication for the accumulation of capital.[36] Political decisions are oriented to the smaller structures of the states (nation-states, city-states, empires) within the world-economy, and those states cannot be understood outside the context of the development of the world-system.

31. Ibid., 47–48.
32. Wallerstein, *World-Systems*, 17.
33. Wallerstein, *Modern World-System I*, 8.
34. Wallerstein, *Capitalist World-Economy* 68.
35. Ibid., 10–11.
36. Wallerstein, *Historical Capitalism*, 51.

Utilizing Wallerstein's model of word-system perspective, Frank is more interested in proposing a concept of the development of underdevelopment. According to the model of underdevelopment, the economic structures of contemporary underdeveloped countries are the result of involvement in the world-economy. If Wallerstein focuses more on the relation between core/semi-periphery/periphery within the structure of the world-system, Frank recognizes it in terms of metropolis-satellite in the colonial context. According to Frank, the socio-economic complexities of Latin America have been capitalist since the Conquest Period. Extra-economic coercion to maximize various systems of labor service was intensified in the plantations of the West Indies. This economy was based on a mode of production that was constituted by slave labor. In the mining areas slavery and other types of forced labor were intensified.

According to Frank, Marx's concept of historical, "primitive accumulation" of capital is limited because Marx did not consider the connection between the colonized mode of accumulation and the industrial revolution. For Marx a primitive accumulation constitutes the point of departure for his study of capitalism rather than being regarded as the result of the capitalist mode of production in the context of colonialism.

Frank's major concern is to analyze the exchange relations between the metropolis and the satellites in the world process of capital accumulation. He attempts to undertake a dialectical analysis of the worldwide historical process of capital accumulation between the development of metropolis and peripheral underdevelopment in light of a single process.[37] A historical and primitive accumulation of capital was a consequence of this single process of world economy. Developing his perspective of the world- system, Frank argues that capitalism has generated the creation of underdevelopment in Latin America. The capitalist world-system was born when Columbus discovered America.

Third World economists focus on colonialism in the sixteenth century as a consequence of world-economy system and insist that triangle trade brought major contributions to the industrial development of capital in Europe which was the primary driving force to the industrial revolution. In this argument, capitalist European world-economy emerged in the sixteenth century, from the creation of a world-embracing commerce and market. The Christian mission played a formative role. This perspective requires a study of Christian mission and colonialism in the sixteenth century in the next chapter.

37. Frank, *Accumulation*, xii.

1

Colonialism and the Historical Development of Capitalism

THE FIRST STAGE OF the journey toward capitalism was marked by the conquest and pillage of America (sixteenth century), while the second stage was marked by the rise and affirmation of the bourgeoisies (seventeenth and eighteenth century). These elements of capitalism fused into a powerful mix, propelling European states toward the territorial conquest of the world. Based on this unique fusion of state and capital, capitalism became identified with the state, thus triumphing.[1]

What Western history calls "the great discoveries" initiated the first stage described above. In 1486, Bartholomew Diaz "discovered" and traveled around the Cape of Good Hope, and in 1492, Christopher Columbus "discovered" America. In 1498, Vasco da Gama arrived in India after a nine-month voyage around Africa. Thus began a great hunt after wealth in the form of trade and pillage, with which the church's missionary efforts became entangled. Following the return of Columbus with reports of the New World, the Council of Castile (established under Queen Isabella in 1480) met. Adam Smith characterized the action of Castile as follows: "The pious purpose of converting inhabitants to Christianity sanctified the injustice of the project. But the hope of finding treasures of gold there, was the sole motive which promoted them to undertake it . . . It was the sacred thirst of gold . . ."[2]

1. Arrighi, *Twentieth Century*, 11.
2. Cited in Beaud, *History of Capitalism*, 18.

Hernán Cortés, conqueror of Mexico, confessed: "We Spanish suffer from a sickness of the heart for which gold is the only cure."[3] In 1519, the pillage of the treasure of the Aztecs in Mexico began; and subsequently, in 1534, the pillage of the Incas in Peru. According to Columbus, "one who has gold does as he wills in the world, and it even sends souls to Paradise."[4] A staunch Catholic, Columbus's stated mission was conversion of the pagans to Catholicism. However, the pagans were killed or enslaved. Hans Konig's *Columbus: His Enterprise*, writes:

> We are now in February 1495 . . . Of the five hundred slaves, three hundred arrived alive in Spain, where they were put up for sale in Seville by Don Juan de Fonseca, the archdeacon of the town. "As naked as the day they were born," the report of this excellent churchman says, "but with no more embarrassment than animals . . ." The slave trade immediately turned out to be "unprofitable, for the slaves mostly died." Columbus decided to concentrate on gold, although he writes, "Let us in the name of the Holy Trinity go on sending all the slaves that can be sold."[5]

MISSION AND ECONOMIC SYSTEM

Genoese capitalism prepared the way for future participation in the trade between Seville and Castile's colonial empire. The establishment of the Casa di San Giorgio in 1407 played an important role in the organization of the Genoese capitalist class in light of the political impasse between the power of money and the power of the sword. The Genoese predominance in trade underlined the course of sixteenth-century Spanish development. The Portuguese prince, Henry the Navigator, the most famous of the precursors and inspirers of the great discoveries, was obsessed with the idea of the Crusade. Queen Isabella of Castile was the most successful of the entrepreneurs of the discoveries and was the leader of a new crusade for expanding the territorial domain of Christian and Castilian power. The expulsion of the Jews took place during her reign. In the violent baptism of the Moors of Granada, the powers entrusted to the new Inquisition represented a reaction against the Muslim pressure. They intensified religious fervor and intolerance in Spain. The trans-oceanic expansion of Iberian

3. Ibid.

4. Ibid., 19.

5. Konig, *Columbus*, 82.

commerce in the late fifteenth and early sixteenth centuries was promoted by entrepreneurial agency that was held by an organic relationship of political exchange. It entailed an Iberian aristocratic component. In the fifteenth century, material expansion of the first Genoese systematic cycle of accumulation came along with Iberian rulers.[6]

Genoese capitalists sponsored an expedition across the Sahara in 1447 and two voyages along the West African coast in the 1450s in search of African gold. By 1519 the power of Genoese capital played a critical role in the election of Charles V, the king of Spain (1525), as emperor of the Holy Roman Empire. The German electoral princes would never have chosen Charles V if the Augsburg house of Fugger had not financially helped him. Genoese merchant bankers were in tandem with the Fuggers and the Weslers in Germany.[7] The Weslers took possession of Chile while the Fuggers did the same thing in Venezuela.

Las Casas reported about the German merchants: "They raged much more cruelly [at the Indians] under them than all the barbarians I have already mentioned [i.e., the Spaniards]; more bestially and furiously than the bloodiest tigers and the angriest wolves and lions. In their avarice and greed they were much more frantic and deluded than all those who came before, they devised even more abominable ways of extracting gold and silver, they set aside all fear of God and the king and all shame before men . . ."[8]

The Genoese merchants were capable of converting the intermittent flow of silver from America to Seville into a steady stream, making themselves indispensable to the king of Spain.[9] Beside Spain and Portugal, it is pivotal to bear in mind that the capital-owning families of Upper Italy and Upper Germany played a major role in the universal expansion of capital accumulation in the first phase of the capitalist world system.

From the seventeenth century on, slaves became the main trading commodity between Europe and Africa. Europe's conquest and colonization of North and South America and the Caribbean islands from the fifteenth century onward created an insatiable demand for African laborers, who were deemed more fit than indigenous people to work in the tropical conditions of the New World. The other European colonies soon adopted the system of sugar plantations successfully used by the Portuguese in

---

6. Arrighi, *Twentieth Century*, 119, 121.

7. Ibid., 122–23.

8. Duchrow, *Europe*, 5.

9. Arrighi, *Twentieth Century*, 126.

Brazil, which depended on slave labor. Sugar cultivation began on the Mediterranean islands, then later moved to the Atlantic islands. Then it crossed the Atlantic over to Brazil and the West Indies. Slavery followed the route of the sugar.[10]

In 1496, when not one ounce of the gold was left, the Spaniards cut out estates for themselves in which the Amerindians were still living. The Indians became their property. The Spaniards used a system known as *encomienda* instead of slave plantations. The *encomienda* differed from slave plantation in that the *encomienda* in Hispanic America was a direct creation of the Spanish Crown and its ideological justification was Christianization. The Spanish king assigned land and Indians (*repartimientos*) to the conquerors and entrusted them with evangelization (*encomienda*).

Although the stated goal was evangelization, the chief functions of *encomienda* were to supply a labor force for the mines and cattle ranches, to raise silk, and to supply agricultural products for the *encomenderos* and the workers in towns and mines. The *encomiendas* in Hispanic America were soon transformed into capitalist enterprises by legal reforms, degenerating in practice to slavery.[11] Pope Alexander VI acted as Supreme Liege Lord for the Spanish and Portuguese conquistadors. Most of the Indians never converted to what Columbus called "our Holy Faith," but instead experienced cultural and racial genocide.

Economic development in Europe and underdevelopment in the colonized countries were two sides of the same coin, resulting from holy mission and colonialism. The Indian on the *encomienda* was more poorly treated than the slave, largely because of the insecure social situation. The Indians who worked on gold washing received a sixth of its value. This payment, called the *sesmo*, was made collectively to the Indians, not paid to individual Indians.[12] In the sixteenth century (1450–1640) a European capitalist world economy came to exist in an enlarged but weakened form, drawing its strength from colonial exploitation.

According to the model of world-system, slavery and feudalism were in the periphery, wage labor and self-employment in the core, and sharecropping in the semiperiphery. These three zones had different modes of labor control, so the flow of the surplus enabled the capitalist system to come into being.[13] The periphery (eastern Europe and

10. Wallerstein, *Modern World-System*, 1:88.

11. Sanderlin, *Witness*, 3–4.

12. Wallerstein, *Modern World-System*, 1:94.

13. Ibid., 86–87.

Hispanic America) did forced labor (slavery and coerced cash-crop labor). The semiperiphery developed an in-between form (sharecropping) as a widespread alternative.[14]

Spain brought together the sword and the cross, by combining them with the economic search for gold and silver. Moving from the Caribbean areas to New Spain (Mexico) and later the Peruvian region, the Spanish encountered the societies of the Aztecs and the Incas. In spite of the fact that the Incas of the Peruvian area were at the time united as a theocratic empire with strong economic, political, and religious foundations, a devastating consequence of this encounter with the Spaniards meant social disintegration and deculturation. Consequently, many indigenous people (perhaps six million) died of malnutrition, dietary changes, new illness, armed conflict, and forced labor.[15] Capitalism flourished by establishing the division of labor and exploiting the innocent victims of the forced slavery within the framework of a world-economy. The church was an ideological weapon of death and violence in sanctioning colonialism.

LAS CASAS'S CRITIQUE OF THE COLONIAL SYSTEM

In the period of the colonial tragedy, we know the story of the Spanish Dominican friar Bartolomé de Las Casas (1484–1566), who wrote his account of this painful chapter in the history of mission and colonialism. His book *The Devastation of the Indies: A Brief Account*[16] (written in 1542) is one of the major witnesses (published in 1552). Las Casas was born in 1484 in Seville and came to the newly discovered Indies. As a teenager he was involved in helping the family business there for which his father acquired some land from Columbus. He was given an *encomienda* and participated in expeditions to seize Indians as slaves.[17]

However, the *encomienda* system would later become a central target in Las Casas's rigorous critique and confrontation with the Spanish rule. Other Dominicans such as Pedro de Córdoba and Antonio de Montesinos had already begun to denounce this system of injustices. In response to the cruelty and abuse during the conquest in Hispaniola (present-day Haiti and the Dominican Republic), the Dominican vicar Pedro de Córdoba

14. Ibid., 103.

15. Bevans and Schroeder, *Constants*, 175.

16. Las Casas, *Devastation*.

17. Traboulay, *Columbus and Las Casas*, 48.

chose Antonio de Montesinos to deliver a powerful sermon condemning the perpetrators and the *encomienda* system. In the sermon he stated:

> Because of the cruelty and tyranny you use with these innocent people. . . . On what authority have you waged such detestable wars on these people, in their mild, peaceful lands . . . Know for a certainty that . . . you can no more be saved than Moors or Turks who have not . . . the faith of Jesus Christ.[18]

Las Casas was ordained as a priest in Rome in 1507, and returned to the New World. In 1514 he underwent a profound conversion from his previous colonial lifestyle and decided to give up his own *encomienda*. From then on he began to denounce the mistreatment of the indigenous, beginning with his first sermon (August 15 of the same year). The biblical text for his sermon on Pentecost Sunday, Ecclesiasticus 34:18, triggered a profound spiritual crisis. "Unclean is the offering sacrificed by an oppressor. . . . The Lord is pleased only by those who keep to the way of truth and justice. The Most High does not accept the gifts of unjust people . . . The one whose sacrifice comes from the goods of the poor is like one who kills his neighbor."[19]

COLONIAL DISCOURSE AND THE HUMANITY OF THE OTHER

In the first half-century after the European arrival in the Americas at Hispaniola, Las Casas witnessed the barbarity of the conquistadors and colonists through their enslavement and genocide. His book depicts the unfair treatment that the indigenous people endured during the Spanish conquest of the Greater Antilles, particularly the island of La Hispaniola.

Spaniards behaved like ravening wild beasts, "killing, terrorizing, afflicting, torturing, and destroying the native peoples . . . never seen or heard before."[20] One of the massacres took place in a large city called Cholula, which had more than thirty thousand people. The Spaniards decided to perform a massacre—a chastisement in their language—only to make themselves feared.[21]

European modernity emerged with Columbus's voyage to the Amerindian territories. It developed through the period of Reformation, the

18. Bevans and Schroeder, *Constants*, 176.
19. Las Casas, *Only Way*, 20.
20. Las Casas, *Devastation*, 29.
21. Las Casas, *Indian Freedom*, 226–27.

Renaissance, the scientific revolution, and the Enlightenment. In the initial stage of modernity, the ideology of colonialism and conquest occupied a significant place for understanding the primitive accumulation of capital in relation to the industrial revolution in western Europe. The dialectic of colonialism was built upon the subjugation, oppression, and exclusion of the subaltern people in the periphery. This colonial dialectic was undertaken by political-military dominion and economic exploitation and by controlling the history of the colonized. In the dominating dialectics of colonialism the colonizer speaks, guides, and interprets for the colonized. The Spanish constructed the class of people known as Amerindians by dominating their culture and life, and by identifying them as subhuman. The alterity was created and established.

Christian religion served the empire by extending religious frontiers, upholding the political, economic interest of the empire. In this context it is essential to review Las Casas's confrontation with Juan Ginés de Sepúlveda (1489–1573), one of Spain's most important humanists.

Sepúlveda, a proponent of modernity, attempted to undertake the religious, intellectual justification for conquest by proposing the Christian doctrine of just war and the Aristotelian logic of slavery. Sepúlveda justified wars against Indians. His justification was that Indians had indulged idolatry and committed sins against nature. The Indians' supposed "natural rudeness" and "inferiority" supported the Aristotelian notion according to which some people were natural slaves by birth. He applied Aristotle's notion of natural servitude to a specific and entire race of people. The enslavement was created by European modernity.

Against the colonial claims, Las Casas's vision was rooted in the biblical God of mercy and justice. For Las Casas all humans were created equal. Against the logic of colonialism, Las Casas made the case that not all indigenous people are irrational, or natural slaves. In his *Apologética historia sumaria*, written after the debate with Sepúlveda, Las Casas insisted that the indigenous people had excellent, capable minds and were endowed by nature with the three kinds of prudence—monastic, economic, and political—precisely as named by Aristotle. As for political prudence, the Indians showed themselves as very prudent peoples governing their republic justly and prosperously. In terms of the rules of natural reason, they had even surpassed the most prudent of all, the Greeks and Romans.[22]

22. Ibid.

Evangelization and the Gospel of Peace

Las Casas's evangelization comes along with respect for the humanity of the Indians. According to Las Casas, God's free grace should be applied to every race and every tribe. God gave the Indians the mind and place to live in.[23] Las Casas wrote that they were very clean and docile, having intelligent minds and open to receiving Christian faith. In hearing the gospel, they were eager to participate in the sacraments of the church.[24] "Their society is the equal of that of many nations in the world renowned for being politically astute."[25] However, he also noted that there were some corrupt customs, which should be healed by the gospel.[26]

For Las Casas, true evangelization is to be undertaken in a way that divine providence leads the human to fulfill its natural purpose in a gentle, coaxing, and gracious way. This leads to a living faith under the universal command of Jesus Christ (Matt 28:19–20). Paul, in his letter to the Romans (10:17), points to the Christian way of teaching people in a gentile, coaxing, and gracious way.[27]

The Spirit of Christ is a gentle Spirit (Luke 9:55–56; Isa 61:1). "He will not break the half-broken reed, nor snuff out the dimly burning wick" (Isa 42:3). Christ wanted to teach humility and compassion, which filled Christ and overflowed from him. The way of humility, peace, and rejection of worldliness draws people to moral life better than force of arms.[28]

Las Casas's concept of divine providence (or predestination, Rev 7) is connected with Paul's notion of the mystical body of Jesus Christ and the church. Divine providence must have been at work in the nations of the Indians, naturally endowing them with a capacity for doctrine and grace and graciously furnishing them with the time of their calling and conversion. The Indians underwent cruelties and injustices under the greedy Christians. God has remembered the Indians. The final judgment in Matt 25:31–46 is fundamental in the thought of Las Casas who acknowledges the dignity of the heathen.[29]

---

23. Las Casas, *Only Way*, 63.
24. Las Casas, *Devastation*, 29.
25. Las Casas, *Only Way*, 65.
26. Ibid., 66.
27. Ibid., 68.
28. Ibid., 79, 96.
29. Gutiérrez, *Las Casas*, 259, 271.

Las Casas promotes the principle of evangelization for invitation to faith "not by war but by peace, by good will, kindness, generosity, credibility, by charity from the heart."[30] The Indians are scourged Christs who were killed untimely and innocently.[31] A few years before his death (July 18, 1566), Las Casas wrote his law will and treatment : "I testify that it was God in his goodness and mercy who chose me as his minister . . . on behalf of all those people out in what God calls the Indies. . . . For almost fifty years I have done this work, back and forth between the Indies and Castile . . . All that the Spaniards perpetrated against those [Indian] peoples . . . was in violation of the holy and spotless law of Jesus Christ . . . such devastation, such genocide of populations, have been sins, monumental injustice!"[32]

POSTCOLONIAL INTERPRETATION AND LIBERATIVE DISCOURSE

There is a debate about the legacy of Las Casas. Some scholars argue that Las Casas's solidarity with Amerindians must be seen only in light of the discussion of human rights rather than in light of anticolonialism. According to their argument, Las Casas supported the missionary aspects of the colonial enterprise and acknowledged that God ordained the Spanish crown to the tutelage, bringing temporal and spiritual benefit to the natives in the New World. Las Casas never talked about the end of the colonial enterprise in the Americas.

Against this argument, other scholars vie with this colonial interpretation of Las Casas, emphasizing Las Casas's fight against the colonial policy and its dehumanizing economic system.

The different perspectives on the legacy of Las Casas in a postcolonial and liberative context bring us to examine a postcolonial hermeneutic. The postcolonial ethos undergirds a Third World perspective, considering "liberation as an emancipatory metastory" and also as a potent symbol for those whose rights are circumvented and put in abeyance.[33] The postcolonial ethos lays bare representation, identity, and a reading posture that emerges among the former victims of colonialism. It is connected to "the minority voices in the first world: socialists, radicals, feminists,

30. Ibid., 163.
31. Gutiérrez, *Las Casas*, 95.
32. Las Casas, *Indian Freedom*, 9.
33. Sugirtharajah, *Asian Biblical Hermeneutics*, 15.

minorities."[34] A hybridized identity, which is a consequence of colonialism, is taken as "a wider and more complex web of cultural negotiation and interaction, forged by imaginatively redeploying the local and the imported elements."[35]

Following in the footsteps of Foucault, Edward Said made a groundbreaking contribution to promoting a postcolonial critique in terms of challenging colonialism and imperialism. His study of *Orientalism*[36] attempts to demystify Europe's cultural representation of the Orient that was undertaken during the colonial period. The colonialist knowledge and representations of the Orient created, represented, and colonized the Orient. The homogenization and essentialization of the Orient was an object of European ideology, discourse, and invention.[37] One can no longer sidestep empires and the imperial context in the studies of culture and imperialism. Imperialism or colonialism is undergirded by ideological formations as well as by forms of knowledge that are associated with Eurocentric domination.[38]

The postcolonial imagination forms cultural identities as contrapuntal ensembles, rather than essentializations, because "no identity can ever exist by itself and without an array of opposites, negatives, oppositions."[39] Contrapuntal reading is a strategy of reading a text with an understanding of what is involved, for instance, when a colonial sugar plantation is seen as important to maintaining a particular style of life in England. The contrapuntal reading of the text takes into account the process of imperialism as well as that of resistance on the part of those who were colonized.[40]

This reading perspective may become an important factor in the debate involved in the legacy of Las Casas, because it will illuminate his standpoint as a Spanish Catholic. Hardt and Negri argue that Las Casas's concept of equality was built on the Christian idea of conversion, caught in a Eurocentric view of the Americas. Their poignant argument that "Las Casas is really not so far from the Inquisition"[41] sounds unfortunate and controversial.

---

34. Ibid., 16.
35. Ibid., 16–17.
36. Said, *Orientalism*.
37. Ibid., 4–5, 104.
38. Said, *Culture and Imperialism*, 9.
39. Ibid., 52.
40. Ibid., 66, 194, 259.
41. Hardt and Negri, *Empire*, 116.

Unlike the postcolonial reading of Las Casas, Gutiérrez portrays Las Casas as the inspiration of liberation theology.[42] In confrontation with the Spaniards' exploitation of the Amerindians, Las Casas saw in the Indians the "other" who was different from Western culture. His respect for people of other cultures and religions separated evangelization from a way of subjugating or converting the Indian nations to European culture. The only way to authentic evangelization lies in persuasion and dialogue.[43] Throughout his life, the witness of Las Casas serves as a preeminent symbol of the spirit of liberation theology.

According to Gutiérrez, a logic of "natural servitude" held that those who were born as slaves by nature subject to those who were destined to dominate. The logic of so called "just war" was waged in the name of rectitude, justice, and utility by declaring that the colonizers provided a greater benefit to the supposed barbarians. The colonial claims of superiority, divine providence, and missionary evangelism became the religious, ideological midwife in collaboration with the rule of the Spanish empire. Military conquest formed the most efficacious method of converting Indians to Christianity. In contrast to colonial discourse, Las Casas advocated for a God who invariably sides with the otherness of the victim. In the struggle of Las Casas against colonialism, the right to life and freedom, the right to be different, and the perspective of the poor were inextricably connected in his experience of God in Jesus Christ who stands in solidarity with the Indian.

APPRECIATION AND CRITIQUE

Postcolonial intellectuals are vigilant in unraveling the deep-seated layers of colonialist patterns of knowledge, power, dominion, and resistance through archaeological-genealogical excavation of the colonizing mind. Eurocentrism resides at the heart of European cultural and political economy which have been expanded throughout the many centuries of colonialism and neocolonialism.

The postcolonial act of deciphering residual colonialism implies a discursive and physical, even violent resistance to imperialism, imperial ideologies and attitudes. It deconstructs their continual reembodiment in

---

42. Gutiérrez, *Las Casas.*
43. Ibid., 456.

the fields of politics, economics, history, and theological and biblical studies. It promotes an alternative way of perceiving and restructuring society.[44]

However, postcolonial reading tends to idealize hybridized identity, fixing their standpoint in a dualistic pattern of the colonizer and the colonized. The mechanism of the colonizer produces a mechanism of the colonized. The postcolonial reading tends to sidestep a critical analysis of the internal, domestic complexities of the periphery in the field of politics, economics, and culture. The role of indigenous leaders, upholding their interest in collaboration with the colonizer, can be seen in political, economic, and cultural interplay as well as discursive power and ideological-religious apparatus.

In contrast to Hardt and Negri, Las Casas himself insisted that the natives were not "undeveloped potential Europeans," and Christian conversion was not the only path to their freedom. The God on the side of the victim and the equality of humanity are at the heart of Las Casas. Las Casas's discourse against the *conquistadors* and the *encomenderos* must be apprehended as the potential for anticolonial discourse that can challenge Eurocentric representational logic of the other. For Las Casas the indigenous people were the subjects of their own history, and they were not subhumans.

La Casas's discourse, based on the God of the victim, was directed against the European sin of exclusion which totalized the different into the sameness built on the European logic of Enlightenment and exclusion. For Las Casas, equality, far from meaning modernity's logic of "sameness," denoted recognition of the other.

If equality leads to respect for the other, the sameness leads to totalization (or reduction) of the other to one's identity. The logic of sameness was rather the logic of enslavement and exclusion. Indigenous people could think and express their experience with God within their social, cultural context and various religious and linguistic circumstances. Self-respect for the local culture, tradition, and history must be held within the prophetic horizon of the biblical narrative. This is because understanding the history of colonialism is not to be measured by the standard of the interest of "here and now," but must be judged and evaluated in the context of its own time. In the conversation between the history of Las Casas and our present history, a prophetic component must be appreciated and incorporated into our social locality in protest to the neocolonial reality. At the same time, a critical distance can be taken from the limitations and

44. Said, *Orientalism*, 17.

setbacks of colonial history (even in the case of Las Casas). Thus, Las Casas remains inspirational for the sake of an appropriation of anticolonial solidarity with the other in the present social reality and history.

MERCANTILE CAPITAL, TRIANGLE TRADE, AND CHRISTIAN MISSION

In Spanish colonialism and mission in Latin America we have seen that the banking and commercial houses of Northern Italy and Northern Germany were allied with the imperial house of Hapsburg as a political and military support for their pursuit of profit. The military cost of extending this empire exceeded its economic capacity (over-stretching of the empire), because enormous profits in interest on their loans were paid to the banking houses. Furthermore, the Spanish economy had weakness and limitations in lavish wasting of riches stolen from the colonies. Since 1566 Holland had been rebelling more and more against the sovereign power of Spain owing to heavy tax burden and its attempt at re-Catholization.[45]

Mercantilism was the dominant school of thought throughout the early modern period (from the sixteenth to the eighteenth century). It was a system of state-regulated exploitation through trade which was essentially the economic policy in the age of colonialism. It carefully regulated colonial trade with the principle of "buying cheap and selling dear."[46] The principal benefit of foreign trade was the carrying off of the surplus produce of the colonies and labor.

The discovery of America benefited Europe by opening a new and inexhaustible market to all the commodities of Europe. The savage injustice of the Europeans was ruinously and destructively perpetrated against colonies. Its trade theories acquired meaning as applied to the exploitation of a dependent colonial system.[47]

Mercantilism helped create infamous trade patterns such as the triangular trade in the North Atlantic, in which raw materials were imported to the metropolis and then processed and redistributed to other colonies. Triangular trade, or triangle trade, is a historical and economic term for trade among three regions. Firstly, the slave ships sailed from a European port with a cargo of manufactured goods to Africa. The slave ship, when it arrived in Africa, sold its cargo for slaves. Secondly, ships sailed from

45. Duchrow, *Europe*, 13.
46. Dobb, *Studies*, 209.
47. Ibid., 204.

Africa to the New World. Slaves were traded on the plantations in exchange for a cargo of raw materials, which were returned to Europe. This was the third leg to their home port to complete the triangle.[48]

The production of sugar cane for rum, molasses, and sugar, the trade in black slaves, and the extraction of precious metals established considerable sources of wealth for Spain throughout the sixteenth century. The flow of precious metals came to Europe in the sixteenth century, opening its civilization. Spain's acquisition of the Americas would later repeat itself in Britain's occupation of India and China or the French empire in Indochina. The English East India Company was created in 1600. England asserted itself as a maritime and colonial power by opposing Spain at the end of the sixteenth century, Holland in the seventeenth century, and France in the eighteenth century.

According to Adam Smith, the policy of Europe regarding colonies has done nothing for the prosperity of the colonies. The folly of hunting after gold and silver mines and the injustice of coveting the possession of a colony established the chimera project.[49] The monopoly of the colony trade has kept the rate of profit in British trade higher than its natural course, changing the direction of British trade.

The trading-capitalist phase of mercantilism in the seventeenth and eighteenth century based on monopolistic trading companies was supported by powerful nation-states such as Holland, England, and France. In England, mercantilism reached its peak during the Long Parliament (1640–1660). British mercantilism thus mainly took the form of efforts to control trade, and put a wide array of regulations in place by encouraging exports against imports.

Merchant and manufacturing capitalism developed considerably in Holland. Its strength rested on three pillars: the Dutch East India Company, the Bank of Amsterdam, and the merchant fleet. Six chambers of merchants gathered together in 1602 to form the Dutch East India Company. The company enjoyed a monopoly on trade with India, where it practiced the *mare clausum* (closed sea), forbidding India to the English, the Portuguese, and the French. In 1621 the Dutch West Indies Company was created. Holland defended the principle of the *mare liberum* (open sea) except in its own colonies, where it imposed the *mare clausum*.[50]

---

48. Frank, *Dependent Accumulation*, 14–17.

49. Smith, *Wealth of Nations*, 747, 760, 722.

50. Beaud, *History of Capitalism*, 25.

The Navigation Acts (1651) expelled foreign merchants from England's domestic trade. The Navigation Acts were a series of laws that restricted the use of foreign shipping for trade between England (after 1707 Britain) and its colonies, which started in 1651. Consequently, these were a factor in the Anglo-Dutch Wars, later, fueling the flames of the American Revolutionary War. The American colonies were forbidden to export woolen goods while tobacco and sugar were only exported to England or to other colonies.[51]

The transatlantic triangular trade operated during the seventeenth, eighteenth, and early nineteenth centuries. In the colonial phase regarding Europe's trade and the church's mission in Africa and Latin America, it is important to consider other prophetic voices along with Las Casas—for example, the Jesuits in Paraguay through the example of self-denial and asceticism (as the film *The Mission* shows), John Eliot (1604–90) in North America through his compassion for the Indians, the Herrnhuts in the eighteenth century, and the self-liberation of the slaves under Toussaint Louverture in French Saint-Domingue (present-day Haiti) between 1791 and 1798.[52]

However, the Protestant churches began to establish missionary societies along with trading companies. The ideological basis for the state-supported money-making economy finds its underpinning in Thomas Hobbes for mercantilism's absolutist phase and John Locke for its constitutional phase. Max Weber argued that capitalism has a special affinity with Protestantism, especially Calvinism, when it comes to the doctrine of election, the work ethic, thrift and Calvinist rationality in Holland, England, and especially Puritanism in the US. Weber's sociological study of the legacy of reformation deserves attention in regard to capitalist development and his analysis of disenchantment of the world and modernization. Martin Luther (1483–1546) and John Calvin (1509–1564) can be seen as contemporaries of Las Casas (1484–1566).

51. Ibid., 205.

52. Duchrow, *Europe*, 18–20.

2

The Protestant Ethic and the Spirit of Capitalism

MAX WEBER (1864–1920) RAISED an important yet controversial thesis, arguing that there is a selective affinity between Protestantism and the spirit of capitalism. In his sociological analysis, a Western form of rationality finds its echo in Protestant innerworldly asceticism. Calvin's theology of predestination is revealed as the ideological seedbed for creating a religious-ethical worldview conducive to the rise of capitalism. Calvin endorsed the charging of interest on loans and the relaxation on commerce. This chapter deals with Weber's sociological evaluation of Martin Luther and John Calvin and includes Weber's sociological study of Protestant religious ethics. It is certain that we also find in Calvin's writings a counterbalance to capitalism and a demand for social justice. However, the Puritan colonizers of New England pushed Calvin's ethical view (associated with the notion of predestination) to the extreme. Although we acknowledge the different social context between Calvin of Geneva and later Calvinists in North America, later Calvinists followed the reformer of Geneva in this respect.

CAPITALISM AND RATIONALITY

In *The Protestant Ethic and the Spirit of Capitalism*, Weber argues that there is a selective affinity between a certain doctrine of vocation associated with salvation and the conduct of life necessary for the accumulation of capital through commercial activity. Weber argues that the development of the Capitalist spirit was best understood as part of the development of rationalism through a process of economic survival of the fittest. This particular ethos of capitalism was lacking outside the Western world.[1]

A rationalized work ethic is coupled with the ideal of Christian asceticism. Without it, capitalism could not have developed as it did. Weber portrayed Benjamin Franklin as a typical representative of the spirit of capitalism. From Franklin's sayings—"time is money," "credit is money," and "money is of the prolific, generating nature"—Weber acknowledged a character of an ethically fashioned maxim for the conduct of life Franklin's moral attitudes were associated with utilitarianism which generated a logical deduction: Honesty is useful, because it assures credit. Punctuality, industry, and frugality are virtues.[2] The opponent of the spirit of capitalism was designated as economic traditionalism. A person with the spirit of traditionalism wished to live as he or she used to live and to earn that purpose. However, for the spirit of capitalism, labor became an end in itself, as did vocation, which was necessary to capitalism. It overcomes economic traditionalism.[3]

Weber further argues that the impulse to acquisition, or the pursuit of profit, gain or money has nothing to do with capitalism. This impulse is common to all conditions of people at all times and places. Unbridled avarice has no resemblance to the spirit of capitalism. Rather, capitalism is a restraint, or rational tempering of the irrational impulse or unlimited greed for gain. Thus Weber defines capitalism as "the pursuit of profit, and forever renewed profit, by means of continuous, rational, capitalistic enterprise."[4] The pursuit of profit is expected from utilizing opportunities for exchange. If the pursuit of capitalist acquisition is rational, the corresponding action is organized in regard to capital calculations. In every form of capitalist undertaking, the calculations and estimates affect the degree of rationality of capitalist acquisition. Capitalism or capitalist undertakings in this sense have existed in all the civilized countries of the world.

Nevertheless, the process of rationalization in the field of technique and economic organization determined the ideal of life of modern bourgeois society. Labor in the service of rational organization has undoubtedly

1. Weber, *Protestant Ethic*, 17–19.
2. Ibid., 51–51.
3. Ibid., 63.
4. Ibid., 17.

appeared as representative of the capitalist spirit. It was rationalized on the basis of rigorous calculation, in sharp contrast to the privileged traditionalism of the guild craftsman and the adventurers' capitalism. It was oriented toward the exploitation of political opportunities and irrational speculation.[5]

No country or age has ever experienced such absolute and complete dependence of its whole existence (the political, technical, and economic conditions of its life) on a specially trained organization of officials as has Western modernity. The most important functions of the everyday life of society came under the control of government officials who were technically, commercially and legally trained.[6] The same is true of capitalism. The West has developed capitalism in different types, forms and directions than have appeared elsewhere: "the rational capitalistic organization of free labor"[7] is not known outside the modern West.

The peculiarly modern Western form of capitalism has been influenced and developed by technical possibilities whose rationality depends on the calculability of technical factors, such as modern science based on mathematics and rational experiment applied to the capitalistic interests.[8] Seeing capitalism as a rational organization of labor, Weber has attempted to grasp the influence of certain religious ideas on the ethos of the economic system, or the development of an economic spirit. He deals with the relationship between the spirit of modern economic life and the rational ethic of ascetic Protestantism. Weber's sociological interpretation of Protestantism deserves attention.

Protestant Asceticism and the Capitalist Ethos

For Weber, Luther's concept of vocation, or calling, is not consistent with the spirit of capitalism. Luther's concept is traditional, and makes it difficult to establish a fundamental connection between worldly activity and religious principle. Luther saw the division of labor forces in contrast to Adam Smith. The fulfillment of worldly duties is the only way to live acceptable to the will of God in which every legitimate calling has the same worth in the sight of God. Luther's justification of worldly activity may be regarded as a platitude. Luther saw the main issue of vocation and work as

5. Weber, *Protestant Ethic*, 76.

6. Ibid., 16.

7. Ibid., 21.

8. Ibid., 24.

the thankful response to God's gracious salvation by faith. This view leads us to the service of one's neighbor within the framework of one's secular vocation. Weber does not regard Luther's position as similar to the spirit of capitalism embodied within a life orientation such as Franklin's.

Weber further argues that Luther's struggle against the Fuggers was based on his theological concept of vocation, which favored traditionalism. Luther's statements against usury revealed the predatory nature of capitalist acquisition; however, Weber regards Luther's critique as backward from a capitalist perspective.[9]

After the conflict known as the peasant rebellion, Luther tended to affirm that the objective historical order of things was to be regarded as the direct manifestation of the divine will. Luther's concept of calling, remaining traditionalistic, requires that the individual must accept the divine ordinance by accommodating to it. This position of Luther's, according to which each individual should remain in the station and calling in which God placed them, kept the worldly activity within the confinement of the established station of life. This economic traditionalism restrained Luther from establishing a new, fundamental connection between worldly activity and religious idea.[10]

However, unlike Luther, Calvin marked a new chapter in the ethical consideration of labor. Calvin saw work as the key task of a Christian who gives the glory to God alone. This so-called work ethic was co-opted by the bourgeois class to mean labor as an abstraction and finally wage labor. Calvin's theology of election in its subsequent development of Calvinism and the Puritan sects has underlined the spirit of capitalism. In short, every person had the divine obligation to work—regardless of the kind of work and the kind of economy. Indirectly, Calvinism contributed to what Weber characterizes as the "religious foundation of worldly asceticism."

Weber takes issue with the Calvinist doctrine of predestination as the most characteristic dogma in the Netherlands, England, and France of the sixteenth and seventeenth century. According to the Westminster Confession of 1647, by the decree of God, and for the manifestation of God's glory, some people and angels are predestinated into everlasting life, and others are foreordained to everlasting death (chapter III, "Of God's Eternal Decree"). Calvinist dogma contradicts Luther's theology of grace in his *Freedom of a Christian* and in the Augsburg Confession. For Calvin this *decretum horribile* is derived from the logical necessity of his theology.

9. Ibid., 83.
10. Ibid., 85.

Even Christ died only for the elect. This eliminates salvation through Word and sacraments.[11]

The influence of the doctrine of predestination is obvious in the elementary forms of conduct and attitudes toward life among Calvinist communities. The elected Christian lives in the world only to increase the glory of God by fulfilling God's commandments to the best of his/her ability. Paradoxically, the doctrine of predestination became foundational for the idea that it is necessary to prove one's faith through worldly activity. The social activity of the Christian is solely activity in *majorem gloriam Dei* which is shared by labor in a calling in service of the mundane life.

The emphasis on the absolute transcendence of God, which was different from the inward emotional piety of Lutheranism, led to ascetic action. Only the elect have the *fides efficax* and are able by virtue of regeneration and the resulting sanctification to increase the glory of God by good works. Good works are indispensable as a sign of election, becoming the technical means for removing the fear of damnation. The *possessio salutis* (the possession of salvation) becomes conditional on them. As a matter of fact, "God helps those who help themselves."[12] The Calvinist doctrine of double predestination and work ethic led to the ascetic action of Puritan morality in the sense of methodically rationalized economic-ethical conduct. The genuine Puritan even rejected all signs of religious ceremony and established an entirely negative attitude to all the sensuous and emotional elements in culture and in religion. It led to one of the roots of individualism. In this development, Puritanism is called the staunchest champion of the capitalistic ascetic movement.[13]

The Puritans had promoted the rationalization of the world through the elimination of magic as a means to salvation. Puritans ethically reinterpreted Descartes' principle *cogito ergo sum*, "I think, therefore I am," into "I work, therefore I am."[14] According to Weber, Calvinists were the seedbed of Capitalist economy and individualism. In the Calvinist view, the attainment of riches as a fruit of labor in a calling signaled God's election and blessing. For the later Puritans the process of sanctifying life could almost take on the character of a business enterprise. This methodical quality of ethical conduct distinguished Calvinism from Lutheranism,

---

11. Weber, *Protestant Ethic*, 102, 104.
12. Ibid., 115.
13. Ibid., 96, 105.
14. Ibid., 117, 8.

in that for Lutherans God's grace of justification stands out without ethical cooperation.[15]

THE PURITAN WAY TO RATIONALIZATION

In the course of subsequent Calvinism, the idea that is positive to worldly morality was added to the ethic founded in the doctrine of predestination: that is, a necessity of proving one's faith in worldly activity—thereby an aristocracy with its indelible character was established.[16] The concept of ascetic Protestantism results in the rationalization of ethical and economic conduct of life. A consequence was the doctrine of proving one's election which appeared in the case of the Calvinist Baptists. The Baptist denomination along with the strict Calvinists accomplished the religious rationalization of the world in the most extreme form. The influence of Calvinistic asceticism surrounded the Baptist sect in England and the Netherlands. The strict morality of the Baptists had followed the path prepared by the Calvinistic ethic.[17]

Weber deals with the relationship between asceticism and the spirit of capitalism. His sociological interest lies in examining the sense of methodically rationalized ethical conduct in Calvinism. However, Lutheranism was based on the doctrine of justifying grace. It lacks a psychological sanction of systematic ethical conduct in promotion of the methodical rationalization of life.[18] Against this direction, Calvinism based on practical sanctification appeared to be closer to the hard legalism and the active enterprise of bourgeois-capitalistic entrepreneurs.[19]

The high religious valuation of restless, continuous, systematic work in a worldly calling was regarded as the highest form of asceticism. At the same time, it was the surest and most evident proof of rebirth and genuine faith. This faith-type has a selective affinity to the spirit of capitalism. Richard Baxter, a Presbyterian and an apologist of the Westminster Synod, was the embodiment of Puritan ethics. His *Christian Directory* was the most complete compendium of Puritan ethics with emphasis on the discussion of wealth and its acquisition. His condemnation of the pursuit of money and goods was undertaken for the activity in service to increase

15. Weber, *Protestant Ethic*, 124–25.

16. Ibid., 121.

17. Ibid., 148–49.

18. Ibid., 128.

19. Ibid., 139.

the glory of God. Franklin's saying "time is money" was taken in a way that the lost hour was a lost opportunity to labor for the glory of God. We must work hard in our calling. Unwillingness to work was symptomatic of the lack of grace.[20] Baxter expressed that the providential purpose of the division of labor was known by its fruits, which were structured more than in Adam Smith's emphasis on the division of labor.[21] What God demanded was rational labor in a calling so that Puritans put emphasis on the methodical character of worldly asceticism. This was different from Luther's concept of calling which God has irreducibly assigned to the individual.[22]

In the concept of the usefulness of calling and its favor in the sight of God an important criterion is found in private profitability. God shows the elect a chance of profit, so that the elect must follow the call by taking advantage of this opportunity given by God. Thus the elect may work to be rich for the glory of God. Wealth as a performance of duty in a calling is actually enjoined. The emphasis on the ascetic importance of a calling provided an ethical justification of the modern specialized division of labor.[23] A religious consciousness of God's chosen people plays a central role in the general attitude of the Puritan. This gratitude for one's consciousness of God's chosen people penetrated the attitude of the Puritan middle class toward economic life and influenced the development of a capitalistic way of life.[24] The pursuit of riches for their own sake was condemned as covetousness or search for mammon. However, the attainment of wealth regarded as a fruit of labor in a calling was a sign of God's blessing. The religious valuation of restless, continuous, systematic work in a worldly calling was accepted as the highest means to asceticism and the surest and the most evident proof of rebirth and genuine faith. This aspect becomes the mechanism for the expansion of the spirit of capitalism. The inevitable consequence was accumulation of capital through ascetic compulsion to save, which in turn made possible the productive investment of capital.[25]

English Mercantilists of the seventeenth century acknowledged the superiority of Dutch capital to that of the English, because newly acquired Dutch wealth did not seek to transfer itself to feudal habits of life, investment in land, but was available for the possibility of capitalist investment.

20. Ibid., 158–59.
21. Ibid., 161.
22. Ibid., 162.
23. Ibid., 163.
24. Weber, *Protestant Ethic*, 166.
25. Ibid., 172.

In the early history of the North American Colonies there was the sharp contrast between adventurers and the middle class outlook of the Puritans. The adventurers wanted to establish plantations and live as feudal lords. However, the influence of the Puritan outlook extended and favored the development of a rational bourgeois economic life, remaining the cradle of the modern economic person.[26]

The leaders of Calvinism were the most passionate opponents of the type of politically privileged commercial and colonial capitalism which upheld the alliance of church and state with the fiscal-monopolistic form. Against this type, the Calvinists placed the individualistic motives of rational legal acquisition in terms of one's own ability and initiative. The Puritans (Prynne, Parker) rejected all connection with the large-scale capitalistic courtiers and projectors, by calling them an ethically suspicious class. One of the fundamental elements of the spirit of modern capitalism, which was rational conduct on the basis of the idea of the calling, was born from the spirit of Protestant asceticism, the content of the Puritan worldly asceticism.[27]

The Puritan wanted to work in a calling. When asceticism was carried out of monastic cells into everyday life, it began to dominate worldly morality and shape the modern economic order. This economic order, which was bound to the technical and economic conditions of machine production, determined the daily lives of all the individuals born into this mechanism. According to Baxter, the care for external goods should only lie on the shoulders of the saint like a light cloak. This cloak can be thrown aside at any moment. However, according to Weber, this cloak becomes an "iron cage."[28] The idea of religious and ethical duty in a calling "prowls about in our daily lives like the ghost of dead religious beliefs." In the Puritan divines, the pursuit of wealth tends to become associated with purely mundane passions giving it the character of sport.[29]

REFORMATION AND ECONOMIC ISSUES

According to Weber, a consequence of Western civilization is disenchantment with the world; where a Protestant ethic juxtaposed with a purposive form of rationality and instrumental reason, it resulted in lost meaning

26. Ibid., 174.
27. Ibid., 180.
28. Ibid., 180–82.
29. Ibid., 182.

and an "iron cage." Weber does not insist that reformers promoted the spirit of capitalism. Rather Weber hoped to demonstrate that the Calvinist doctrine of predestination nevertheless contained incentives in this direction.[30]

In the tradition of Ritschl and Karl Holl, Luther's concept of vocation has been interpreted as indifference to the spirit of capitalism. According to Troeltsch, Luther demanded obedience toward all natural ordinances which God created. Lutheran ethics dealt with the natural moral law contained in the Decalogue and aimed to show how ethical knowledge was useful in the following ways: (1) a preparation for repentance, (2) preservation of social order, (3) providing the basis of reason for the idea of the existence of God and of the moral government of the world, and finally (4) merging of the natural, moral knowledge into the unity of the Christian idea of love.[31] A Lutheran concept of natural law was entirely conservative, because Lutherans saw that society was shaped and produced by divine providence in the natural development of history. All order and welfare depended upon unconditional obedience toward authorities, glorifying whatever authority may happen to be dominant in a given time and context. Divine sanction on the status quo! Luther's Catechism must be read to see how the Christian ruler as God's representative was to serve the cause of love and faith, by using the office with all strictness, and in might and right. The Lutheran church was concerned only with the salvation of the soul and the interior individualist life of religion. Thus the Lutheran Church has never advanced further than the ideal of charity.[32]

In Weber's and Troeltsch's evaluation, Luther's antagonism toward the great merchants of his time should not be seen as prophetical or biblically grounded; rather, they argue that it was claimed as a part of the spirit of capitalism in an economic traditionalistic sense. Luther, on account of lack of ethical rationalism, was not capable of establishing "a new or fundamental connection between worldly activity and religious principle."[33]

Against this evaluation, a socialist economist, Fabiunke argues that Luther took the decisive step away from feudal Catholicism toward bourgeois-reformed Protestantism by recognizing the economic reality at the time of early capitalism.[34] A socialist criticism of Luther says that his

30. Bendix, *Max Weber*, 58.

31. Troeltsch, *Social Teaching,* 527.

32. Ibid., 529, 552, 568.

33. Weber, *Protestant Ethic*, 85.

34. Chung, *The Spirit of God Transforming Life*, 161–62.

dynamic understanding of theology and economy suffered from its natural scientific or moral confinement. Production, distribution, exchange, and consumption were valid, in Luther's theology, as a direct natural connection. From this perspective, Fabiunke regards Luther as an ethical thinker who was concerned for the poor in the period of early capitalism.[35]

Generally, the church's relationship with the poor has been understood only as a question of ethics or human charitable action, not as theology proper. Against the Lutheran doctrine of vocation in its traditional sense, however, Luther himself affirmed the significance of economic life in his theological reflections on God in the first commandment. Here we perceive that there is an inseparable connection between Luther's confessional theology and economic justice. Luther had to face the economic situation when early capitalism started to advance the property-money economy into more and more spheres of life.

Considering Luther's theological integration of the economic sphere, Weber and Fabiunke tend to sidestep Luther's prophetic theology of biblically grounded economic justice. Luther prophetically criticized the "Christian character" of capital accumulation at his time, clearly seeing the political-economic alliance between the Catholic Church, Charles V, and the Fuggers. Luther was more keenly aware of the irrational and negative side of early capitalism than Weber who acknowledges only the rational side of capitalistic organization. Luther's prophetic stance against mammon in the period of early capitalism constituted an essential motive for his church struggle with economic justice. The ethical issues of economic life come from our confessional and dogmatic engagement with God. Along this line we are suspicious of Weber's characterization of Luther as an economic traditionalist who failed "to establish the fundamental connection between worldly activity and religious principles." On the other hand, Fabiunke's thesis about the independent autonomy of the economy must be reversed, because he misunderstands Luther's concept of economy as God's "independent order" of creation through the so-called doctrine of two kingdoms. Where Luther dealt with economic issues in terms of the seventh commandment, he challenged the economic arena, because the economic realm should not be accepted as independently autonomous.

35. Fabiunke, *Luther*, 118–24.

Martin Luther: God versus Mammon

The question of God versus mammon in relation to the economy is for Luther—as with the Bible—inseparably bound up with the impact of economic structures and behavior on human community. As we have seen, the first table of the law relates to the second table, and vice versa (that is, the first commandment to the seventh commandment). Property and money are the very foundational elements of capitalism. Luther dealt with capitalism as a theological question. In his exposition of the seventh commandment, "You shall not steal," he described the social-ethical consequences of idolatry.

His critical stance against usury penetrates his theology from his early position in his "Small and Great Sermon on Usury" (1519/20) and "Trade and Usury" (1524) until the later writing of "Admonition to the Clergy that They Preach against Usury" (1540). Luther's texts on economic issues were written in the context of emerging capitalism, particularly on the problem of interest (usury) and the emerging international, monopolist trading and banking companies (Fugger, Wesler, etc.) during the Genoese-Spanish cycle of capital accumulation. This makes it necessary to first look at Luther's theological issue involved: the alternative of "God versus idol," or "God versus mammon." Contrasting God with mammon, Luther contends: "This is the most common idol on earth."[36] Idolatry is primarily "a matter of the heart."[37] It occurs when one places one's trust in something other than God as the source of life and wholeness. Although one has piled up great riches, these have turned to dust and blown away.[38] In his exposition of the seventh commandment, Luther states: "They all misuse the market in their own arbitrary, defiant, arrogant way, as if it were their privilege and right to sell their goods as high as they please without any criticism."[39]

Within the exposition of the seventh commandment, Luther makes a distinction between petty thieves and super-thieves. The former pilfer more locally and less significantly, while the latter are more politically and systematically significant, robbing and pilfering from whole countries. Here Luther's theological critique of the financial practices in broader scale becomes visible. Far from being picklocks and sneak thieves, the

36. Kolb and Wengert, *Book of Concord*, 387.
37. Ibid., 388.
38. Ibid., 391.
39. Ibid., 418.

super-thieves are called armchair bandits and highway robbers. "They sit in their chairs and are known as great lords and honorable, upstanding citizens," robbing and stealing "under the cloak of legality."[40] The free public market turned into nothing but a carrion pit and a robber's den. "The poor are defrauded every day, and new burdens and higher prices are imposed."[41]

According to Luther, doing good works against social and economic injustice and its violent structure is heartily acceptable and pleasing to God: "God lavishes upon them a wonderful blessing, and generously rewards us for what we do to benefit and befriend our neighbor."[42] Seen in Luther's time of church struggle, Weber's characterization of Luther on the whole line of traditionalistic backwardness remains specious and questionable. As Weber wrongly states, "Ethical principles for the reform of the world could not be found in Luther's realm of ideas. . . . Hence the world had to be accepted as it was, and this alone could be made a religious duty."[43]

Luther's concept of calling has little to do with fate, nor is it adapted to the status quo of economic reality. Luther's teaching of justifying grace was deeply connected with his notion of the justice of God.

As in the First Testament, we see the connection between idolatry and death mechanisms. Luther says the same not only about those who charge interest but also about trading companies when they manipulate prices through monopolies "just as if they were lords over God's creatures and immune from all the laws of faith and love."[44] The church also fell for this semblance of virtue, as did the theologians. Hence, Luther calls the Catholic theologian John Eck (1486–1543) a "plutologian" (expert on wealth), not a theologian, and says of the Roman Church: "Basically the whole spiritual governance is nothing but money, money, money. Everything is geared to money making. . . . "[45]

For Luther, the reality of early capitalism was not merely the subject matter of individual capitalists. Rather it subordinated everything to the coercion of the system through impoverishment, and functions—with the force of the idol system—as the domination structure. Mammon is, therefore, a concept with which Luther described and analyzed structural

40. Ibid., 417.
41. Ibid., 418.
42. Ibid., 420.
43. Weber, *Protestant Ethic*, 160.
44. "Trade and Usury," LW 45:270.
45. Marquardt, "Gott oder Mammon," 193.

injustice in the economic process of capital accumulation. Luther clearly discerned the process character of the system, and he portrayed the restless, independent expansion of capital and its development toward the domination of social history by way of the devouring capital. Self-generating capital in the economic free market system devoured the peasants and the citizens. Self-generating capital and its devouring function denoted the blind coercion of the modes of production, which became manifest in the logic of the laissez-faire system.

Luther argues that, like the devouring capital, the usurers were eating our bread and drinking our wine. They lived off the bodies of the poor. The world became one big whorehouse where the big thieves hang the little thieves.[46] Luther challenged pastors to condemn usury. Aware of the "Christian character" of capital accumulation, Luther observes "how skillfully Sir Greed can dress up to look like a pious man if that seems to be what the occasion requires, while he is actually a double scoundrel and a liar."[47]

Luther's treatise "Admonition to the Clergy that They Preach against Usury" (1540) was a classic example for the church's engagement with economic justice, including Luther's critique of colonialism. In parallel with Las Casas, Luther was a key figure to clearly discern the function and effect of the capitalist process, and prophetically to denounce its reality embedded within Christendom's ideology. Luther's critique of the powerful in mercantilist, monopoly capital is imbued with his confessional statement about God. The big banking and trading companies were increasingly pervading the whole of society—the system of the devouring capital. The decisive point of Luther's analyses and interpretations was the affirmation that the economic institution of the transnational banks and trading companies as such is in conflict with the will of God. Luther's Reformation initiated a concept of economic justice transcending a traditional idea of charity.[48]

JOHN CALVIN AND ECONOMIC ETHICS

It is argued that the capitalism of Geneva was incorporated into the later development of a Calvinist ethic. Calvin's cooperation with the economic administration of the State demonstrated an inner connection between

46. LW 21:180.

47. LW 21:183.

48. Linbeck, *Beyond Charity*.

economic progress and moral elevation.[49] The Protestant ethic of the calling was stamped with the Calvinistic adaptation of the capitalist system; it was rendered as a sign of the assurance of election and became service in one's calling. However, we do not need to neglect Calvin's anti-mammon stance in his political economic ethic.

Calvin had in mind the situation of refugees who came to Geneva needing financial assistance before they could make a profit in business themselves. Calvin allowed only productive credit for business purposes, not usury credit. Usury credit should not be used for living on interest. The rate of interest must not exceed a maximum. It must be fixed legally according to the needs of the situation. In Geneva, economic life was regulated in accordance with these principles. We find the protocols of the council and of the Consistory full of the fight against usury and the exploitation of the poor. Calvin's economic ethic, in the face of the modern development of capitalism, showed a tendency toward merging into a form of Christian social humanism.[50]

Calvin's scattered thoughts on the problem are best summed up in his commentary on Ezekiel 18:7–8. God wishes the good offices of life to be reciprocal, because God commands the individual not to oppress anyone. God has united people in the bonds of mutual society so that they must mutually perform good offices for each other.[51] Calvin states that to restore the pledge to the debtor (Ezek 18:7) is restricted to the poor and the needy since God forbids taking a pledge of a widow or a poor individual. The destruction of the poor person's house, which is forbidden by God, would be a type of robbery or violence. The Hebrew name "usury" is given to that which gnaws and consumes the miserable by degrees. The avaricious person uses many secret kinds of usury with many disguises. The prophet condemns increase by making a profit at the expense of others. Because usury is odious, no usurer is tolerated even in the profane state. The usurer must be expelled from all interaction with the fellow human. To take usury is almost the same as murder. Usury and interest must be blotted out from the memory of human beings.[52]

Calvin's concern about social economic life was an expression of biblically grounded Christian faith. He critically and analytically examined mundane problems in the light of biblical faith. Our faithfulness to the

---

49. Troeltsch, *Social Teaching*, 2:643–44.

50. Ibid., 649.

51. Calvin, *Commentaries on Ezekiel*, II. 224.

52. Ibid., 227–28.

gospel moves the Christian life toward community and solidarity with those in need. In line with the purpose of economic goods and human work Christian community must serve the common good of neighbors and society. Human work was basically assigned by God. The purpose of human occupations was useful and in service of the common good by sharing of the common benefits and seeking solidarity with humanity. The criterion of good work lies in benefiting the community and standing in service for the commonwealth. God will punish and chastise the cruelty of the rich who exploit the poor and do not compensate them for their labor. Calvin also was very critical of idlers and good-for-nothings. A refusal of one's vocation was an offense to God. Human work in a secular calling became creative and liberating, rather than an occasion of pain.[53]

In a sermon on Deuteronomy 24:14, Calvin denounced the exploitation of the poor by the rich. Calvin was keenly aware that self-interest or selfish desire drives people to exploit their fellow humans. God often uses the disobedience of workers as a means of judging and chastising exploiters. Calvin was not opposed to nonviolent protests and strikes. "What greater violence can we find," he writes, "than that which by hunger and poverty starves those who feed us by their labor? . . . We must note that Saint James adds that the cry of the poor reaches up to the ears of God so that we may know that the wrongs done to the poor will not remain unpunished."[54]

Calvin acknowledges the division of labor and commerce in a positive way concerning the parable of the talents. The goal of commerce was to promote what people need for mutual intercourse and solidarity, little to do with fraud and dishonesty. Calvin denounced speculation, cornering, and monopolizing as the principal forms of a vitiated and distorted economic order. In his exposition of 2 Cor 8:13–15, Calvin states that according to God's will there should be proportions and equality among human beings. Calvin understands Paul's term "equality" as equality of proportional right in Aristotle's sense.[55] There may not be some in affluence while others are in indigence. Concerning the system of proportional right in the church, this mutual contribution produces a befitting symmetry, although gifts are distributed unequally. Each individual is to provide for the needy according to his means.

53. Biéler, *Social Humanism of Calvin*, 45–46.

54. Ibid., 49.

55. Calvin, *Commentary on Corinthians*, 294.

Consequently, no one has too much or too little. We find an example of this equality in Exodus (16:18); Moses prohibited his fellow Israelites from hoarding it, either from excessive greed or from distrust. Riches heaped up at the expense of one's brethren are accursed and will soon perish in connection with the ruin of the owner. It is unlawful for the rich to live in greater elegance than the poor. Observing equality, no one is to be allowed to starve, and no one is to hoard their abundance at the cost of defrauding others.[56]

To restore the genuine function of the economic relation, Calvin spoke in favor of the intervention of the state in terms of regulating commercial and traffic operations; it should facilitate the process of trade and regularity of exchange for the commonwealth. In this regard, the task of the civil government sees to it that "men breathe, eat, drink and are kept, his property safe and sound, and "that honesty and modesty may be preserved among men."[57] In Geneva the state was openly involved in economic enterprise as it regulated buying and selling and making contracts for the protection or search of the common good of society. What is unique in Calvin's economic ethic is his consideration of the ancient Jewish law (Jubilee Year) in which a periodic redistribution of lands and liberation from debts should be well kept. Thus property never became a source of social oppression through individual hoarding and general involvement in debt. Riches are far from desirable in Geneva, rather they would be pernicious. The sumptuary laws inspired by Calvin's economic ethic were introduced in Geneva by Calvin's successors.[58]

Calvin's model of the redistribution of the manna among the Israelites maintains that the rich are the ministers of the poor, and the poor are the receivers of God, the vicars of Christ, or the proxies or solicitors of God.[59] Private property is really private, but it should be used for the common good of society. Insisting on the mutual communication of wealth within society, Calvin runs toward mutual emancipation and solidarity—the rich from selfishness and the poor from slavery. Calvin's economic and ethical way has little to do with the possessive market individualism or Puritan asceticism that Weber envisioned in the case of Benjamin Franklin or Richard Baxter. Calvin's economic concern is expressed in terms of *de chacun selong ses capacities à chacun selon ses besoins* ("from each according to ability, to each according to need"). As St. Paul states, "The one who had

56. Ibid., 297.

57. Calvin, *Institutes* 2. IV.XX.13.

58. Graham, *Constructive Revolutionary,* 110–15.

59. Biéler, *La Pensée,* 327.

much did not have too much, and the one who had little did not have too little" (2 Cor 8:15). The church's participation in the economic order is to distribute private property in the service of social humanism, encouraging the intervention of the state in this direction.[60] In his commentary on 2 Cor 8:15 Calvin argues that the rich must consider that their abundance, whether inherited or procured by industry and effort, should not be used in intemperance or excess. But their wealth must be used in relieving the necessities of the poor.

In our discussion of two reformers, it is obvious how strongly they looked at the Scripture and only accepted restricted elements of a capitalist form of economy with many cautionary rules. Capital accumulation and possessive market individualism are not simply accepted but linked to tight conditions. Any judgment is oriented to the living conditions of the weak. The state is invoked to offer a counterweight to the autonomy of the money-accumulation mechanism. The church is called to corporately reject and offer resistance to what is not compatible with biblical rules and social justice in the public sphere. The legacy of Reformation can inspire the Protestant church today to promote the church's mission and evangelization in the spirit of economic justice and solidarity with the poor.

CRITICAL EXAMINATION OF WEBER'S SOCIOLOGY OF RELIGION

Weber defines sociology as a science whose object is to interpret the meaning of social action. Thereby, sociology gives a causal explanation (in terms of selective affinity) of the relationship between the action and the effects. Weber's interpretive sociology which aims to interpret meaning takes a rational form by reliving an experience. Rational certainty in the interpretation of the meaning of social action can be intellectually understood in its entirety. Every interpretation of a rationally directed purposive action entails the highest possible extent of certainty as compared to the emphatic certainty, which is experienced in one's relived imagination. A sociological model of an ideal type enables one to understand the real action.

When the type (or an ideal type) is constructed according to a fully rationally purposive action, it is to be understood with complete certainty. An interpretive strategy reads: "It is not necessary to be Caesar in order

60. Ibid., 336, 354.

to understand Caesar."[61] Weber relates ideas and interests in terms of the concept of selective affinity. There is no preestablished correspondence between the content of an idea and the interests of those who follow. By a selective process of elements, Weber finds their relevance in an affinity between the autonomous role of ideas and the origin of modern capitalism.

An interpretive grasp of meaning (or pattern of meanings) is constructed scientifically for the pure or ideal type, which is called ideal-typical meaning. The ideal types of systems "exhibit the internal coherence and unity which belongs to the most complete possible adequacy on the level of meaning."[62] Human action is effected by the rational pursuit of economic goals. An ideal-typical model is constructed on the assumption of a fully rational pursuit of a goal. In this light Weber has attempted to examine the relationship between Calvinistic Puritanism and the capitalist spirit. Western rationalism is preceded by religious rationalization by way of the spread of purposive-rational action orientations into the economic and administrative spheres of life.[63]

Weber wanted to conceive of the modernization of Western society as the result of a universal-historical process of rationalization. In dealing with the process of disenchantment by the analysis of the history of religion, Weber likes to use Friedrich Schiller's phrase "the disenchantment of the world." In the institutionalization of purposive-rational action, an administration operating in such purposive-rational way is calculable. In a universal-historical perspective, the progress toward the bureaucratic state and administration according to rationally established laws and regulations is closely related to modern capitalist development. The existence of a legal and administrative system can function rationally, calculated like the expected performance of a machine.[64]

Religious Rationalization and Ethical Conduct of Life

Weber focuses on understanding the influence of certain religious ideas on the development of an economic spirit, or the ethos of an economic system. Weber's study *The Protestant Ethic and the Spirit of Capitalism* demonstrates the connection of the spirit of modern economic life with

61. Weber, *Selections,* 8.
62. Ibid., 23.
63. Habermas, *Theory of Action,* 1, 157, 167.
64. Weber, *Economy and Society,* 1394.

the rational ethics of Protestantism. Weber's approach has implication for the study of culture since his use of the term ethos emphasizes that each individual's participation in the society involves a personal commitment both to the ethical conduct of life and to the economic and ideal interests of a particular status group.[65]

His interpretive sociology has no intention to replace a one-sided materialist interpretation of cultural and historical causes with an equally one-sided idealist interpretation. Sociological method becomes interpretive to create meaning of the ideal type in the analysis of sociocultural process of modernization. Material and ideal interests in religious interpretation of the world also rule and shape human ethical-economic conduct. Although both material and ideal interests are equally possible, neither of them must be the conclusion of social research and investigation.[66]

There is an interplay between ideas and interests at the level of society as well as at the level of culture. In this process of interplay the universal-historical process of disenchantment marches on. In the modern West, there exists a completely different form of capitalism. The rational capitalist organization of free labor and its enterprise is directed to the opportunities presented by the market; it goes along with the separation of the household from the place of work as well as the practice of rational bookkeeping.[67] Religious rationalization is traced with a view to the rise of the capitalist economic ethic. Thus we may recognize in Weber's sociology that the ethical rationalization of worldviews entails a rationalization of legal consciousness as well.[68]

The emergence of capitalism in the West is characterized by the bourgeois enterprise coupled with the rational organization of free labor. An essential condition of the rationality is the calculability of the technically decisive factors which are the foundations of exact calculation.[69] Social rationalization is institutionalized in the capitalist enterprise in which a labor force is integrated into a systematically organized production process. A legal system and a state administration ensure the calculability for capitalist business and enterprise. A state apparatus provides sanctions for the law and further institutionalizes purposive-rational action orientations in public administration. In the study of the Protestant ethic, an ethic of religious conviction systematizes all spheres of life and

65. Bendix, *Max Weber*, 260–61.

66. Weber, *Selections*, 172.

67. Ibid., 336.

68. Habermas, *Theory of Communicative Action*, 1:199.

69. Weber, *Selections*, 338.

grounds purposive-rational action orientations in a value-rational way. Institutionalization of purposive-rational action resulted from the ethical rationalization of worldview.[70]

According to Sombart, the genesis of capitalism is distinguished concerning the satisfaction of needs and acquisition which are the two great leading principles in economic history. In the case of the satisfaction of needs, the attainment of goods is necessary to meet personal needs. In the case of acquisition, a struggle for profit is the end of controlling the form and direction of economic activity. The economy of needs is identified with economic traditionalism. In accordance with Sombart's concept of acquisition, Weber describes the spirit of modern capitalism as the ethos seeking profit rationally and systematically as embodied in the example of Benjamin Franklin.[71]

Weber maintained that the institutionalization of purposive-rational economic action was explained in terms of the Protestant vocational ethic and then the modern legal system. A modern vocational culture was identified as the implementation of an ethic of conviction which generated important consequences for establishing the capitalist enterprise. Nevertheless, Weber's study of the capitalist spirit is methodologically restricted with emphasis on an analysis of the motivational and institutional embodiment of religious ideas (investigation from above). It needs to relate an analysis of external factors (colonialism) and internal economic dynamics (investigation from below) to the study of the relationship between religious ideas and material interests. A type methodology of selective affinities between the Protestant ethic and the spirit of capitalism states that the methodical conduct of life in Calvinism penetrated all spheres and phases of life, rationalized in this everyday life and dominated for the glory of God on earth. This ethical rationalization has brought forth innerworldly asceticism as well as the methodical conduct of life in the early capitalist enterprise.

At issue in Weber's sociology of religion is not the ethical doctrine of a religion, but the form of ethical conduct upon which premiums are placed. Such conduct forms one's specific ethos in the sociological sense. Its specific ethos is the ethos of the modern bourgeois middle classes. This conduct in the world of Puritanism is a certain methodical, rational way of life, paving the way toward the spirit of modern capitalism. The premiums are placed upon proving oneself before God in the sense of attaining salvation. Not the guild, but the methodical way of life of the ascetic sects gave

---

70. Habermas, *Theory of Communicative Action*, 1:219.

71. Weber, *Protestant Ethic*, 64.

birth to the modern bourgeois capitalist ethos; it legitimated the economic individualist impulses of the modern capitalist ethos.

RESPONSIBLE ETHIC AND POLYTHEISM

In "Religious Rejections of the World and Their Directions," Weber further argues that the religious ethic of brotherliness that the prophetic religions had developed comes into contradiction with the unbrotherly, innerworldly orders of life. The ethics of brotherliness became the fundamental imperatives of all ethically rationalized religions: to help widows and orphans in distress, to care for the sick and impoverished brother of the faith, and to give alms.[72] The more the world of the modern, rational, capitalist economy follows its own immanent laws, the less it becomes accessible to a religious ethic of brotherliness.

At this point Weber's critique of Protestantism is not negligible. Puritanism renounced the universalism of love, deviated from the direction of a universalist brotherhood. It rationally bound all work in the world to serving God's will by testing one's own state of grace. Puritanism accepted the routinization and objectification of the economic cosmos. With the whole world, it devalued the economic cosmos as creaturely and depraved. At bottom, Puritanism renounced the idea that salvation was a goal attainable by everybody. Salvation is renounced in favor of a groundless and only particular grace. In fact, this standpoint of unbrotherliness is no longer a genuine religion of salvation.[73] The ascetic ethic of vocation was regressed with its egocentric foreshortening, particularism of grace, and conformity to the unbrotherliness of the capitalist economy. The more rationally the idea of salvation is construed, the more the imperatives issue from the ethic of reciprocity among neighbors. Externally, they are heightened into a communism of loving brethren, while internally to the disposition of caritas, that is love for the sufferer, for one neighbor, for humankind, and finally for one's enemy.[74]

However, the Protestant ethic is a distorted, highly irrational embodiment, arguing that the commandment of God should be imposed upon the world by means of violence. The world is subject to violence and ethical barbarism. This vocational ethic resists the obligation of the religious ethic of brotherliness in the interest of God's cause. The salvation

72. *From Max Weber*, 330.

73. Ibid., 332–33.

74. Ibid., 330.

aristocracies of Puritanism contradict the genuine ethic of brotherliness, which feels responsible before God for the souls of all. An organic social ethic that is dominated by a cosmic, rational demand for brotherliness is in contrast to the mystic and more sharply to the idea of calling in innerworldly asceticism.[75]

Unfortunately, Weber did not manage to develop this critical-universalistic side of the Christian ethic of brotherliness as an alternative to a rationally conceptualized ethic of calling. Rather, he followed his analysis of the subsequent fate of the Protestant ethic of calling in the course of capitalist development. Insofar as the Protestant ethic of calling fulfills the necessary conditions for the motivational basis of purposive-rational action,[76] it entails the fashioning of an environment that threatens to finally ruin the rational side of the Protestant ethic. Ethical religiosity has appealed the rational knowledge and followed its own autonomous and innerworldly norms. However, rational knowledge had to reject this claim. Thus there is an irreconcilable opposition between the cosmos of natural causality and the postulated cosmos of ethical causality. The intellect also created an unbrotherly aristocracy, which is based on the possession of rational culture and independent of all personal ethical qualities.[77] Nevertheless, as an ethical sociologist Weber attempts to demonstrate the limits of the religious ethic of brotherliness as an ethic of conviction.

Weber made arguments for the superiority of ethics of responsibility over against ethics of conviction. Conduct of life can be oriented toward an ethic of ultimate ends or toward an ethic of responsibility. This distinction of Weber's does not mean that an ethic of ultimate ends is identical with irresponsibility and an ethic of responsibility with unprincipled opportunism. The adherent of an ethic of ultimate ends goes to pieces on the problem of the justification of means by ends; it suddenly ends in a chiliastic prophet. He or she cannot endure under the ethical irrationality of the world: undeserved suffering, unpunished injustice, and hopeless stupidity. "From good comes only good; but from evil only evil follows."[78] In fact, an ethic of ultimate ends and an ethic of responsibility are not in absolute contrasts, but in complementary relationship. The ethic in unison constitutes a genuine person who can have a calling for politics. A mature

75. Ibid., 338.

76. Habermas, *Theory of Communicative Action*, I. 228.

77. *From Max Weber*, 355. See further Habermas, *Theory of Communicative Action*, 1:229.

78. Ibid., 122.

person is aware of responsibility for the consequences of his/her conduct while really feeling such responsibility with heart and soul.[79]

Weber diagnoses critically the development of capitalist society since the late eighteenth century in the thesis of a loss of meaning and a loss of freedom. Weber finds inspiration in the voice of the elder Mill who said that if one proceeds from pure experience, one arrives at polytheistic values. This is shallow in formulation and sounds paradoxical, and yet there is truth in it.[80] The world of the ancient was not yet disenchanted of its gods and demons, and we are likewise enthralled nowadays, albeit in a different sense. "Only the bearing of man has been disenchanted and denuded of its mystical but inwardly genuine plasticity."[81]

Weber sees the sign of the age in a new polytheism. The struggle among the gods takes on the depersonified, objectified form of an antagonism in the irreducible orders of value and life. The rationalized world has become meaningless. Over these gods and their struggles fate holds sway. A new polytheism is related to the thesis of a loss of meaning, that is, the experience of nihilism Nietzsche had dramatized. Reason was split up into a plurality of value spheres and threatened to ruin its own universality.[82] Before "the stream of immeasurable events," which "flows unendingly towards eternity" and constitutes "the eternally inexhaustible flow of life,"[83] human beings can discover and choose gods rather than search for the one God directing the flow.

As Weber further argues, the grandiose rationalism of an ethical and methodical conduct of life has dethroned this polytheism in favor of the 'one thing that is needful.' However, "many old gods ascend from their graves; they are disenchanted and hence take the form of impersonal forces."[84] They strive to gain power over human life, resuming their eternal struggle with one another. Rebellion against these gods would amount to Christianity's deconstruction of polytheism in favor of the one thing that is needful. Gods and demons hold sway over the world and the gods are equal. Rebellion against them makes things worse.

In the rise of a new polytheism, in which the struggle among the gods assumes the depersonalized and objectified form of antagonism, Weber sees the sign of the age. Over these gods and their struggles among

79. Ibid., 127.

80. Ibid., 147.

81. Ibid., 148.

82. Habermas, *Theory of Communicative Action*, 1:247.

83. Weber, *From Max Weber*, 147.

84. Ibid., 148–49.

irreducible orders of value and life, it is fate—not science—that holds sway. Weber's formulation of a new polytheism accounts for the loss of meaning associated with Nietzsche's experience with nihilism. The practical rationality, which binds purposive-rational action orientation in a value-rational manner, can find its place only in the personality of the solitary individual. Out of the loss of the substantial unity of reason comes an inevitable struggle with the polytheism of depersonalized gods and demons.

An attempt to send the old gods back to their graves would be likened to an attempt at establishing heaven on earth. This millennial, socialist attempt will fail; it amounts to transforming earth into hell. For Weber, good can produce evil just as evil can produce good. In other words, there is an unbridgeable gap between "be" and "ought to be" in which a teleological idea of historical progress is rejected. When the old, disenchanted gods reappear in the form of impersonal powers locked in conflict with one another, Weber sees a clash, not only between classes, but also between worldviews. Disenchantment with religious-metaphysical worldviews is coupled with the emergence of modern structures of consciousness and has brought progress and liberation as well as the inevitable bondage of the iron cage. It is certain that Weber conveys an impression of speaking out against the pessimistic prediction of a reification of the subsystems into an iron cage in his late essays ("Politics as a Vocation," "Science as a Vocation," "Religious Rejection of the World and Their Directions"). Nonetheless, Weber's endorsement is an acknowledgment of the powerful reality of impersonal forces and polytheism rather than de-dramatizing and transcending the reality of lordless powers or the iron cage.

According to Weber we do not know who will live in this cage in the future, whether at the end of this tremendous development new prophecies will arise, or whether there will be a powerful rebirth of old ideas and ideals.[85] Weber has expectations for the last men of this cultural development: "Specialists without spirit, sensualists without heart; this nullity imagines that it has attained a level of civilization never before achieved."[86]

Weber's pessimism is seen paralyzed in his evaluation of religious ideas and ethical conduct, so he remains an individual liberalist in matters pertaining to socioeconomic reform in contrast to the reformers critically engaged in the public sphere for the sake of the gospel and the fragile, the vulnerable, and the oppressed.

---

85. Weber, *Protestant Ethic*, 182.
86. Ibid.

3

Political Right and
Economic Freedom

IN THE PREVIOUS TWO chapters we discussed the historical genesis and
development of Capitalism within the framework of the world-economy,
colonialism, and the rationalization process. Tracing the economic movement of Christian theology and mission, a critical study was undertaken
in regard to Christian mission and colonialism in the New World and
also Weber's thesis of the Protestant ethic and capitalist spirit. Along with
the capitalist development of world-economy and sociological analysis
of religious ideas, it is necessary to examine how closely the philosophical ideas of individual rights, civil society, and freedom have been intertwined with the economic individualism of capitalism.

The next few chapters will deal with political theory and economic
analysis which will serve as background material for further consideration
of the church's role and responsibility in the final chapter and the epilogue.
This chapter begins with the Western intellectual tradition of civil society
and economic theory of individualism and market in terms of Hobbes,
Locke, Rousseau, and Hegel.

THOMAS HOBBES AND POSSESSIVE MARKET SOCIETY

Thomas Hobbes (1588–1679) was an English philosopher who conceptualized the social, political, and economic conditions of British society in
light of a social contract. *De Cive* was the first elaboration of his political

view, *Leviathan* was the second. The English Civil War broke out in 1642. When the Royalist party began to decline in the middle of 1644, there was an exodus of the king's supporters to the European Continent. Many came to Paris and were known to Hobbes who stayed there.

The company of the exiled royalists led Hobbes to produce an English book to set forth his theory of civil government in relation to the political crisis resulting from the war. The State, according to Hobbes, may be regarded as a great artificial "man" or monster (Leviathan). However, the first effect of his publication of *Leviathan* was to sever his link with the exiled royalists in Paris, forcing him to appeal to the revolutionary English government for protection. The secularist spirit of his book greatly angered both Anglicans and French Catholics. His book *Leviathan* was published in London in 1651, and established the foundation for most of Western political philosophy from the perspective of social contract theory. Hobbes' doctrine is a vindication of the absolute rights of the sovereign power. His account of human nature as self-interested cooperation has proved to be an enduring theory in the study of the market society.

LEVIATHAN AND SOCIAL CONTRACT

In *Leviathan*, Hobbes set out his doctrine of the foundation of states and legitimate governments—based on social contract theories. Much of the book is occupied with demonstrating the necessity of a strong central authority to avoid the evils of discord and civil war. Hobbes' account of the social contract is deduced from his view of human nature. The restless desire of everyone for assurance has led to most complete insecurity.

Hobbes postulates what life would be like without government, a condition that he calls the state of nature. In the state of nature, each person would have a right, or license, to everything in the world. A general inclination of humankind implies a perpetual and restless desire for power until power will cease only in death. This inevitably leads to conflict, a "war of every man against every man" (*bellum omnium contra omnes*).[1] Because the condition of the human being is a condition of war of everyone against everyone, there can be no security for anyone. Everyone should strive for peace, but when one fails, one may seek and use the advantages of war. Contract without the sword is mere word, having no strength to secure an individual at all.[2]

1. Hobbes, *Leviathan*, 105.
2. Ibid., 107, 113, 139.

According to Hobbes, the only way to establish a common power is to confer all the powers and strength upon one man or one assembly of people; this may reduce all wills, by plurality of voices, into one will. This is more than consent or concord; rather, it is a real unity of them all with the same person which is made by covenant of everyone with everyone. As Hobbes states, "I Authorize and give up my Right of Governing my selfe, to this Man, or to this Assembly of men, on this condition, that Thou give up thy Right to him, and Authorize all his Actions in like manner."[3]

The multitude so united in one person is called a commonwealth, *civitas* in Latin; this is the generation of the great Leviathan or of the mortal God. To this we owe our peace and defense under the immortal God. When this one person uses the strength and means of all for their peace and common defense, the person is called sovereign, entailing sovereign power greater than all the subjects. In the sovereignty is the foundation of honor.[4]

The titles of honor, appointment of order of place and dignity, execution of the laws, etc, are the rights which make the essence of sovereignty. The power of coining money, disposing the estate and persons of infant heirs, having preemption in markets, all other statute prerogatives including the protection of the subjects may be transferred by the sovereign.[5] For the standpoint of struggle in the market, Hobbes advocates for the political necessity of a sovereign ruler. If the market society is not degenerated into the struggle of all against all, a single sovereign force is needed. Sovereignty is indivisible and unlimited, and the power of the authority cannot be limited by appeal to the law of nature, the church or the voice of conscience. Law must be obeyed because it is the command of the sovereign.[6]

At this point we attend to the economic foundation of Hobbes' political theory. Hobbes' economic view was explored by Macpherson, who argues that *Leviathan* can only be properly understood when the relationship between the economic facts of England in Hobbes' time and its political system is taken into account.[7] Hobbes writes, "Honorable is whatsoever possession, action, or quality, is an argument and signe of Power. . . . Riches, are honorable; for they are Power. . . . Covetousness of

3. Ibid., 143.

4. Ibid., 143–44, 153. Cf. Ryan, "Hobbes," in *Cambridge Companion*, 208–45.

5. Hobbes, *Leviathan*, 152.

6. Ibid., xxviii.

7. Macpherson, *Political Theory*.

great Riches, and ambition of great Honours, are Honourable; as signes of power to obtain them . . ."[8]

From this statement of Hobbes, Macpherson acknowledges the essential characteristics of the competitive market. Human desire in striving for unlimited power over others is only tenable for those who are in a universally competitive society.[9] He argues that England at Hobbes' time was "essentially a possessive market society,"[10] or a bourgeois market society. Possessive market society is defined as the society in which human labor becomes a commodity. Where human labor has become a market commodity, market relations shape and permeate all social relations. This possessive market society is similar to the concept of bourgeois or capitalist society used by Marx, Weber and Sombart; it is in contrast to a society based on custom and status as well as in contrast to a society of independent producers.[11] Hobbes' political theory is associated with this economic foundation of possessive market society. However, Hobbes in his political analysis of society sidesteps "the centripetal force of a cohesive bourgeois class within the society."[12]

The human being is identified as a calculating individual motivated by desire and its fulfillment. Humans are vulnerable to the struggle of all against all, owing to differing types and degrees of desire. To escape this state of war, people in the state of nature accede to a social contract and establish a civil society. Civil society or possessive market society has two essential features: "the pre-eminence of market relations and the treatment of labor as an alienable possession."[13] In this society individuals are economically free agents; they make contracts enforced by custom or law. All individuals act rationally in the economic sphere; some have unsatisfied appetites for pleasure or power while some are better endowed than others.[14] English society in the seventeenth century was the basis for shaping and erecting Hobbes' political theory.

In contrast to Macpherson's argument, Hobbes also argued that in England in 1650 people earned their living from agriculture based on the old communal arrangements (restricting farming to traditional crops

8. Hobbes, *Leviathan*, 70–71.

9. Macpherson, *Political Theory*, 38, 45.

10. Ibid., 62.

11. Ibid., 48.

12. Ibid., 56.

13. Ibid., 48–49.

14. Ibid., 46–53.

and ancient methods).[15] However, it is certain that mercantilism was the dominant school of thought throughout the early modern period (from the sixteenth to the eighteenth century). Domestically, this led to some of the first instances of significant government intervention and control over the economy. Internationally, mercantilism encouraged the many European wars of the period and fueled European colonialism. Mercantilism helped create trade patterns such as the triangular trade in the North Atlantic. Colonies were sources of raw materials and exclusive markets for developing English society as a possessive market society.

From the beginning of the seventeenth century, England was engaged in colonial expansion. The British East India Company was created in 1600. The English sovereigns down to 1650 established and enforced the law of contract, coined money, and charted colonial adventures toward Asia. All values and even the concept of justice began to be reduced to a market society. The emerging class of bourgeoisie would endorse absolutism and also object to it according to their common interest. A model of the possessive market society which underscores Hobbes' political theory of the sovereign state can be sharpened in the economic transition of English society toward the industrial revolution and burgeoning colonialism. A mercantilist is required in the development of a possessive market society.

In chapter 24 of *Leviathan* Hobbes regarded labor as a commodity. The superfluous commodities supply the wants at home, by importation of foreign goods—either by exchange, just war, or labor. Human labor is a commodity exchangeable for benefit; the commonwealth increased in power, partly by the labor of trading and partly by selling the products made from materials brought in from other places.[16]

Hobbes recognized that human labor becomes a "commodity" exchangeable for benefit in his time, and further colonial trade belongs to the commonwealth. Individuals distribute that which they can spare and transfer their property mutually one to another, by exchange and mutual contract. The commonwealth appoints all kinds of contracts between subjects as to "buying, selling, exchanging, borrowing, lending, letting, and taking to hire."[17]

According to Hobbes, society is a population beneath a sovereign authority, to whom all individuals in that society cede their natural rights

15. Letwin, "Foundations" in *Hobbes and Rousseau*, 143–64.

16. Hobbes, *Leviathan*, 209–10.

17. Ibid., 213–14.

for the sake of protection. Any abuses of power by this authority are to be accepted as the price of peace. The self-perpetuating sovereign (an assembly or a monarch) permits the economic battle for wealth and power by non-violent means. Everybody can seek power over others without destroying the society. Hobbes' political, economic concern must not be misunderstood as a model of today's welfare society.[18]

The "long" sixteenth century (1450–1640) was the first formative stage of the capitalist world economy. The British East India Company started to bring return on investment in the form of plunder and tribute from India; no other investment could ever have generated such profit in comparable size, industrial or otherwise. The English metal industries expanded rapidly during the Genoese-led financial expansion of the late sixteenth and early seventeenth centuries.[19] This picture of English society is a model similar to the society in which Hobbes lived. In particular, the doctrine of separation of powers is rejected: the sovereign must control civil, military, judicial, and ecclesiastical powers. There is no property without sovereignty. The necessity of a sovereign to guarantee contracts corresponds to Hobbes's notion of the calculating individuals involved in mercantilist-bourgeois enterprise.

His political economy justifies colonialism by just war; a relationship between metropolis and colonies is established so that the right of colonies (saving honor and league with their metropolis) depends on their license by which the sovereign authorized them to be planted.[20] As to the constitution of the state Hobbes was an absolutist. As to the economic policy of government he was on the threshold from mercantilism to possessive market society. Hobbes was indifferent to the fact that the policy of Europe regarding colonies brought nothing to the prosperity of the colonized.

JOHN LOCKE AND THE SOCIAL CONTRACT

John Locke (1632–1704) is widely regarded as one of the most influential Enlightenment thinkers, classical republicans, and contributors to liberal theory. He is called the theorist of the English Revolution of 1688 and also a main source of the ideas of the American Revolution of 1776. Locke's religious background was Puritan and his political sympathy was with Parliament, for which Locke's father fought in the Civil War. The year 1660

18. Ryan, "Hobbes," in *Cambridge Companion*, 235.

19. Arrighi, *Twentieth Century*, 209–10.

20. Hobbes, *Leviathan*, 216.

saw the restoration of the Stuarts, but not in the sense of the early Stuart absolutism. This year was a watershed in English political experience and event; troubles lay ahead. Intellectuals such as Descartes in his *Discourse on Method* and Newton in *Principia Mathematica* (1687) generated much of the change in the intellectual and scientific world. Locke was an ardent reader of their works.

Locke composed the bulk of the *Two Treatises of Government* to defend the Glorious Revolution of 1688, and also to counter the absolutist political philosophy of Thomas Hobbes. The *Second Treatise* was directed against the line of argument for absolutism that Hobbes' *Leviathan* represented. When the book appeared, a victorious bourgeois revolution of 1648–49 culminated in the Glorious Revolution of 1688. This revolution reduced the king to a constitutional monarch who was put in place by Parliament. It promulgated the fundamental right of *habeas corpus* (1679) and the Bill of Rights (1689) that emphasized human equality before the law with Parliament as the representative of the people and the guarantee of private property.

England was in a phase of founding its empire in rivalry with Spain and the Netherlands. English immigrants were in the process of conquering North America. England acquired the monopoly of global slave trading between Africa and Spanish America. Given the colonial expansion and international trade, a new political theory was needed. Early in the eighteenth century Locke's books were circulated in the colonies. This influence is reflected in the American Declaration of Independence, as well as state Declarations and Constitutions. Locke's individualism, his glorification of property rights, and his love of conscience remain indelible factors interwoven into the political, economic and social fabric of American life.[21] In political theory and practice the American Revolution drew its inspiration from the parliamentary struggle of the seventeenth century and Locke's political theory. Locke's *Second Treatise of Government* (1690) marks his thinking of property, democracy, and human rights.

In the study of Locke, the dimension of radicalism can be seen in one's engagement with revolutionary action which constitutes an important part of political activity.[22] However, in 1671 he was a major investor in the English slave-trade. This conflict between his writings and his economic activities has led to accusations of hypocrisy. His concern for liberty could seem to extend only to English capitalists.

21. Locke, *Second Treatise* xx.
22. Ashcraft, *Revolutionary Politics*, xvii.

LOCKE'S POLITICAL THEORY AND CIVIL SOCIETY

Locke grounded his political theory on social contract theory. Thomas Hobbes saw that humankind would be in a constant state of war and insecurity without the restraints of government. However, Locke believed that human nature was characterized by equality, freedom, reason, and tolerance. The rationality ascribed to humankind was the common rule and measure that God has granted.

Locke states that "all men are naturally in, and that is a state of a perfect freedom to order their action and dispose of their possessions and persons, . . . within the bounds of the law of nature, without asking leave or depending upon the will of any other man."[23]

This state of equality is reciprocal without subordination or subjection. The reason which is the law of nature teaches that all humankind is equal and independent. According to Locke, humankind was free, independent, and equal in the enjoyment of inalienable rights, liberty, and property. Property was a natural right which preceded civil society and is not created in it. Through labor on gifts of nature, the individual creates property, and cannot be deprived of it by government. "By property I must be understood here, as in other places, to mean that property which men have in their persons as well as goods."[24] In this interpretation of human nature, the state of nature had little to do with the condition of war or anarchy. In contrast, "men living together according to reason, without a common superior on earth with authority to judge between them, is properly the state of nature."[25]

Government must be limited in its powers and based on social consent. The agreement is undertaken between free individuals, not between rulers and ruled as in the case of Hobbes. To avoid the state of war, human beings put themselves into society and quit the state of nature. Civil society is, as a polity with institutionalized authority, a perfection of what already applied in the state of nature which accordingly, underlies civil society. Government is an essential part of civil or political society. The government and civil society come into existence with each other. A political authority asserts the law of nature in civil society. In a natural state all people were equal and independent, and everyone had a natural right to defend life, health, liberty, or possessions. However, there are transgressors of the

23. Locke, *Second Treatise*, 4.
24. Ibid., 98–99.
25. Ibid., 13.

law. The state of war is a state of enmity and destruction. Insofar as we discover an enmity and kill a wolf, a person outside the common law of reason can be treated as a beast or prey, with force and violence to destroy him/her.[26] The bourgeoisie are assumed by Locke to be advocates for peace against aggression. The opponents who are in resistance to the bourgeoisie expansion are declared to be those without human rights.

RIGHTS OF PROPERTY AND THE AMERICAN COLONIES

From the Puritan tradition Locke regarded poverty as a sign of moral shortcomings. The poor must be helped from a superior moral footing. The poor were not full members of a moral community. Being less than full members, they were subject to the jurisdiction of the political community. They were not of civil society, although there were in that society.[27]

Those who have renounced the reason which God has given to humankind as the common rule and measure may be destroyed or killed as one of the wild savage beasts.[28] Such an offender has quit the principles of nature and became a noxious creature. This implies that the conqueror may appropriate the property of the conquered in a legal way. It justifies a right to forced labor through slavery. "A king of a large and fruitful territory [in several nations of the Americas] feeds, lodges, and is clad worse than a day-laborer in England."[29] Thus the reasonable Europeans are fully justified in conquering the nations of the Americas.

According to Locke, the European conquerors came to North America with peaceful intentions. These peaceful conquerors may treat the whole population like wild animals, and destroy them on the basis of the law of nature. God has placed the law in the human heart. Now a biblical concept of natural law or natural theology is misused to turn John Locke and the English bourgeoisie into representatives of humankind. Everyone knows that the Lord shall judge. Since there is no Judge on earth, the appeal lies to God in heaven.[30]

Locke's reference of the Last Judgment refers to the power beyond critique. Power as such becomes the prime criterion insofar as it appeals to Locke's law of nature. The war waged by this power is by definition a just

26. Ibid., 11.

27. Macpherson, *Political Theory*, 227.

28. Ibid., 8.

29. Ibid., 25.

30. Ibid., 14, 100.

war in the name of defending the law of reason and humankind. It legitimizes forced labor by promoting just war to those who are outside the law of reason. If the political organization of civil society is not grounded in the law of nature, representatives of civil society should enter into a state of war. In the name of the law of nature, humankind, and the law of reason, the bourgeois representatives are entitled to appropriate the wealth of the whole world. "The perfect condition of slavery" . . . "is nothing else but the state of war continued between a lawful conqueror and a captive."[31]

Therefore, slavery is legitimate so that the indigenous peoples of North America can be unconditionally expropriated. "The conquerors and conquered never incorporate into one person under the same laws and freedom."[32] Native Americans can also be colonized with the use of force. All this violence becomes legitimate as a consequence of the natural equality of all people. The equality of all human beings, according to Locke, does not contradict the legitimacy of forced labor through slavery.

> The power a conqueror gets over those he overcomes in a just war is perfectly despotical. He has an absolute power over the lives of those who, by putting themselves in a state of war, have forfeited them. [33]

Guaranteeing property does not come into conflict with declaring that the indigenous people can be expropriated without restriction. A liberal interpretation of human rights entails the consequence of eradicating the rights of the other.

Locke believed that human beings are owners of their own person (including labor). Property precedes government and government cannot dispose of the estates of the subjects arbitrarily. This is the law of nature which "wills the peace and preservation of all mankind."[34] The offender of the law of nature becomes dangerous to humankind, because he/she is a noxious creature. The rule of reason and common equity are the measure that God has to set to the human action for mutual security. Crime lies in transgressing the law of nature, indifferent to the right rule of reason. Reason commonly given to people in the world by God must be used "to the best advantage of life and convenience."[35]

31. Ibid., 16.
32. Ibid., 101.
33. Ibid., 102.
34. Ibid., 6.
35. Ibid., 17.

In the colonial context, slaves, captives taken in a just war, are subjected by the right of nature to the absolute dominion and arbitrary power of their masters. These slaves forfeited their liberties, losing their estate, while being in the state of slavery.[36] The conqueror has a despotic right over those captives in the war. The conqueror's losses are to be paid from the possession of the conquered and the enslaved. Locke's principle—all people are equal by nature—paradoxically justifies the forced labor in the name of the law of reason and the related just war. Locke's notion of social contract excluded slaves, and challenged the divine right of kings and absolutism. However, he also justified and legitimized a despotic power to the point where the reality of world conquest is upheld in the name of the law of nature and reason. There is no possibility of contract in a genuine sense of mutual respect and recognition between the conquerors and the indigenous people.

Locke stressed that inequality had come about by tacit and voluntary agreement on the use of money, not by the social contract establishing civil society or the law of land regulating property. Locke insisted that human beings by a tacit and voluntary consent found out a way to possess property in exchange for gold and silver. This may be hoarded up without injury to anybody. The use of money enables the industrious, rational agent to retain the right to accumulate by making the natural limit of the state of nature invalid. The validity of the use of money started in a state of nature, equated with the right to the accumulation of wealth and increase of property.

A social contract which underlines civil society is regarded as secondary to the consent on the use of money.

> This portage of things in an inequality of private possessions men have made practicable out of the bounds of society and without compact, only by putting a value on gold and silver, and tacitly agreeing in the use of money; for, in governments, the laws regulate the right of property, and the possession of land is determined by positive constitutions.[37]

Locke anchored property in labor, but in the end, he upheld the unlimited accumulation of wealth. His idea was based on the principle that money can answer all things. The chief end of civil society is the preservation of property.[38] For Locke, free men, those who enter into the social contract,

36. Ibid., 47.

37. Ibid., 29.

38. Ibid., 47–48.

are the members of the nobility, the clergy, the gentry, the commercial and financial bourgeoisie, and particularly the enlightened landowners. The ideas of Locke are those of an enlightened bourgeois, which explained their success among the ruling classes of England and Holland, and in the following centuries.

Social Contract and the Critique of Early Capitalism

Democracy, freedom, the social contract—these new ideas began to be found in Jean Jacques Rousseau (1712–1778), whose concept of them was different from Locke and also Hobbes. His writing influenced the revolution of 1776 in North America and that of 1789 in France, which may be considered the two most influential political events of the eighteenth century. The American Revolution marked the first major step in the collapse of the colonial empires after Columbus's discovery of the New World. The French Revolution signaled the first major step in the collapse of the hereditary monarchies.

Rousseau and the Social Contract

Rousseau's concept of social contract finds its place in the political context described above. The first chapter of the *Social Contract* opens: "Man was/ is born free, and everywhere he is in chains." "To renounce one's freedom is to renounce one's status as a man, the rights of humanity and even its duties." Rousseau's solution is read in the *Social Contract*.

> What man loses by the social contract is his natural freedom and an unlimited right to everything that tempts him and that he can get; what he gains is civil freedom and the proprietorship of everything he possesses.[39]

In "Discourse on the Origin of Inequality" (usually called *Second Discourse*) Rousseau argued that a scientific approach to the nature of a human being is the only means left. Such a scientific approach removes a multitude of difficulties hiding knowledge of the real foundations of human society.[40] However, civilization is not natural. To the extent that

---

39. Rousseau, *Social Contract*, 46, 50, 56.
40. Rousseau, *First and Second*, 93.

civil societies are not natural, humanity in the state of nature before the foundation of civil societies had no recognition of legal or moral obligations. That is "wandering in the forests, without industry, without speech, without domicile, without war and without liaison, with no need of his fellow-men, likewise with no desire to harm them."[41]

Unlike Hobbes, Rousseau saw that a human being was good by nature, but isolated and solitary. This nature made people happy and good while the society depraves them making them miserable. Humanity becomes wicked by its institutions, and this idea leads to skepticism of progress and civilization. Rousseau's pessimistic view of the history of progress becomes obvious in "Discourse on the Science and Arts" (*First Discourse*) composed after the illumination of Vicennes.[42] Here, the enlightenment project was attacked, because it linked science and technology as a way of improving the human condition. Advancement in the sciences and arts has destroyed virtue while strengthening slavery in all times and places.[43] Ancient political thinkers talked about morals and virtue while our contemporary thinkers talk only of business and money.[44]

Since human beings were originally isolated, they are basically selfish. However, their stupidity and independence kept the selfishness from vanity or wickedness. The natural goodness is based on instinct or feeling, instead of reason, since the reason is bound to civil society and civilization. Natural goodness and freedom are grounded in the state of nature before civil society corrupted humankind. A human being is born free in the state of nature, but he/she is in chains everywhere in the civil society. The origin of civilized governments must have been a social contract that was freely accepted by every individual. Every existing society can be rejected in the name of nature and freedom. A human being *was born* free and everywhere he/she *is* in chains.

Seen in light of the past tense, there has been evolution from the natural freedom of the state of nature to the slavery of civil society. The trend of history is toward corruption and despotism. All existing governments are chains which can be transformed into legitimate institutions. In fact, the theme of social contract is not the eradication of the chains, but its legitimization. A search for the political structure has consequence in issuing an indispensable dominion in the state of society in the name of

41. Ibid., 137.

42. Rousseau, *Social Contract*, 8.

43. Rousseau, *First and Second*, 36–40.

44. Ibid, 50–51.

rationality and righteousness. It is called *Republica*. If Hobbes's concept of Leviathan serves to establish the security of the bourgeoisie, Rousseau attempted to secure the regeneration of the freedom of those who are transformed to state citizen. Freedom as an infallible good of human being, the definition of its essence, must be the content of the social contract. For Rousseau it should not be abandoned as in the case of Hobbes.[45]

In the two *Discourses* the emphasis is on the transition from freedom to slavery. In *Social Contract* focus is rather given to what makes this transition legitimate. Rousseau admits that "the social order is a sacred right that serves as a basis for all the others."[46] This dialectical approach can be outlined: natural freedom and the social contract. Since the people are by nature free –because freedom is the quality of becoming a human being—there are by definition no moral, rational, or political laws governing human behavior in the state of nature. From this assumption it follows that all social obligations must result from an agreement between individuals. The social contracts created a civil society with morally binding laws and duties. Civil society resulted from a voluntary agreement between naturally free and equal individuals. Like the law of gravity, the clauses are determined by the nature of the act of forming a civil society.[47]

It operates everywhere the same, everywhere tacitly accepted and recognized. Political right, which denotes a legitimate reason for obeying a government and laws, creates social obligation. The right of the strongest may exist in the state of nature. When it degenerated into a state of war, such a right cannot produce legitimate obedience. A right in the proper sense must create an obligation that is rationally binding by conscience.

CIVIL SOCIETY AND THE GENERAL WILL

The social contract is defined and based on principles of political right. Principles or universally valid rules are discovered by human reason. Political right means standards of obligation or duty, making it reasonable for one individual to obey another. It implies a legitimate reason for obeying a government and laws; it does not come from nature. Accordingly, slavery cannot be natural, nor become a legitimate convention or agreement. To renounce one's freedom is to renounce one's status as a human being, the

45. Fetscher, *Rousseau*, 103–4.
46. Rousseau, *Social Contract*, Book I, ch. I.
47. Ibid., Book I, ch. VI.

rights of humanity, and its duties.[48] However, Rousseau argues that the only legitimate society is based on a "total alienation of each associate, with all rights, to the whole community."[49] For Rousseau, if some rights were left to private individuals, the association would necessarily become tyrannical or ineffectual.[50] For better understanding of the relationship between the individual and the community, Rousseau introduced the concept of the general will (*volonté générale*). As he asserts,

> Each of us puts his person and all his power in common under the supreme direction of the general will; and in a body we receive each member as an indivisible part of the whole.[51]

In *Second Discourse*, Rousseau described the fundamental compact of all government as a common opinion. This is an act of will in which the people have united all their wills into a singular one.[52] For Rousseau, a community is a Republic governed by an assembly in which each citizen has a vote. In the eighteenth century the term sovereign in France generally meant the King or absolute Monarch. At issue for Rousseau is that the concept of sovereignty must be defined as an attribute of the entire body. He presented the sovereignty of the people, the general will, as unalterable, indivisible, and infallible, if it is well informed. And thus it became sacred and inviolable. He distinguished the sovereign from the government, because the government receives the orders from the sovereign. The product or power of the government must be equal to the product or the power of the citizens, who are sovereigns on the one hand and subjects on the other.[53] Thus the exercise of political power by individual leaders must be subordinate to the freely expressed will of the people as sovereign. The social contract is not identified as the alienation of such a right to individual rulers.

The general will implies that a popular assembly could make decisions by binding each individual member. An act of general will presupposes an egalitarian community in which each citizen has a right to vote and the actions of the whole assembly have an equal effect on every individual. For a decision to be legitimate, every citizen must vote on it. It

48. Ibid., Book I, ch. IV.
49. Ibid.
50. Ibid.
51. Ibid.
52. Rousseau, *First and Second*, 169.
53. Rousseau, *Social Contract*, Book III. ch.1.

must also affect every citizen equally. The general will can create socially binding duties, so the concept of general will transforms the traditional concept of the common good into a requirement of popular sovereignty.

The general will is proposed as the ideal of the civil state. Distinguishing the will of all from the general will, Rousseau states that the latter considers only the common interest. The former considers private interest as a sum of private will.[54] The general will is an ideal model, an abstraction; it is also easily subverted by private interests, the will of all and it is to be paraded under the banner of the common good. The will of the people is the sovereign will which is general both in relation to the State—considered as a whole—as well as in relation to the government—considered as part of that whole.[55] The general will is expressed in a process of dynamic interaction of individual wills within the rule of law. However, Rousseau's liberal ideas are said to achieve themselves in terms of totalitarian means. In my view, it is essential to assume that Rousseau's totalitarian passages are grim while his love of freedom and equality is so intense.[56]

Democracy as a form of government fascinated Rousseau. "If there were a people of Gods, it would govern itself democratically. Such a perfect government is not suited to men." A true democracy in the strict sense of the term has never existed and never will exist. It is contrary to the natural order that the majority govern and the minority is governed.[57] Hostile to absolutism, Rousseau gives the impression of reserving direct democracy for small states, and he seems to prefer instead the lesser evil of an elective aristocracy (in some ways, our representative democracy). A very small State, in which the people are easily assembled and each citizen can easily know all the others, prevents a multitude of business and knotty discussion. In this small democratic State there is little or no luxury. Luxury as the result of wealth corrupts both rich and poor; the one by possessing while the other by coveting.[58]

DEMOCRACY AND ECONOMIC JUSTICE

Compared to the aggressive egoism of Hobbes and rational egoism of Locke, Rousseau preferred democracy and a republican or egalitarian

54. Ibid., Book II, ch. iii.

55. Ibid., Book III, ch. ii.

56. Mcmanners, "Social Contract" 294–95.

57. Ibid., Book III, ch. IV.

58. Ibid.

small form of government. Sovereignty of the people, the general will, and freedom, were all the great themes of the bourgeois revolution. In this revolution there were also the great themes of the popular movements— sovereignty of the people, direct democracy, and freedom—in place. In the initial stage of the French Revolution people quoted and commented on Montesquieu, but in the final analysis, people spoke only of Rousseau. It is certain that the name Rousseau was connected with the ideal of the French Revolution: freedom, equality, and brotherhood. Nevertheless, he did not believe that a revolution in France could be a democratic revolution and establish the republic. In this regard he remained a pessimist. As a moral philosopher he believed in egalitarian democracy and propagated it. Rousseau's influence on the French Revolution needs to be understood in the general spirit of the time which was related to other political theorists. It would be a specious argument to overemphasize an ongoing appeal of French revolutionary groups to Rousseau.[59]

For Rousseau the administration of the government might be best done by a limited number rather than by the whole body of citizens. He was a democrat who conceived of legislative rule by the whole body of citizens. However, such democracy is for gods, not for human beings.[60] He was also a republican or a champion of popular sovereignty. He saw that the task of social policy was preservation of the middle petit classes (farmer and handicraft); these are the ideal and practical class basis for the Republic state order. This is not only the necessary presupposition for the establishment of the legitimate Republic, but also the condition for its preservation. It must be conserved through the law and policy measurement of government.[61]

Throughout his writings and life, Rousseau berated wealth and the wealthy. Rousseau had a heart for the poor and a sense of justice, challenging the arrogance, injustice and stubbornness of the rich. We may recognize the Christian command of loving the neighbor in Rousseau's social theory. At issue is not property or capital accumulation, but the life of humanity.[62] In *Social Contract*, Rousseau argues that the fundamental compact substitutes a moral and legitimate equality. They all become equal through convention and by right.

59. Fetscher, *Rousseau*, 263.
60. Ibid., Book III, ch.4.
61. Fetscher, *Rousseaus*, 12, 224.
62. Vossler, *Rousseaus*, 367–68.

> Under bad government, this equality is only apparent and il-
> lusory. It serves merely to maintain the poor man in his misery
> and the rich in his usurpation. In fact, laws are always useful
> to those who have possessions and harmful to those who have
> nothing.[63]

In light of the general will, Rousseau attempts to clarify the issue of political economy at the governmental level. The general will which is in favor of the common good "tends toward the preservation and welfare of the whole and of each part."[64] The general will is the source and supplement of all the laws. The legislator's first duty is to make the laws conform to the general will.[65] Thus Rousseau established the general will as the first principle of public political economy and the fundamental rule of government. The first rule of public economy is that administration should be in conformity with the laws. Insofar as law is abused, it serves the powerful as an offensive weapon and as a shield against the weak. Here "the pretext of the public good is always the most dangerous scourge of the people."[66] Providing for the public needs becomes an evident consequence of the general will.

In the societies, where accumulated wealth always facilitates the means to accumulate greater wealth, wealth is detrimental to those who have nothing to acquire anything. In the *Second Discourse*, Rousseau links the problem of inequality and the question of property. Regarding the right of property, Rousseau asserts that it is "the true basis of civil society and the true guarantee of the citizens' engagements."[67] He concludes in his *Discourse*:

> It is manifestly against the law of nature, in whatever manner it
> is defined . . . that a handful of men be glutted with superfluities,
> while the starving multitude lacks necessities.[68]

However, Rousseau did not advocate the abolition of private property. He held the right of property to be the most sacred of all the rights of the citizens, while limiting this right through taxation and by changing the rights of inheritance. It is important to find the public capital or treasury

63. Rousseau, Book I, ch. IX. Footnote.

64. Ibid., 212.

65. Ibid., 216.

66. Ibid., 221.

67. Ibid., 225.

68. Rousseau, *First & Second*, 181.

which is sufficient for the upkeep of the magistrates and other officers and for all public expenses.

As Rousseau critically observes, the social confederation protects the immense possessions of the rich and barely lets the poor wretch enjoy the hut that they built with their own hands.

> Money breeds money . . . All that the poor man pays is forever lost to him, and remains in, or returns to, the hands of the rich.[69]

Commerce and industry attracted all the money from the countryside to the capitals. These rendered the tail more burdensome rather than making it more bearable by an abundance of money. The important task of the government is to prevent extreme inequality of wealth in terms of removing the means of accumulating it from everyone.[70]

For Rousseau, true liberty is never destructive of itself. Liberty without justice is a veritable contradiction. A free people obey the laws, but they have magistrates, not masters; thanks to the laws, they do not obey human individuals in the administration of government.[71] In light of freedom and equality, Rousseau argues that "with regard to wealth, no citizen should be so opulent that he can buy another, and none so poor that he is constrained to sell himself."[72] Thus Rousseau envisions "moderation in goods and influence on the part of the upper classes and moderation in avarice and covetousness on the part of the lowers classes."[73]

HEGEL, THE FRENCH REVOLUTION, AND CIVIL SOCIETY

In comparison with Rousseau, Hegel addressed the French Revolution only as a philosophical concept. He elevated revolution to the primary principle of his philosophy. Celebrating the ideals of the revolution, Hegel attempted to overcome its negative side of terror through his philosophy as the critique of revolution.[74] It is certain that Hegel did not see the result of the French Revolution as the realization of freedom, but as the

---

69. Rousseau, *Social Contract*, 232.

70. Ibid., 221.

71. Rousseau, *Social Contract*, 32.

72. Rousseau, *Social Contract,* Book II, ch. XI.

73. Ibid.

74. Habermas, *Theory and Practice*, 121.

establishment of a new despotism. His mode of interpretation took the course of revolution as a necessary historical development.[75]

According to Hegel, the Jacobin terror undertook a negation of abstract freedom for the sake of absolute freedom. However, Napoleon was welcomed by Hegel as the conqueror of the French Revolution and the protector of its order. He was hailed as the patron of the new bourgeois legal code. Along with him the principle of reason had become reality in which freedom of all human beings as persons was legally ensured.[76] Hegel conceptually legitimated the revolutionizing of social reality without justifying the revolutionaries such as Robespierre.

In the chapter on the "objective spirit," in his *Phenomenology of Mind*, Hegel reflected on the reality of the French Revolution in light of absolute freedom and terror.[77] Absolute freedom was realized in the French Revolution as a dialectical moment rather than the final accomplishment. The direct realization of the universal (or general) will culminated in the terror. The substance of absolute freedom put itself on the throne of the world without any power of resistance. In this absolute freedom all social ranks or classes were effaced and annulled.[78] There was left for universal freedom only negative action: the rage and the fury of destruction. Death was the sole and only work and deed accomplished by universal freedom. It was the most cold-blooded and meaningless death of all, only cleaving a head of cabbage or swallowing a draught of water. The terror of death was the direct appreciation of the absolute freedom in its negative nature.[79] This was Hegel's interpretation of the dialectical meaning of the terror which transpired in the French Revolution.

According to Hegel, the French Revolution (1789) has its origin in the Reformation in Germany (1517) and is elevated to the moral philosophy of Kant and Fichte in German idealism. Hegel concurred with Rousseau's theory of social contract. The wisdom of the government is the intelligence of the universal will, because it is the individual embodiment of the universal will. When the government constitutes itself as a specifically determinate will and opposes the universal will, it can become nothing but fraction. As the direct necessity of the overthrow the government has committed a crime against the universal will. It shows the guilt

---

75. Marcuse, *Reason and Revolution*, 91.

76. Habermas, *Theory and Practices*, 188.

77. Hegel, *Phenomenology*, 343–50.

78. Ibid., 344, 348.

79. Ibid., 346, 347, 348.

of the will opposing itself to it.[80] Freedom and reason are seen in light of the universal will.

However, Hegel's political philosophy was quite complicated as his position advanced. In 1816 Hegel, the principal of a high school in Nuremberg, was appointed to a professorship of philosophy at the University of Heidelberg. The next year he became chosen as Fichte's successor at the University of Berlin. With this appointment he began to be considered by many to be the official philosopher of the Prussian State. Napoleon was still for Hegel the historical hero fulfilling the French Revolution. For Hegel a social order built on the rational autonomy of the individual fulfilled the principle of reason in society. The freedom of each individual was embedded in life-and-death struggle for which the terror of 1793 became an example. The revolutionary terror of 1793 remained an acute warning for Hegel to defend and protect the existing social order with all available means. Hegel envisioned a state governed by the standards of critical reason and guided by universally valid law. The rationality of law was the life of the modern state. However, this concept of the modern state should not be reclaimed to support the total state of the Nazis. Hegel's position against National Socialism was affirmed convincingly by Marcuse, Ritter, and Habermas.[81]

With this modern state in mind, Hegel went on to say that the social-contract hypothesis did not become valid. Rousseau's theory of the state and society presupposed an original state of humanity. According to Hegel, Rousseau elevated the will and the spirit of the particular individual in one's peculiar caprice to the substantive and primary basis in society. For Hobbes the absolute state described in *Leviathan* did not hold to preserve the interests of the rising middle class. [82]

Hegel maintained that within the state the family was first developed into civil society; and the Idea of the state disrupted itself into these two moments, family and civil society. The Idea of the state has actuality and a self-dependent organism: the constitution or constitutional law and international law. The Idea of the state as the Universal Idea is the mind giving itself its actuality in the process of world history.[83] Law is materialized in the protection of property through the administration of justice. Hegel followed Locke's concept of property which included the basic rights of

---

80. Hegel, *Phenomenology,* 347.

81. Habermas, *Theory and Practices,* 193.

82. Marcuse, *Reason and Revolution,* 186, 188.

83. *Hegel's Philosophy of Right,* § 259, 160.

the individuals (their lives, liberties, and estates). Human equality for Hegel meant an equal right of all to property. All the organizations and institutions of civil society were established for the protection of property. The freedom of the society is the right of property.[84]

Placing the state over civil society, Hegel called the state the realization of freedom; the state is an independent and autonomous power, in other words, the march of God in the world. Hegel's deified state stands in contrast to the civil society. The state paves the space for realizing reason and freedom. However, in the civil society reason is distorted by the blind necessity of the economic process. Freedom is perverted through competition of conflicting private interests. Civil society is ruled by the state in Hegel's thought.[85]

For Hegel, philosophy did not provide any guideline for revolutionizing praxis; it gave a lesson only to those who misused the philosophy as an inspiration for political action. Hegel's dictum on the *ex post facto* argued that political theory was not aimed at "instructing the state what it should be like, but rather instead how the state—the moral universal—should be known."[86] Hegel's Cassandra-like warnings can be seen in his attack on the English Reform Bill. In France voting rights were democratized and in England an electoral reform became an impending reality. Hegel warned of the power of the people and opposed seeking "its strength in the people and bringing about a revolution instead of a reform."[87]

CIVIL SOCIETY AND ECONOMIC ISSUES

Unlike his later glorification of the state, Hegel early on developed his political notion of civil society in connection with economic issues. In the *System of Morality* (1802) and the lectures of 1803–1806 in Jena, Hegel worked on refining the concept of modern bourgeois society in critical examination of the economic theory of his time. By way of the economic studies social labor gained weight with the social system. The civil society became an arena for humanity's emancipation from the state of nature. The struggle for recognition would lead to a system of social labor and to emancipation from the state of nature.[88]

84. Marcuse, *Reason and Revolution*, 206.

85. Ibid., 215–16.

86. Habermas, *Theory and Practices*, 179.

87. Ibid., 189.

88. Ibid., 187.

Hegel differed from the Anglo-Saxon understanding of liberalism. According to Hobbes and Locke, rights in the civil society existed as a means of preserving private and material property. The American Founding Fathers like Jefferson and Madison followed in the footsteps of Hobbes and Locke. However, Hegel saw rights as recognition of human status and dignity.

Hegel's philosophy of labor, whose foundations were laid down in the *System of Morality*, developed in the *Realphilosophy*, firmly established in the *Phenomenology of Mind*. This perspective continued to be defended in the *Philosophy of Right* and the *Science of Logic*. In his *Aesthetics* Hegel described the contrast between poverty and wealth and the alienation of all classes of society resulting from this contrast. Within the industrial formation

> the constant reflection of a ceaseless dependence has been eliminated, and man is all the more remote from all the risks of earning his living because it no longer appears to him as his own work. All that surrounds him is no longer his own creation but is . . . produced . . . by others than himself.[89]

Here, Hegel's interest was in uncovering the negative side of this system rather than emphasizing its positive one. The modern society appeared as necessity, not as liberty; the individual finds its place according to the capital tied to the labor power. The specific wants of individuals are satisfied by one's abstract labor. The system of civil society built on capital and labor power generated inequalities in a spectacle of excess, misery, and physical and social corruption.

According to Hegel, individual wants produced the relations of people. To the extent that the wants are prepared and procured, large fortunes are amassed. On the other hand, a repartition and limitation of the work of the individual laborer occurs, consequently leading to dependence and distress in the artisan class. A large number of people sunk below the standard of living which was essential for the members of society. They lost the sense of right, rectitude and honor. A pauper class arose and wealth accumulation fell into the hands of a few.[90]

In the *System of Morality*, Hegel dealt with a dialectical system of needs and satisfaction. The various social institutions and relations were described as a system of contradicting forces which originated from the

---

89. Mandel, *Formation,* 156.

90. Marcuse, *Reason and Revolution,* 205.

mode of social labor. The mode of labor transformed the particular work of the individual into general labor, or abstract and quantitative labor; this labor was pursued for the gratification of personal wants and produced commodities for the market. This dimension increased inequality of people and wealth. Because society was not capable of overcoming the antagonism, Hegel proposed a concept of the true community in terms of great discipline and military preparation. The aim of the state was to suppress the increasing antagonism of individualist and possessive market society.

In the civil society the contradiction, according to Hegel, was inherent in the economic structure, and social order was based on the system of general, abstract, and qualitative labor, and antagonistic interests. Social integration of wants transpired through the exchange of commodities. This social order governed by blind economic mechanism brought Hegel to conceive of a string and independent state as an alternative to the irreconcilable contradiction of the modern civil society.[91] Here Hegel saw the capitalist economy as an autonomous self-regulating system in reference to the intervention of the government in its power to combat the inequality and destruction of the capitalist society.

In the *System of Morality*, Hegel stated that commerce was the highest point of universality in economic life. He conceived of concentration of capital in terms of merchants' capital. In the discussion of money, the structure of capitalism culminated in trade.

> The ruling principle of the merchant class then is the realization of the identity of the essence and the thing: a man is as real as the money he owns; . . . the essence of the matter is the matter itself; value is hard cash. . . . But this money which bears the meaning of all needs is itself only an immediate thing) . . . The outlook of the merchant is this hard-headedness in which the particular is wholly estranged and no longer counts . . . the bill must be honored whatever happens—even if family, wealth, position, life are sacrificed.[92]

Hegel recognizes the problem of the pauper class and worries about the negative aspect of a social system grounded in its irreconcilable contradiction; this social reality is embedded within the excess of wealth generating excess of poverty and paupers. Civil society contains three moments: the system of needs (the mediation of need and one's satisfaction

91. Ibid., 58–61.
92. Ibid., 336.

through the work and the satisfaction of the needs of all others); the protection of property through the administration of justice; the police and the corporation (care for particular interests as a common interest).[93]

Hegel's limitations lay in his political philosophy about the state over against the civil society. Here Hegel generalized and leveled the social contradiction between the rich and the poor for the sake of the self-regulating state with utmost discipline and authority through administration of justice, the police, and the corporation. The empirical reality of the state was declared to be rational. Nonetheless, there is an essential component in Hegel's dialectical logic of labor directed toward emancipation of those who are burdened in the economic field. The division of labor has generated abstract labor and the commercial exchange generated abstract enjoyment for the satisfaction of the needs of all. The contract became the principle of bourgeois commerce. Possession was transformed into property, ensured by universal recognition. At this point Hegel kept in mind that the moment of emancipation still lay in labor.[94]

Hegel articulated the decisive importance of labor in the process of humanization; it became obvious when Hegel wrote his 'Robinsonade' of master and servant in the *System of Morality*. In Hegel's social model of master and servant the starting point is Hobbes' *bellum omnium contra omnes* in order to conceptualize the dialectical relationship between the master and the slave. The subjugation of some people by others gave rise to the condition of mastery and servitude. The master relates to the product through labor of the slave. The slave working on them, the master gets enjoyment and satisfaction in the products. The satisfaction of the master is dependent on the slave who labors. Labor restraining the slave's desire shapes and fashions the thing for the enjoyment of the master. [95]

Hegel regarded this alienation to be rooted in human nature in a society. But he did not see that the contradiction could lead to elimination of this alienation through a transformation of the social structure, once a certain level of development of the productive forces has been reached. In this connection the well-known dialectic of master and slave is resolved not by the actual abolition of servitude, but merely by the declaration that spiritually the slave becomes freer than his master. Hegel's dialectic of master and slave, his view of labor, finds an inspiration in Karl Marx's critique of alienated labor in capitalist society. A critical study of Hegel

93. *Hegel's Philosophy of Right*, §188, 126.

94. Ibid., § 194, 128.

95. Hegel, *Phenomenology*, 111.

and Marx will continue later in chapter five. Chapter four will deal with the self-regulating principle of market, industrial revolution, colonial expansion of British capitalism in India and China, and Marx's controversial theory of the Asiatic mode of production.

4

Industrial Capitalism and the Self-Regulating Market

MAX WEBER'S SOCIOLOGICAL ANALYSIS of the affinity between Calvinism and capitalism finds its evidence in Holland and England. The political-economic development in the British context, including enclosure and mill, led to the industrial revolution. Industrial capitalism came into full swing with the self-regulating market. Along with the development of industrial capitalism, colonial trade played an indispensable role in connection with Christian mission. This chapter entails a critical study of the industrial revolution and British colonial economic policy in India and later China, including the opium wars to which Christian mission was linked. This chapter further includes a critical study of the Marxist view of the Asiatic mode of production under a Eurocentric guise concerning capitalism and colonial rule, and also Adam Smith's view on free market and colonial economy. First, enclosure and mill deserve attention in our study of industrial capitalism and self-regulating market.

ENCLOSURE AND THE MILL

Enclosure, called a revolution of the rich against the poor,[1] broke down ancient law and custom to promote the rich's improvement at the price of social dislocation. Common land was land which was owned by one person, but over which other people had certain traditional rights, such

1. Polanyi, *Transformation*, 35.

as arable farming, or mowing meadows for hay, or grazing livestock.[2] In England and Wales, enclosure ended the use of open fields for farming and the parallel system of common meadows. It also enclosed a large proportion of the common pastures in the lowlands, restricting commons to rough pasture in mountainous areas and in relatively small parts of the lowlands. In an official document of 1607, we read: "The poor man shall be satisfied in his end: Habitation; and the gentleman not hindered in his desire: Improvement."[3]

Enclosure had been taking place at least from as early as the thirteenth century. Many earlier enclosures were undertaken by those who made fortunes in trade or in government service. They sought prestige by the possession of the soil. In the first half of the eighteenth century the old-land aristocracy had lost much in the civil wars and reasserted its claim to its former place in society. Encouraged by low rates of interest, noblemen mortgaged their estates and bought more land. They took initiative to practice enclosures.[4]

By about 1780 the enclosure movement had culminated in England which induced the quasi-liquidation of the class of independent peasants. They were replaced by big capitalist farmers working with wage labor.

> Poor and needy persons, many of whom have the charge and burden of wives and many children to support, and who have nothing but what they can get by the work of their hands.[5]

Enclosure by Act began to take effect after 1760, hastening the expropriation of poor peasants. Squatters who were living on the commons were driven off. Impoverished peasants who owned tiny patches of land could not bear the costs of enclosure and were unable to live on the poor lands they received. The rich individuals' joy increased while the poor's decayed.[6]

Enclosure drove people from the land, contributing to the process of the industrial revolution. The process of enclosure has sometimes been accompanied by force, resistance, and bloodshed. It remained among the most controversial areas of agricultural and economic history in England. The rich landowners used their control of state processes to appropriate public land for their private benefit. They robbed the poor of their share

2. Ibid., 34.

3. Ibid.

4. Ashton, *Industrial Revolution*, 25.

5. Mandel, *Marxist Theory*, I. 117.

6. Beaud, *History of Capitalism*, 64.

in the common, tearing down the houses which the poor had long regarded as theirs and their heirs. They turned them into a mob of beggars and thieves. This created a landless working class that provided the labor required in the new industries developing in the north of England. Enclosure was a plain enough case of class robbery. The years between 1760 and 1820 were the years of wholesale enclosure.

James Watt's (1736–1819) patenting of the steam-engine in 1769 and the application of this engine to cotton-manufacturing revolutionized the progress of industrial capitalism. It is certain that Watt's invention and development of the steam engine was financed by profits from the mercantile triangular trade. Technical advances took place in other aspects of textile production and in other industries. With this energy power, a system of machines went into operation which necessarily resulted in an organization of production and of work rhythms; it involved a new discipline for the laborers who served the machines.

Spinning mills were installed in brick buildings four or five stories high. The workers were subject to inflexible regulations and the pitiless movement of a mechanism drove them like gear-wheels without a soul. Entering a mill was like entering barracks or a prison. The machine was the starting point for the industrial revolution, replacing workers by mechanisms operating within a system of machinery. The steam-engine superseded the earlier motive-power and set the labor power in motion as a single motive power.[7]

The manufacturer had to instruct, train and above all discipline the inexperienced workers. The need for the activities of the laborer was increased to conform to the rhythm and the movements of the machine process. A coercive and disciplinary force over the laborer perpetuated the growing dependence of labor on capital. The new machinery led to an equalization of labor, reducing the task of the laborer to the exercise of vigilance and dexterity.[8]

According to Michel Foucault, the integration of the body into systems of efficient and economic controls was ensured by the procedures of discipline and regulatory control of the population. Numerous and diverse techniques were exploited to achieve the subjugation of bodies and the control of populations which marked an era of bio-power (power over life); this bio-power which invested life plays an indispensable role in the development of capitalism. Its success was achieved in terms of the

7. Marx, *Capital I*, 308, 370–71, 378.

8. Dobb, *Studies*, 259.

controlled insertion of bodies into the machinery of production. In the development of capitalism, the accumulation of people is adjusted to that of capital.[9]

The country folk had been crowded in the industrial towns of England, being dehumanized into slum dwellers. "Under the slack and scrap heaps vomited forth from the satanic mills," social conditions in the period of the industrial revolution were referred to as "a veritable abyss of human degradation."[10] From 1825 onward, the building of railways enabled the triumphal march of machine production and the capitalist mode of production. Linking town to country, commodities, set at low prices by big factories, penetrated into the far corners of all countries. This transition transformed labor power into a commodity and the means of production into capital.[11]

The creation of the mill in the eighteenth century established capitalism as a distinctive mode of production. Its development was based upon an accumulation of wealth from two principal sources: 1) the traditional extortion of peasant surplus labor, and 2) extreme colonial exploitation taking diverse forms: pillage, forced labor, slavery, unequal exchange, colonial tax, and so on. The development of markets (domestic and worldwide) and the expansion of exchange made an increase in production necessary. This development was done first in the traditional forms of production (manufacture, work in the home) and then with new techniques and within the framework of the energy-powered mill. The bourgeoisie was formed from the wealthy from the banking and commercial sectors, from dealers and manufacturers who had become rich. This new ruling class everywhere cultivated a key word: "freedom." The freedom in question was above all economic freedom. It was freedom of trade and of production, as well as freedom to pay for labor power at the lowest possible price. It was to defend itself against workers' alliance and revolts.

Free trade and work for wages in the form of "Manchester Capitalism" proved to be more profitable than mercantile protectionism and slavery. The market system became the sole director of human life and the natural environment. Human beings would die as the victims of social dislocation through vice, perversion, crime, and starvation. Nature was reduced to its elements, and neighbors and landscapes were defiled. Rivers were polluted, military safety jeopardized and the power to produce

9. Foucault, *History of Sexuality I*, 139–40.

10. Polanyi, *Transformation*, 39.

11. Mandel, *Marxist Theory I*, 118–20.

food and raw materials was destroyed. Although labor, land, and money markets are essential to a market economy, no society could stand the effects of such a system brought by the ravages of this satanic mill.[12] Once elaborate machines and plants were used for production in a commercial society, and once the impact of the machine used for production in a commercial society was established, the idea of a self-regulating market was bound to take shape.[13]

At the end of the nineteenth century the colonizers of Black Africa and Oceania repeated what their slave-trading ancestors had done for assembling a mass of slave labor. What mattered this time was not sending this labor over the ocean to the plantations of the New World. Rather it employed this labor on the spot in capitalist agricultural, mining or industrial enterprises in order to produce the surplus value which was indispensable to the life of capital.[14]

THE INDUSTRIAL REVOLUTION AND COLONIAL TRADE

The Industrial Revolution–the term used by Engels in his *Condition of the Working Class in England in* 1844 and popularized by Arnold Toynbee–was a period from the 18th to the 19th century (1760–1830). Major technical changes augmented the productivity of labor in agriculture, manufacturing, and mining. Transport had a profound effect on the socioeconomic and cultural conditions starting in England. This economic scene in the first three-quarters of the nineteenth century caused an abnormally rapid increase of the proletariat along with widening investment and market growth to an unprecedented measure. Fresh sources of raw material were exploited and new markets were opened; new methods of trade were devised, capital increased in volume and fluidity. A banking system came into being.

Previously, the growth of capitalist industry was fettered by the narrowness of the market. These barriers were swept away at the Industrial Revolution so that capital accumulation and investment widened its horizons, affecting supply of labor, productivity and markets in interconnection.[15] This Industrial Revolution subsequently spread throughout Europe, North America, and eventually the world.

12. Polanyi, *Transformation*, 78.
13. Ibid., 39–40.
14. Mandel, *Marxist Theory, I,* 126.
15. Dobb, *Studies,* 257.

Whether such a series of changes should be called the "Industrial Revolution" can be in dispute. The changes were not merely industrial, but also social, cultural, political, and intellectual. The system of capitalism had its origin before 1760 and attained its full development long after 1830. Economic progress was characterized by the essential fact of continuity rather than the sudden breakup of revolution. The phrase "Industrial Revolution" has been used in the circle of historians, becoming common speech.[16]

However, the European view of the "Industrial Revolution" is challenged by the perspective of the unified world economy and system, in other words, the standpoint of horizontally integrative macrohistory. The Eurocentric view of the rise of capitalism produced a microhistorical, even parochial outlook. It is important to view a comprehensive and globally interconnected reality of world economy at both a vertical and horizontal level. Horizontally integrative history searches for globally interrelated historical phenomena by mapping historical parallelism. According to Joseph Fletcher,

> to find interconnections and horizontal continuities of early modern history, one must look underneath the surface of political and institutional history, and examine developments in economics, societies, and cultures of the early modern period.[17]

Doing horizontally integrative macrohistory, Frank takes issue with the Eurocentric view of the industrial revolution.[18] According to Frank, the real world during the period from 1400 to 1800 was very different from what Eurocentric history and classical social theory have alleged. Europeans obtained wealth from the gold and silver mines found in the Americas through the slave plantations in Brazil, the Caribbean, and the North American South. The slave trade itself supplied and ran these plantations. Europeans made more money by selling their products to people in the Americas. However, European products were not salable in competition with Asia. According to Adam Smith, the market of Europe had become more extensive since the discovery of America which made a most essential contribution. America and the English colonies were altogether

16. Ashton, *Industrial Revolution*, 2.
17. Fletcher, "Integrative History," 38.
18. Frank, *ReOrient*, 248.

a new market which opened up a new and inexhaustible market to all commodities of Europe.[19]

Furthermore, Smith recognized the advanced economic reality in Asia:

> The improvements in agriculture and manufacture seem likewise to have been of very great antiquity in the provinces of Bengal in the East Indies, and in some of the eastern provinces of China . . . Even those three countries [China, Egypt, and Indostan], the wealthiest, according to all accounts, that ever were in the world, are chiefly renowned for their superiority in agriculture and manufactures . . . [Now, in 1776] China is a much richer country than any part of Europe.[20]

Britain and Western Europe had to compete primarily with India and China as well as west Asia. We observe that the technological developments of the industrial revolution were already in Asia. According to Arrighi, the main historical link between the three moments of the industrial expansion in the fourteenth, sixteenth/early seventeenth, and late eighteenth centuries in England was integral to an ongoing financial expansion by restructuring and reorganizing the capitalist world-economy. From the start England was incorporated in the capitalist world-economy.[21] Industrial revolution would not be possible without an extensive foreign market, so it can be seen in centuries-long industrial expansion.

COLONIAL TRADE EXPANSION AND BRITISH RULE IN INDIA

Europe was for centuries dependent on India for its most valuable products and consumption. India had the advantage of a less expensive and more skilled workforce, in contrast to the impoverishment of Europe.[22]

With respect to British colonial trade, the British East India Company was an early English joint-stock company that was formed initially for pursuing trade with the East Indies. It ended up trading mainly with the Indian subcontinent and China. After a rival English company challenged its monopoly in the late seventeenth century, the two companies were merged in 1708 to form the United Company of Merchants of England

---

19. Smith, *Wealth of Nations*, 416.

20. Ibid., 20,348,169. Cf. Frank, *ReOrient*, 279.

21. Arrighi, *Long Twentieth Century*, 209.

22. Wallerstein, *World-System*, 3, 24.

Trading to the East Indies. The English East India Company had received its charter in 1600 and other English companies even earlier.

However, throughout the seventeenth century the Dutch VOC (*Verenigde Oost-Indische Compagnie*), chartered in 1602, was the greatest success of the revival in foreign trade which the English imitated. The Dutch chartered companies were both beneficiaries and instruments of the ongoing centralization of Amsterdam, so they played a decisive role in the rise of Amsterdam to the status of world financial center. A large, profitable joint-stock company like the VOC had risen in defeat of the old Genoese or in competition with the new British high finance. From around 1610–20 to around 1730–40, the upper strata of the Dutch merchant class occupied a leading role in the European capitalist economy. Dutch brutality took place in enslaving indigenous peoples and in using violence to break the indigenous resistance to the policies of the Company. Such a record of brutality stood in parallel with the crusading Iberians throughout the extra-European world.[23]

The spread of multiple mercantilisms in the late seventeenth and early eighteenth centuries created a condition unfavorable to the Dutch economy on a world scale. Mercantilism reestablished the territorialist principle of economic self-sufficiency in the form of national economy-making. The Dutch, under the pressure of territorialist interests, were drawn into the struggles with disastrous consequences. In the war following from the American rebellion, the Dutch took sides with France against Britain. The British retaliated viciously; in the course of the fourth Anglo-Dutch War (1781–84), Dutch seaborne power was annihilated. The defeat in the war and the following Batavian Revolution and Orangist counter-revolution hastened the displacement of Amsterdam by London "as the financial entrepôt of the European world-economy."[24]

Throughout the eighteenth century, London took the position of the revival center of high finance from Amsterdam. London emerged as the new governing center of world finance and became the phoenix rising from the ashes of the Dutch crisis of 1780–83. The British regime had taken the Dutch world-scale processes of capital accumulation one step further by internalizing production costs.[25]

The commercial expansion was tremendous. The development of triangular trade and of shipping and shipbuilding led to the growth of the

---

23. Arrighi, *Twentieth Century*, 155.

24. Ibid., 143.

25. Ibid., 159.

great seaport towns. The slave and sugar trade made Bristol the second city of England in the eighteenth century. When Bristol was outstripped in the slave trade by Liverpool, it turned its attention from the triangular trade to direct sugar trade. The capital accumulated by Liverpool from the slave trade poured into the hinterland to fertilize the energies of Manchester. Manchester goods for Africa were taken to the coast in Liverpool slave vessels.

The East India Company (EIC) established under Elizabeth I effectively began its rule in India in 1757, which lasted until 1858. Following the events of the Indian Rebellion of 1857, the British Crown assumed direct administration of India in the new British Raj under the Government of India Act of 1858. The Company itself was finally dissolved on 1 January 1874. The Company long held a privileged position in relation to the English, and later the British, government. Control over India meant a command over financial and material resources including military power. As a result, it was frequently granted special rights and privileges, including trade monopolies and exemptions. Furthermore, the company's military force began to expand in the 1740s in response to the disintegration of the Mughal Empire.

Between 1845–49 and 1870–75, British exports of railroad iron and steel were more than tripled and those of machinery increased nine-fold. During the same period, British exports to Central and South America, the Middle East, Asia, and Australasia increased some six-fold. The outcome of this acceleration in the material expansion of capital can be called the globalization of the capitalist world economy. Through new military conquistadors, the entire globe was integrated into an entirely new economic world.[26]

The British industrial interest became more and more dependent on the Indian market. With railroads, steamship, and the opening of the Suez Canal in 1869, India was transformed into a major source of cheap food and raw materials (tea, wheat, oil seeds, cotton) for Europe. India also was transformed into a major remunerative outlet for the products of the British capital goods industry and its enterprise. In the late nineteenth and early twentieth centuries, the large surplus that the British earned from India became pivotal for the enlarged reproduction of Britain's world-scale process of capital accumulation.[27]

---

26. Hobsbawm, *Age of Capital*, 32.

27. Arrighi, *Twentieth Century*, 263.

Up to the eighteenth century, the economic condition of India was relatively advanced. India's failure in the economic field was caused from the very onset by the ruthless and systematic rule of the British and despoliation of India. The East Indian Company and the British Parliament followed a selfish commercial policy. It discouraged Indian manufacturing in the early years of British rule in order to promote the rising manufacturers of England. The immediate harm which was done to India's economic potential was exceeded by long-term crippling. Even more lasting damage was inflicted upon the people of India.[28] Indian masses in the second half of the nineteenth century not only died of hunger because of the exploitation by Lancashire; but also perished in large numbers because of the demolition of Indian villages.

The actual source of famines was the free marketing of grain which was combined with local failure of incomes. The new market organization of labor and land broke up the old village.

> The term "exploitation" describes but ill a situation which became really grave [for the Indian producers] only after the East India Company's ruthless monopoly was abolished and free trade was introduced in India.[29]

According to Marx,

> all the civil wars, invasions, revolution, conquests, famines strangely complex, rapid and destructive as the successive action in Hindustan may appear, did not go deeper than its surface. England has broken down the entire framework of Indian society, without any symptoms of reconstitution yet appearing.[30]

In the early 1850s, Marx took to journalism, contributing to the New York Daily Tribune. Marx's articles attracted German refugee readers in North America. In his article "The Future Results of British Rule in India" Marx argued that England had to fulfill a double mission in India; one is destructive, while the other is regenerating. In other words, England annihilated the old Asiatic society, while laying the material foundations of Western society in Asia. The British became the first conquerors superior, inaccessible to and not succumbed to Hindu civilization as compared to previous conquerors who became Hinduized. The British rule in India was hardly anything beyond destruction.

28. Baran, *Political Economy*, 147–48.
29. Polanyi, *Transformation*, 160.
30. Marx, "British Rule," 313.

Nevertheless, according to Karl Marx, the work of regeneration began through the heap of ruins imposed by the British sword and was strengthened and perpetuated by the electric telegraph. The native army was organized and trained by the British drill-sergeant and became the condition for Indian self-emancipation. The free press became a new and powerful agent of reconstruction. Steam brought India into regular and rapid communication with Europe, vindicating it again from its isolated position and stagnation.

India was actually annexed to the Western world. The establishment of a net of railways entailed the exclusive way, according to Marx, for British colonialists to extract the cotton and other raw materials at diminished expenses for their manufacturers. Thus the railway-system would become the forerunner of modern industry in India.[31]

Marx scornfully quotes Mr. Campbell, who was influenced by the prejudices of the East India Company. Campbell avowed

> that the great mass of the Indian people possesses a great industrial energy, is well fitted to accumulate capital, and remarkable for a mathematical clearness of head, and talent for figures and exact sciences.[32]

The railway–system would dissolve the hereditary divisions of labor tied to the system of the Indian castes; this system had played a detrimental role as a decisive impediment to Indian progress and Indian power. Thus, the Indians would not reap the fruits of the new elements of society scattered by the British bourgeoisie. It would be so until the ruling classes in England could be supplanted by the industrial proletariat or when the Hindus could grow strong enough to throw off the English yoke.[33] In the British rule over India, Marx observed that "the profound hypocrisy and inherent barbarism of bourgeois civilization"[34] is revealed. This colonial form confiscated in India the dividends of rayahs—those who had invested their private savings in the Company's own funds. The trade was taken up in the murder and prostitution which was perpetrated in the temple of Juggernaut. The British colonialists were "the men of Property, Order, Family, and Religion." The colonial rule of the British bourgeoisie

31. Marx, "Future Results," 334–35.
32. Ibid., 335.
33. Ibid.
34. Ibid.

resembles a "hideous pagan idol, who would not drink the nectar but from the skulls of the slain."[35]

Marx argues that without the British Empire India would not have achieved the necessary social transformation. It threatened the idyllic village communities which had always been the scene of oriental despotism and brought an end to "stagnatory and vegetative life." "Whatever may have been the crimes of England she was the unconscious tool of history in bringing about that revolution."[36] Marx's intransigent Occidentalism remains questionable; however, his view of British rule in India still spoke out against the Eurocentric notion that the future for every society must follow the European way. We shall have occasion to deal with Marx's own view of Asia in more detail later in this chapter.

The Opium Wars, Rebellions, and Christian Mission

The weakening process of destabilizing the entire economic system culminated in the opium wars and the fall of China. 1839 was the outbreak of the Opium War, ending with the Treaty of Nanking (1842). In 1793 Emperor Quanlong wrote King George III.

> As your ambassador can see for himself, we posses all things. I set no value on objects strange or ingenious, and we have no use for your country's manufactures . . . There was [is] therefore no need to import the manufactures of outside barbarians in exchange for our own produce.[37]

Europe increasingly demanded Chinese silk, porcelain, liquor, and tea. Big profits were made by the merchants and the export duty on opium from India. By 1790 there were fifteen private trading firms in Calcutta which had also expanded eastward to the straits and to China. Since the EIC monopolized tea purchases in Chinathe commodities carried from India to China had to be exchanged in the EIC for low-value goods or for payment itself. The EIC used the extra gains to acquire payment or generate profits, developing an Asian example of triangular trade. According to the triangular trade with China, if the EIC owed an advance to X in Hong

---

35. Ibid., 336.
36. Kee, *Marx*, 273.
37. Frank, *World Accumulation*, 160.

Kong, X could buy cotton or opium from country trader Y and Y would remit to London by bill of exchange on the Court of Directors there.[38]

Following the Battle of Plassey in 1757, the British East India Company pursued a monopoly on production and export of Indian opium. The monopoly began in earnest in 1773. For the next fifty years opium trade would be the key to the East India Company's hold on the subcontinent. British merchants carrying no opium would buy tea in Canton on credit, and they would balance their debts by selling opium at auction in Calcutta. From there, the opium would reach the Chinese coast hidden aboard British ships, then be smuggled into China by native merchants. In 1797 the company further tightened its grip on the opium trade by enforcing direct trade between opium farmers and the British, and ending the role of Bengali purchasing agents. As of 1819, the drug trade boomed. Opium was profitable like gold.

In March 1839 the Emperor appointed a new strict Confucian commissioner, Lin Zexu, to control the opium trade at the port of Canton. His first course of action was to enforce the imperial demand that there be a permanent halt to drug shipments into China. He ordered the confiscation of all stocks of opium. The opium was burnt, but opium continued to be smuggled. When the British refused to end the trade, Lin imposed a trade embargo on the British. In 1839 Lin took the extraordinary step of presenting a letter directly to Queen Victoria questioning the moral integrity of the British government. Citing a strict prohibition of the trade within Great Britain, Lin questioned how it could then profit from the drug in China.

> Where is your conscience? I have heard that the smoking of opium is very strictly forbidden by your country; this is because the harm caused by opium is clearly understood. Since it is not permitted to do harm to your own country, then even less should you let it be passed on to the harm of other countries—how much less to China.[39]

The Opium Wars, also known as the Anglo-Chinese Wars, lasted from 1839 to 1842 and 1856 to 1860. These wars culminated in the dispute of trade and diplomatic difficulties between China and the British Empire. Opium was smuggled by merchants from British India into China in defiance of Chinese prohibition laws.

38. Fairbank, ed., *Cambridge History of China*, 168.
39. Lodwick, *Crusaders*, 27.

After open warfare between Britain and China in 1839, further disputes over the treatment of British merchants in Chinese ports resulted in the Second Opium War. China ratified the Treaty of Tianjin at the Convention of Beijing in 1860, ending the war. The Treaty of Nanking marked the opening of China to the Western influences of the nineteenth and twentieth centuries. Westerners directly took part in plotting and drafting unequal treaties, such as the Sino-British Treaty of Nanking of 1842, the Sino-American Treaty of Wanghea of 1844, the Sino-American and Sino-French treaties of Tientsin of 1858, and the Sino-French Convention of Beijing of 1860.

According to these unequal treaties, Western Catholic and Protestant missionaries could lease land for building their own places of worship in trade ports and enjoyed the protection of local officials. Missionaries could also freely lease or buy land for construction and other purposes in the provinces. Local Chinese officials must treat kindly and protect those missionaries who came to inland regions to preach their religions. Chinese officials must not impose prohibitions on Chinese who professed a religious faith. Many of the missionaries had arrived in China on ships carrying opium.

Following the Opium War of 1840, China declined to a semi-colonial country. During this process Western Protestantism and Catholicism were used by colonialism and imperialism as a tool for aggression against China, and a number of Western missionaries played a part in this war. They participated in the opium trade and in plotting the Opium War unleashed by Britain against China.

Robert Morrison (1782–1834) was the first Protestant missionary of the London Missionary Society (an interdenominational body founded in 1795) and arrived in Canton in 1807. From 1809 to 1815 Morrison worked as translator for the East India Company, participating in dumping opium in China. During the twenty-seven years of service Morrison and his colleagues baptized only ten Chinese, mostly missionary employees and students in Christian schools.[40]

Some missionaries strongly advocated military force by Western powers to make the Qing government open its coastal ports. For the sake of Christian mission they directly participated in the British military activities to invade China. Morrison was joined by other missionaries, notably by Karl F. A. Gützlaff (1803–1851), a Prussian missionary. He succeeded Morrison's son as Chinese secretary to the British authorities

---

40. Hughes, *Invasion of China*, 61.

in Hong Kong. During the first opium war (1841–1842) Gűtzlaff worked as translator and negotiator for the British commander-in-chief. His task was "the communication of reports from the invaders' Chinese spies" acknowledging that a British victory would definitely be an important opening for the sake of Christianizing China.[41] He made plans for the victorious advance of British troops to Nanjing that ended the war. He helped to negotiate the Treaty of Nanking in 1842.In the mission history during this period we read that the Western assumption of moral superiority underlay linking mission with aggressive claims to domination. European centrism led to the beliefs in the superiority of the white race. Mission was regarded to be useful for the advancement of the trading companies or for colonial annexations. In the German context there was an endorsement of a process of making Germany a colonial power with German settlements overseas. A European sense of manifest destiny was expressed in which "the countries of Europe would remain the agents of the world's history and fate until the Last Day."[42]

According to one of the terms of the 1842 treaty, extra-territoriality was to be established; a foreigner did not come under the jurisdiction of Chinese law. The missionaries enjoyed extraterritoriality, and they were not governed by China's laws. The Western powers gave their missionaries in China protection on the strength of the consular jurisdiction they enjoyed. Taking advantage of extraterritoriality, some Western missionaries were backed by the aggressive imperialist forces. The missionaries who were caught travelling beyond legal limits were in the same position as the trader who was caught smuggling opium.[43] They forcibly occupied land, and bullied and oppressed Chinese officials and civilians. In 1842 the Qing authorities sued for peace, which concluded with the Treaty of Nanjing which was negotiated in August of that year and ratified in 1843. In the treaty, China was forced to pay an indemnity to Britain, open four ports to Britain, and cede Hong Kong to Queen Victoria.

The Protestants after 1860 were successful in their penetration of the Chinese interior led by J. Hudson Taylor, the founder of the non-denominational China Inland Mission (CIM). Over 90 percent of all Protestants were British or American.

Once the trade of opium imports was legalized, Britain forced the Chinese government into signing the Treaty of Nanjing and the Treaty

41. Moffett, *History of Christianity in Asia II*, 297.

42. Duchrow, *Europe*, 24.

43. Hughes, *Invasion of China*, 62.

of Tianjin. They are also known as the Unequal Treaties. Many Chinese found these agreements humiliating and these sentiments were considered to have contributed to the Taiping Rebellion (1851–1866). It was one of the cataclysmic events in the history of China.

The leader of the Taiping revolutionary movement, Hung Hsiu-chuan (born January 1, 1814) became the king of Taiping country. He believed that his mission, according to the heavenly authority of the Christian God, was to rule China in order to unite all people in the worship of the one true God. He gained a few converts to the new faith which grew over a relatively short period into a huge revolutionary army. Strict observance of the Ten Commandments and attendance at daily worship were mandatory for the Taiping Army.

To the end of their lives Hung and his fellow leaders held firm to their Christian faith. The Taiping revolutionary movement envisioned a complete reform of China's social, economic, political, and military institutions. This vision was often outlined in the biblical phrase "a new heaven and a new earth" (Rev 21:1). After that the Boxer Rebellion (1899–1901) ensued. Finally the downfall of the Qing Dynasty in 1912 was an end to dynastic China. In the historical perspective, the Taiping movement is regarded as a forerunner of the National Revolution of 1911. Dr. Sun yat-sen proclaimed himself as the successor of Hung and welcomed the few Taiping soldiers remaining to his first revolutionary organization.[44]

EUROCENTRIC VIEW ON ASIA AND ASIATIC MODE OF PRODUCTION

As we have already seen, Marx was undertaking an analysis of Britain's foreign trade and economic situation which had been causing profound upheavals in Oriental society, for instance, the Taiping rebellion in China and the Sepoy mutiny in India. The theory of despotic government in the East explains that the King was the sole proprietor of the land. Adam Smith also wrote of the caste system in ancient Egypt and in India; which was effective because of the division of the country and the hereditary maintenance of the division.[45]

The fundamental characteristic of Marx's AMP (Asiatic mode of production) is the absence of private ownership of the land which was the

---

44. Jen Yu-wen, *Taiping*, 1–9. See further, Moffett, *History of Christianity in Asia II*, 298–300.

45. Smith, *Wealth of Nations*, 62, 645.

actual key to the Oriental heaven. According to Marx, the Indian village community was self-sustaining and included agricultural and handicraft production which connected self-sufficiency to the backwardness of the village. The idyllic village communities had always been the scene of Oriental despotism and formed stagnant and vegetative life. For geographical and climactic reasons, agriculture required hydraulic works in order to prosper. The state concentrated the greater part of the social surplus product for artificial irrigation. Maintaining the appearance of social strata by this surplus, the state constituted the dominant power in society—therefore, the expression of "Oriental despotism."[46]

In *Grundrisse*, Marx took up the question of the original accumulation of capital as a systematic process within the political economy of capitalism. AMP can be seen in connection with Marx's systematic discussion of original accumulation of capital and colonialism. The epochs of the economic formation of society are forms which preceded the capitalist production. One section is subtitled "Concerning the Process which precedes the formation of the capital relation or of the original accumulation."[47]

Concerning forms preceding capitalist production, Marx presupposed three different modes of production: Asiatic, classical antiquity, and Germanic. These different forms became points of departure for the class society. In the Asiatic form, the individual had no property but only possession. Here the real proprietor was the commune so that property was only communal property in land. "The Asiatic form necessarily hangs on most tenaciously and for the longest time."[48] In the Asiatic form the individual never became a proprietor but only a possessor. Slavery and serfdom were only further developments of the form of property resting on the clan system.[49] The individual member of the commune never entered into the relation of freedom, because one was rooted to the spot, ingrown. The original form of the property was direct common property in an oriental form.[50]

According to AMP, the real communities were the only hereditary possessors; the individual was in fact propertyless. In Oriental despotism and propertylessness, the communal property existed as the foundation which was created by a combination of manufacturing and agriculture

46. Marx, *Grudrisse*, 473. See Wittfogel, *Oriental Despotism*.
47. Ibid., 471.
48. Ibid., 486.
49. Ibid., 493.
50. Ibid., 497.

within the small commune. The form of the lordly dominion occurred first in the Slavonic communes and in the Rumanians. This form may extend to the communality of labor in Mexico, Peru, especially among the early Celts, and a few clans of India. These communal conditions were very important among the Asiatic peoples. Means of communication appeared as the work of the despotic regime over the little communes.[51]

In the absence of private ownership of the land, the big landowners and peasant tenants retained two distinct forms of private property in land—the great desideratum. The idyllic village communities were based on the mode of communal ownership, which was the material foundation for Asiatic society. This was also the definite reason of stagnation. Irrigation and large-scale public works undertaken by the state monarch were the foundation of agriculture. The social life of the village communities was little affected by dynastic changes. At the court of the Mogul empire, the village communities had none of the institutional relations of civil society apart from the relations of rent, tax and exchange. Thus, not stagnation of the productive forces, but retarded development proved to be fatal to the nations based on AMP.[52] The relatively underdeveloped class served as the universal servants of the Orient which was different from that of the Western form of slavery or peasant system.

At bottom, Marx reiterates the Eurocentric view of stagnation as the essential feature of Asia. Marx regarded external colonial dominion as inevitable for the abolition of AMP in Indian and Chinese society. European industrial capitalism was encountered in the eighteenth century in terms of the conquest of India or the capital penetration of China. This colonial penetration would cause social revolution in the colonized society. Marx saw such revolution in the case of the Taiping rebellion (1850–66). Nevertheless, Marx would anticipate that an enormous revolution such as the Taiping rebellion would bring a definite impact on capitalist society in Europe. For Marx, anti-colonial struggle was connected with the revolution of the industrial proletariat.

AMP, under the rubric of "pre-capitalist forms of production," was a part in Marx's reflection of the primitive accumulation of capital tied to his view of Spanish colonialism in the Americas. The colonies provided a market for the growing manufacturing, including a vast increment of accumulation ensured by the mother country's monopoly of the market. The colonial system was in almost exclusive possession of the East Indian

51. Ibid., 474.
52. Mandel, *Formation*, 123.

trade and commerce between the south-east and north-west of Europe.[53] "The treasures captured outside Europe by undisguised looting, enslavement and murder flowed back to the mother-country and were turned into capital there."[54]

In Asia capitalism actually arose during the seventeenth-nineteenth centuries. In 1658 Louis XIV of France sent six Jesuits to China on a specifically scientific mission. Leibniz had extensive correspondence with the Jesuits in Beijing. In 1689, Leibniz, in correspondence with the Jesuit Grimaldi, stressed the wealth of information available in China to the observer and asked for more detailed information about the manufacture of metals, tea, paper, silk, 'true' porcelain, dyes, glass, etc. In the 1720s, a Chinese winnowing-machine was sent to France and attracted much attention. Until the 17th century, productivity in European agriculture was severely limited. The 17th to 19th centuries saw a transformation of North European agricultural technology, through the development of the turn-plough with a curved iron mould-board, the seed-drill and the horse-hoe. The transformation of European agriculture coincided with Western scholars' growing awareness of the civilizations of the Far East and in particular China. China made a contribution to Europe's agricultural revolution.[55]

As compared to the historical development of Western Europe, Confucian society or the Confucian mode of production in eighteenth century China cannot be fully explained by a theory of historical materialism which broadly outlines stages of Asiatic, ancient, feudal, and modern bourgeois modes of production. Marx's theory of history and society shows serious limitations and mistakes in regard to non-Western society. If we explain the Confucian society or mode of production, the Confucian society may be located as the most advanced society. That is, a Gentry society coming in between feudal society and capitalist society.[56]

European exceptionalism misrepresented how Asian economies and societies were shaped by participation in the world economy. For the centuries between 1400 and at least 1700 there was nothing exceptional about Europe; rather it remained marginal, benefiting from trade with nations of Asia. AMP is vulnerable to an ideology of Eurocentrism, a part and parcel of Western colonialism and cultural imperialism. The Chinese Ming/

---

53. Marx, *Capital I*, 918.

54. Ibid.

55. Needham, *Science & Civilization*, 581.

56 Eberhard, *Conquerors and Rulers*.

Qing, Indian Mughal, Perisian Safavid, and Turkish Ottoman empires carried much greater political and military weight than Europe. "China is a much richer country than any part of Europe" (Adam Smith).[57]

Sharing third world scholars' critique of the Eurocentricsm of Marx's AMP, I argue that there is still an important insight within that framework in regard to Marx's own analysis of the primitive accumulation of capital in Spain and the New Indies. If we see AMP within the perspective of primitive capital accumulation, it becomes useful in the analysis of the conditions for colonization and colonial penetration of Western capitalism at a global scale. "Asiatic" Mode of Production is a misnomer, as the mode is not indigenous to Asia. Rather it was the result of colonization, and thus applicable to the analysis of any colonized country.I argue that we must read AMP in light of the relationship between the god of Western capitalism and the victims of colonies. Marx denounced "the Christian character of primitive accumulation"[58] which was connected with a critical analysis of British rule and Christian mission in India and China. According to Marx, the "strange God" preached God's self along with the old divinities of Europe on the altar. It "proclaimed the making of profit as the ultimate and the sole purpose of mankind."[59]

POLITICAL ECONOMY AND THE SELF-REGULATING MARKET

Adam Smith (1723–1790), one of the key figures of the Scottish Enlightenment, proposed a foundational concept of political economy in light of the self-regulating market. Although his best known work is *An Inquiry into the Nature and Causes of the Wealth of Nations*(usually abbreviated as *The Wealth of Nations*,)[60] it was in *Theory of Moral Sentiments* that Smith first referred to the "invisible hand" to describe the apparent benefits to society of people behaving in their own interests. His aim in the work was to explain the source of humankind's ability to form moral judgments, in spite of the human's natural inclinations toward self-interest, selfishness, and rapacity.

As he argues,

57. Frank, *ReOrient*, 13.

58. Marx, *Capital I*, 917.

59. Ibid., 918.

60. Smith, *Wealth of Nations*.

> the rich only select from the heap (of the harvest) what is most
> precious and agreeable. They consume little more than the poor;
> and in spite of their natural selfishness and rapacity . . . they
> divide with the poor the produce of all their improvements.
> They are led by an invisible hand to make nearly the same dis-
> tribution of the necessaries of life which would have been made
> had the earth been divided into equal portions among all its
> inhabitants.[61]

Here Smith proposed a theory of sympathy in which the act of observing others made people aware of themselves and the morality of their
own behavior.

However, in *The Wealth of Nations* (published in 1776), Smith tried
to justify the social order based upon the quest after individual interests.
Economic behavior was primarily guided by the fundamental force of self-
interest. The economy as a system in which people interact in markets was
regulated on their own accord without interference from outside intervention. He advanced the idea of the invisible hand in a direction of self-
interest and a self-regulating market. An invisible hand, without intending
it, without knowing it, advances the interest of the society.

> When providence divided the earth among a few lordly masters,
> it neither forgot nor abandoned those who seemed to have been
> left out in the partition. These last, too, enjoy their share of all
> that it produces.[62]

Similarly in the *Wealth of Nations*, he stated that every individual intends
only his/her own security by preferring the support of domestic than that
of foreign industry. Intending only his/her own gain, as in many cases,
every individual is "led by an invisible hand to promote an end which has
no part of his intention."[63]

It is argued that Smith was not a staunch doctrinaire in regard to unfettered free enterprise.[64] Nevertheless, under the banner of conditions of
perfect liberty and perfect competition, he was vulnerable to the wretch-
edness surrounding him. For him competition is economically efficient.
Every individual is continually in search of that individuals' own advantage

---

61. Smith, *Theory of Moral*, 264–65.

62. Ibid., 263–64.

63. Smith, *Wealth of Nations*, 572.

64. Smith, *Theory of Moral*, xii.

by "find[ing] out the most advantageous employment for whatever capital he can command."[65] Smith went so far as to write about the poor.

> In what constitutes the real happiness of human life, they are in no respect inferior to those who seem so much above them. In ease of body and peace of mind, all the different ranks of life are nearly upon a level, and the beggar, who suns himself by the side of the highway, possesses that security which kings are fighting for.[66]

It is argued that Smith did not esteem the invisible hand in which individual exchange in the marketplace leads to the greatest good for society.[67] Nevertheless, it is certain that Smith was not convinced of the encroachment of government on economic activity. Smith's understanding of the human being is grounded in the activity of exchange in the market place: "The propensity to truck, barter and exchange one thing for another . . . is common to all men, and to be found in no other race of animals."[68] The division of labor emerges from a propensity in human nature to exchange. This propensity to exchange is encouraged by self-interest, leading to division of labor. Insofar as that division of labor is occasioned and limited by the extent of the power of exchanging, the rise of market is unavoidable by the use of money. Labor is the real measure and universal standard of exchangeable value in exchange between commodities.[69]

Insofar as every individual does not violate the laws of justice, each individual is left perfectly free to pursue his or her own interest and to bring both industry and capital into competition with those of any other individuals. In this system, the sovereign has only three duties: first, the duty of protecting the society from the violence and invasion of other independent societies (by means of a military force); secondly, the duty of protecting every member of the society from the injustice or oppression of every other member of it, or the duty of establishing an exact administration of justice (upon which the liberty of every individual depends); and thirdly, the duty of erecting and maintaining certain public works and certain public institutions that are not capable of bringing a profit to individuals.[70]

65. Smith, *Wealth of Nations*, 569.
66. Smith, *Theory of Moral*, 265.
67. Rothschild, *Economic Sentiments*, 116.
68. Smith, *Wealth of Nations*, 22.
69. Ibid., 31, 52.
70. Ibid., 879, 901, 916.

In consequence of the division of labor, the great increase of the quantity of work was because of three different circumstances: First, the increase of dexterity in every working individual, secondly, the saving of time, and lastly, the invention of all the machines by which labor was so much facilitated and abridged.[71] A division of labor would affect a great increase in production. However Smith failed to consider that in the progress of the division of labor, one's dexterity in performing a few simple operations is to be acquired only at the expense of one's intellectual and social virtues.

The world of Smith was that of manufacturing capitalism; mills gather together workers with manual skills; the trade to which Smith referred remains at the craft level (fuller, spinner, weaver, dyer, master tailor, shoemaker, carpenter, furniture maker, locksmith, etc). For Smith labor was the real measure of the exchangeable value of all commodities. Smith tied his thinking about productive labor to his analysis of capital accumulation.

Regarding the different employment of capital, Smith stated that capital may be employed in four different ways. First, in procuring the rude produce annually required for the use and consumption of the society; secondly, in manufacturing and preparing that rude produce for immediate use and consumption ; thirdly, in transporting either the rude or manufactured produce to where they are wanted (those of all the wholesale merchants); or lastly, in dividing particular portions of either into such small parcels as suit the occasional demands of those who want them (those of all retailers). All of those four methods of employing capital are necessary to each other.[72]

THE MARKET AND COLONIES

Smith understood the global logic of capital, the logic of accumulation in connection to foreign commerce.[73] What interests us in this context is Smith's view of the colonialism of the New World. He asserted that the discovery of America and the passage to the East Indies by the Cape of Good Hope were the two greatest and most important events in history.[74] In the event of this encounter, all the commercial benefits were sunk and lost in

71. Ibid., 14.

72. Smith, *Wealth of Nations*, 459.

73. Ibid., 474.

74. Ibid., 749, 793.

dreadful misfortune, while the superiority of force on the side of the Europeans committed every sort of injustice in the colonies with impunity.[75]

Smith acknowledged that in consequence of the discoveries of Columbus, the pious purpose of converting indigenous people to Christianity sanctified the injustice of the Christian mission project. The Council of Castile was attracted by the gold, determined to take possession of countries in which the inhabitants were not capable of defending themselves against the colonizers. A method of plundering defenseless natives was justified, and its sole motive was the hope of finding treasures of gold, a thirst for gold. The subsequent Spanish enterprises followed the same motive.[76] According to Smith, a decisive turning point took place in the European discoveries of America and no human wisdom could foresee what benefits or what misfortunes would come from these events.

The fortunes of the conquering west and the misfortunes of the conquered non-west formed a single historical process of a capitalist world-economy. The centrality of colonial force determined the distribution of costs and benefits among participants in the world market economy established as a result of the discoveries. Concerning Smith's theory of colony, Arrighi observes that "the fusion of state and capital was the vital ingredient in the emergence of a distinctly capitalist layer on top of, and in antithesis to, the layer of market economy."[77]

Smith indicated that as the world market economy widened and deepened exchange, it would act as an unstoppable equalizer of relationships of force between the west and the non-west. The inequality of force between west and non-west would increase; world market formation and the military conquest of the non-West proceeded in collaboration. Through opening a new market to Europe, it gave occasion to new divisions of labor, improvement of the productive powers of labor and the increase of its produce in Europe bringing the real revenue and wealth of the inhabitants.

In the disposal of the surplus produce, every European nation endeavored to monopolize the commerce of its colonies. Smith was not ignorant of triangular trade; Great Britain and its colonies became almost the sole market for all the sugar that was produced in the British plantation. Rum, as a very important article, was carried by the Americans to the coast of Africa, from which the Americans brought back slaves in return. British merchants were able to establish an advantageous carrying trade

75. Ibid., 794.

76. Ibid., 711–12.

77. Arrighi, *Long Twentieth Century*, 20.

between the plantations and foreign countries. Great Britain was to be the center of emporium.[78]

The policy of Europe had engaged in "the folly of hunting after gold and the injustice of coveting the possession of a country."[79] The monopoly was the principal badge of the dependency of the colonies upon the mother country. The surplus produce of the colonies was the original source of all increase of enjoyment and industry in Europe which derived from the colonies.[80] Smith's idea of monopoly, surplus produce, and its different degree of exercise may have lead to an explanation of underdevelopment in terms of external factors between mother country and colonies.[81]

Proponents of dependency and underdevelopment find interest in Smith's critique of mercantilist monopoly. Great Britain should voluntarily abandon all authority and dominion over the colonies, leaving them to elect their own magistrates, and enact their own laws.[82] Nevertheless, Smith does not understand that the colonial reality of economic injustice and violence would also have ramifications built on the chaotic and unrestrained logic of the free market.

Driven by a so-called "invisible hand," Smith believed that when an individual pursued his/her self-interest, he/she indirectly promoted the good of society. Self-interested competition in the free market, he argued, would tend to benefit society as a whole by keeping prices low, while still building in an incentive for a wide variety of goods and services. His faith in an "invisible hand" built on the logic of self-regulating market was already defeated by the reality of colonies. In his analysis of colonies, the relationship between developed country and underdeveloped country is emphasized, but his critique is done only for the sake of the principle of the self-regulating market which would also be the driving force for capital accumulation and expansion at a global scale.

Laissez Faire and the Free Market

An economic ideology of laissez faire and the free market was continued in the work of David Ricardo. Ricardo (1772–1823) was an English political economist, often credited with systematizing economics, and was

78. Smith, *Wealth of Nations*, 735.

79. Ibid., 747.

80. Ibid., 752.

81. Frank, *Dependent Accumulation*, 36.

82. Smith, *Wealth of Nations*, 782.

one of the most influential of the classical economists, along with Adam Smith. Ricardo became interested in political economy after reading Adam Smith's *The Wealth of Nations* in 1799.

Ricardo insisted that the free play of the market, that is to say, the law of supply and demand, assures equilibrium; not only economic equilibrium but also equilibrium among the three classes of society (landowners, owners of capital, and laborers). Property, free enterprise, and the free play of the market should ensure the best of all possible worlds. Governmental action was essentially restricted to ensuring order, security, and justice. Beyond this limit, it was a usurpation of conscience, intelligence, and labor, that is, human freedom. For the rest, laissez-faire!

According to Ricardo the mutual benefit from trade (or exchange), exists even when one party or nation is more productive than its trading counterpart in every way possible; such mutual benefit is conditioned upon the fact that each concentrates on the activities where it has a relative productivity advantage. Under a system of perfectly free commerce, each country devoted its capital and labor to such enjoyment by being most beneficial to each other.[83]

Ricardo's most famous work is his *Principle of Political Economy and Taxation* (1817) in which he opened the first chapter with a statement of the labor theory of value. The value of a commodity for exchange depends on the relative quantity of labor necessarily spent for its production.[84] The labor is the foundation of the exchangeable value of all things. Influenced by Ricardo's labor theory of value, Marx later looked for a labor theory as the groundwork for a theory of surplus value. However, Ricardo himself did not search for a theory of exploitation related to surplus value.

The labor theory of value states that the relative price of two goods is determined by the ratio of the quantities of labor required in their production. The employment of machinery and other fixed and durable capital become cause for the rise or fall in the value of labor. There can be no rise in the value of labor without a fall of profits.[85] To the extent that labor becomes foundational for the value of commodities, the comparative quantity of labor is necessary to their production. The power of purchasing is the natural price if not disturbed by any accidental cause. In the market of a large town, the principle which apportions capital to each trade in

83. Ricardo, *Principles*, 81.

84. Ibid., 5

85. Ibid., 18, 21.

the price amount is more active than is generally supposed.[86] With the progress of society the natural price of labor has a tendency to rise, while the natural price of all commodities has a tendency to fall in the progress of wealth and population.[87] The cost of production ultimately regulates the price of commodities rather than the proportion between the supply and demand. It is certain that the proportion between supply and demand affects the market value of a commodity only temporarily.[88]

Ricardo argues that wages should be left to the fair and free competition of the market. They should never be controlled by the interference of the legislature. The poor laws as the legislature intended were not to amend the condition of the poor, but to deteriorate the condition of both poor and rich.[89] According to Ricardo's theory, even if a country could produce everything more efficiently than another country, it would reap gains from specializing in what it was best at producing and trading with other nations. Ricardo believed that wages should be left to free competition, so there should be no restrictions on the importation of agricultural products from abroad. The benefits of comparative advantage are both distributional and related to improved real income. Within Ricardo's theory, distributional effects implied that foreign trade could not directly affect profits, because profits changed only in response to the level of wages. The effects on income were always beneficial because foreign trade did not affect value.

In view of Smith's observation on colonial trade, Ricardo stated that Smith had demonstrated most satisfactorily the advantages of free trade while acknowledging injustice suffered by colonies. Contrary to Smith, Ricardo advocated for an equal privilege of foreign trade under ordinary circumstances between the mother country and the colony.[90] Ricardo's position supported an idea that an international division of labor through free trade would be advantageous to the world as a whole.

> If capital freely flowed towards those countries where it could
> most profitably be employed, there could be no difference in the
> rate of profit, and no other difference in the real or labor price
> of commodities, than the additional quantity of labor required

86. Ibid., 49.
87. Ibid., 52.
88. Ibid., 260.
89. Ibid., 61.
90. Ibid., 229.

to convey them to the various markets where they were to be sold.[91]

Further,

> The same rule which regulates the relative value of commodities in one country does not regulate the relative value of the commodities exchanged between two or more countries . . . In one and the same country, profits are, generally speaking, always on the same level . . . It is not so between different countries.[92]

If capital is mobile, and if the rate of profit is equalized throughout the world, there is no difference between international value and national value. The cost of this factor is self-equalizing without any international competition. However, Ricardo's theory is challenged, because his theory of value cannot apply any longer in international trade.[93]

In Ricardo's theory of labor value, the value of a commodity for exchange in the world of the market depends on the relative quantity of labor which is necessary for its production. The labor affects the value of the commodities. The price is the monetary expression of the value, so that the distribution of produced wealth will be based upon wages. Along with Ricardo, the interests of the workers, the capitalists, and the landowners are in opposition. In his idea of political economy the poor stand in direct opposition to his obvious principle of the fair and free competition of the market. "No scheme for the amendment of the poor laws merits the least attention which has not their abolition for its ultimate object."[94]

It is from Ricardo's theses and from the critique of their weak points that Marx began to develop his analysis of capital in solidarity with those who are poor workers.

THE COLONIES, THE SELF-REGULATING MARKET, AND SELF-LIBERATING LABOR

The history of Dutch colonial administration is "one of the most extraordinary relations of treachery, bribery, massacre, and meanness."[95] Marx introduces W. Howitt's remarks about the Christian colonial system.

91. Ibid., 142–43.
92. Ibid., 139.
93. Emmanuel, *Unequal Exchange*, xi, xxxii.
94. Ricardo, *Principles*, 62.
95. Marx, *Capital I*, 916.

> The barbarities and desperate outrages of the so-called Christian race, throughout every region of the world" in any age of the earth . . . "are not to be paralleled by those of any other race," "they are fierce, untaught, reckless of mercy and shame. [96]

Colonization of suitable regions was envisaged in the 1621 charter of the Dutch West Indian Company (WIC). WIC was controlled by the party of Orangists, Calvinists, Zeelanders, and Southern Netherlander immigrants, and it was involved in conquering all or parts of Brazil. In 1674, the WIC was reorganized as a slave-trading enterprise in contraband trade with Spanish America and in sugar production in Surinam. The English East India Company overshadowed the performance of the VOC. The English East India Company started to bring returns in the form of plunder and tribute from India. The historical significance of the Plassey plunder lay therein.[97]

Malachi Postlethwayt, a staunch mercantilist, asserted that the colonies, because of their prosperity indebted to the mother country, owed gratitude and "all indispensable duty—to be immediately dependent on their original parent and to make their interest subservient thereunto."[98] In this context the ideas of philosophers flourished: evidence, clarity, conformity to reason; a wonderful universe, mechanics following eternal laws established by a supreme being, God, at once all powerful and all knowing; a world based upon natural laws, natural right, and natural morality were to be rediscovered. This world of Western civilization promoted the idea of progress, the development of the mind, knowledge, and enlightenment.

The eighteenth century was usually presented as a century of expanding trade, especially world trade, and of increasing market, agricultural, and manufacturing production, accompanied by rising prices and population growth. This was the century of the strengthening of British capitalism. Capitalism was still mainly colonial, mercantile, and manufacturing. From the new wave of enclosures and the proletarization of the rural masses, along with the cumulative movement of accumulation and technical progress, it was also able to create the conditions for the "Industrial Revolution" of the nineteenth century.

The original meaning of the term proletarian which was linked to fertility and mendacity was a striking expression of economic prejudice. This prejudice was the source both of the crude exploitation theory of

96. Ibid.

97. Arrighi, *Long Twentieth century*, 201, 210.

98. Beaud, *History of Capitalism*, 45.

early capitalism and of a social catastrophe. This perspective was related to the rehabilitation of laissez-faire economy. The term "Industrial Revolution" was now frowned upon as conveying an exaggerated idea of what was essentially a slow process of change.[99]

A gradual unfolding of the forces of technological progress transformed the lives of the people, but many suffered in the course of the change, without doubt. All the ills of social and cultural catastrophe can be seen in regard to the economic liberalism of laissez-faire. The self-regulating market upheld that labor, land, and money were essential to a market economy. Market mechanisms received unparalleled momentum once world commodity markets, world capital markets, and world currency markets were organized under the gold standard.[100]

In the situation of the working class in Great Britain at the beginning of the 1840s, the worker became, in fact, the slave of the property-holding class. Effectually like a slave, the worker was sold like a piece of goods, and rose and fell in value like a commodity.[101] With steam and machinery revolutionizing industrial technology, industrial expansion became the main factor in integrating the market of the whole world into a single world market. The penetration of the East Indies and Chinese markets, the colonization of the Americas and colonial trade created the conditions for the emergence of modern industry. The formation of a single world market entailed a cosmopolitan character, endowing production and consumption to every country.[102]

As the capitalism of the nineteenth century developed, it engendered a brutal confrontation between bourgeois wealth and workers' misery. Social ideas were not the monopoly of socialists. In 1864 English trade unionists, militant French workers, and émigrés from Germany (including Karl Marx), Italy, Switzerland, and Poland created the International Workingman Association in London. The wealth and the power of the bourgeoisie developed on the basis of the dreadful misery of the workers of the nineteenth century. Marx produced the analysis of this capitalist system in order to illuminate the logic of capitalism and its necessary downfall for the sake of the project of liberation: transition, or exodus from the self-regulating market society toward realm of freedom and liberation. Marx's *Capital* was a scientific analysis of the historical capitalism of 1867, which is the topic under investigation in the following chapter.

99. Polanyi, *Great Transformation,* 161.

100. Ibid., 76.

101. Engels, *Condition of Working Class,* 159–202.

102. Arrighi, *Long Twentieth Century,* 251.

5

Sociocritical Dialectics in the Shift from Alienation to Emancipation

THIS CHAPTER IS A study of the limitations and contributions of Karl Marx in the economic field. I shall deal with basic elements in Marx's political economy and his method of historical materialism in reference to Hegel, because Marx's thought cannot be properly understood without Hegel's concept of labor and alienation in civil society. Marx's critique of religion implies his negative evaluation of the role of church mission in the domestic-economic context, as well as in the colonial context. As we have previously seen, Marx's critique of mission and colonialism and his analysis of the Christian character of capital accumulation remains a challenge to the church's responsibility for justice in the context of world economy.

In order to understand Marx's critique of religion it is important to examine his critique of civil society, which is supported by the church. Hegel as the representative of the alliance between state and church, which is utilized by today's neo-liberal theoreticians, comes under investigation at this point. Diverse perspectives on Hegel in the liberative postcolonial context should constitute a counter argument to this neoliberal interpretation of Hegel. Hegel shall be dealt with for the sake of supporting liberative and postcolonial theory.

Karl Marx (1818–1883) owed a great deal to the thought of classical economists who advanced his economic thinking. Since his doctoral study, Marx was under the pressure of his experiences with social problems. Socioeconomic and political problems, such as the treatment of wood thieves in the Rhine provinces of Prussia, the uprising of the Silesian textile workers, the strikes in England, and the class struggle in France, turned him to preoccupy himself with economic studies.[1] We observe that there was a trajectory in Marx's theoretical development: from critique of religion to critique of philosophy; from critique of philosophy to critique of the state; from critique of the state to critique of society, that is, from critique of politics to critique of political economy, leading to a critique of private property.[2]

What Marx attempted to give account of in his *Capital* was the capitalist impulse to growth, characterizing production for private profit and the predominant use of profit for capital accumulation. The concentration of wealth and power in a small number of giant industrial and financial corporations had generated the increasingly universal struggle between capital and labor. Marx laid bare the capitalist mode of production as the laws of motion governing the origin, rise, development, decline, and disappearance of a given social economic formation. Each specific social form of economic organization has its own particular economic laws. In dealing with basic elements of political economy in Marx's thought, focus is drawn toward Marx's concept of labor and alienation in connection with Hegel. Hegel's dialectic between the master and the slave and his concept of human labor remain influential in Marx's economic development.

BASIC ELEMENTS IN MARX'S POLITICAL ECONOMY

Marx referred to his approach as the materialist conception of history. The non-economic features of a society (e.g., social classes, political structures, and ideologies) are seen as co-determining factors upon human economic activity. Human beings are conditioned by a definite development of their productive forces and the relationships corresponding to such forces. In producing the means of subsistence, people produced their actual material life.[3] The modes of production (the Asiatic, the ancient, the feudal, and the modern bourgeois methods of production) can be designated as epochs in the progress of the economic formation of society.[4]

This mode of production is a definite form of individuals' activity. What the individuals are coincides with their production: both with what

1. Mandel, *Formation*, 9–26.
2. Ibid., 10–11.
3. McLellan, *Karl Marx*, 160.
4. Ibid., 390.

they produce and with how they produce.[5] The first historical act is the production of the means to satisfy needs, that is, the production of material life itself. The nature of individuals depends on the material conditions that determine their production. Thereby, productive force determines the nature of society. The history of humanity, according to Marx, is to be studied in relation to the history of industry and exchange.[6]

For Marx, productive forces refer to the means of production such as tools, instruments, technology, land, raw materials, and human knowledge and abilities. The character of the production relations is determined by the character of the productive forces. In each of these social stages, people interacted with nature and produced their living in different ways. The production relations of society arose on the basis of given productive forces and were identified as the economic base of society. Out of the foundation of the economic base arose certain ideological forms: political institutions, laws, customs, culture, ideas, ways of thinking, and morality. These constituted the political/ideological superstructure of society. This superstructure not only has its origin in the economic base, but also in interaction with the character and development of that economic base. The way people organize society is determined by the economic base and the relations that arise from its mode of production.

Humans are inevitably involved in production relations (roughly speaking, economic relationships or institutions), which constitute our social relations. Production relations progress in correspondence with the development of the productive forces. Relations of production help determine the degree and types of the development of the forces of production. The superstructure is ultimately an expression of the mode of production that combines both the forces and relations of production on which the society is founded. Explaining the origins of the capitalist mode of production as a product of history, Marx pointed toward the inevitable historical decline and fall of the social system.

Neither legal relations nor political forms could be comprehended by themselves. They originated in the material conditions of life, the totality of civil society. The autonomy of this civil society, however, has to be sought in political economy. In the social production, people inevitably enter into definite relations, independent of their will; that is, relations of production that are appropriate to a given stage in the development of their material forces of production.

5. Ibid., 161.
6. Ibid., 166.

In his preface to "A Critique of Political Economy," Marx argues that legal relations and forms of state are rooted in the material conditions of life under the civil society. The sum total of the relations of production (rationality, organizational skills, administration) constitutes the economic structure of society, which is the real foundation. Upon this economic foundation the intellectual superstructure rises and definite forms of social consciousness correspond to the economic foundation. The social existence determines human consciousness. At a certain stage wherein the material forces of production in society come into conflict with the existing relations of production, the relations of production in a given society turn into fetters because of excessive development of the productive forces. From this moment on, an era of social revolution begins. The changes in the economic foundation can be explained by such a period of transformation from the contradictions of material life. That is the conflict between the social forces of production and the relations of production.[7]

In this light, Marx also made a profound analysis of the social conditions in which the Homeric epics were written. Marx provocatively states,

> The difficulty we are confronted with is not, however, that of understanding how Greek art and epic poetry are associated with certain forms of development. The difficulty is that they still give us aesthetic pleasure and are in certain respects regarded as a standard and unattainable ideal.[8]

Given Marx's assertion about human consciousness and social existence, there is a tension inherent in Marx's own method. In the statement about the artistic influence and a certain economic stage, we perceive that the artist's products and epic poetry created within the social-material condition still transcend the given social material life. They can become cross-culturally communicable and influential on human life in different times and places. In a socioeconomic connection of human beings with one another, Marx himself hinted at an important role of language, which is as old as consciousness. However, Marx's understanding of language remains completely limited in his entire program of the interpretation of capitalist society. This is because Marx conceptualizes language only as arising from need: the necessity of intercourse with the other.[9] Marx's meager and unqualified notion of language remains a substantial problem

---

7. Ibid., 389–400.

8. Lukacs, *Hegel*, 510.

9. McLellan, *Karl Marx*, 167.

with his economic theory. In fact, Marx left his tension unresolved and his materialist theory of interpretation was doomed to become a theory of economic reductionism.

In contrast to Marx, linguistic interaction is correlated with material life. Discursive act and formation can be seen and analyzed in light of dialectical interplay between economic life, rational organization, institution, and the ideological sphere of superstructure. Human consciousness and existence are linguistically mediated and assembled through personal formation in the family, education, and social integration.

What occupies Marx's concern is not language, but the division of labor. Following in the footsteps of Adam Smith, Marx argued that the division of labor developed spontaneously by virtue of natural predisposition through needs or accidents, as, for instance, in the sexual act or in physical strength. Division of labor became true when a division of material and mental labor appeared. With the division of labor developed, all the contradictions were implicit: the contradiction between the interest of the separated individual or individual family and the communal interest of all individuals in intercourse with one another.[10]

In light of a materialist concept of social history, Marx's theory of interpretation aims at revealing commodity production, capital accumulation and expansion, and market economy in the socio-economic development. All of these are operated by objective economic laws, which stand behind the backs of the producers. Capital is a social relation between people, appearing as a relation between things or between people and things. Capitalism is the capitalist mode of production, which means the seizure of the means of production by capital. All production is supplied commercially through the market.[11]

Marx's analysis of the capitalist mode of production is determined by the fact that the masses of producers have to sell their labor power to the owners of the means of production. These owners are organized into separate firms in competition with each other for the shares of the market, for profitable fields of investment on capital, and for sources of raw materials. The owners of the means of production are compelled to extort the maximum surplus value from the producers for the sake of the accumulation of more and more capital. This inevitably leads to the concentration and centralization of capital, growing organic composition of capital. At this

---

10. Ibid., 169.

11. Marx, *Capital I*, 55.

point, the tendency for the rate of profit to fall is developed, undergoing periodically recurrent crises over production.

Nevertheless, a vision of any sudden and automatic collapse of the capitalist system, which was due to a single economic cause, remains questionable. There is the subjective side related to the collapse of the capitalist system: the emergence of the proletariat. Its organized revolt against the exploitation is the main lever for the overthrow of capitalism. As Marx states,

> the monopoly of capital becomes a fetter upon the mode of production which has flourished alongside and under it. The centralization of the means of production and the socialization of labor reach a point at which they become incompatible with their capitalist integument. This integument is burst asunder. The knell of capitalist private property sounds. The expropriators are expropriated.[12]

What drives Marx's thought is that overproduction in capitalist society leads to social crisis. Radical advancement of the capitalist revolution becomes possible only based on high technological progress, institutionalized rationality, and social systems as we see in light of Marx's interpretation of the interplay between the capitalist mode of production and the intellectual, religious, ideological sphere of superstructure. The advanced social structure and life system already influenced and transformed the consciousness of the working class. Thus, Marx's emphasis on the role of the proletariat in the phase of social revolution is wrongly assumed because they are already integrated into society and the advanced system of capitalism.

At any rate, what guides Marx is a combination of a theory of class struggle and the capitalist mode of production. The commercial crises by their periodical return put on trial, each time more threateningly, the existence of the entire bourgeois society. In these crises, there breaks out an epidemic of overproduction. Back into a state of monetary barbarism, industry and commerce seem to be destroyed. This is because there is too much civilization, too much means of subsistence, too much industry, too much commerce. In order to overcome these crises, the following is created: enforced destruction of a mass of productive forces, the conquest of new markets, and the more thorough exploitation of the old ones.[13]

12. Ibid., 929.
13. Ibid., 226.

In 1844 Marx envisioned a historic mission for the proletariat. The dissolution of society as a particular class is the proletariat "who is, with the categorical imperative, to overthrow all circumstances in which man is humiliated, enslaved, abandoned, and despised."[14]

The mission of the proletariat was to destroy all previous securities for, and insurances of, individual property. The first step in the revolution by the working class was to raise the proletariat to the position of ruling class, to win the battle of democracy. In the beginning this can be affected by means of despotic inroads on the rights of property, finally revolutionizing the mode of production. The proletariat were the grave-diggers of civil society, which the bourgeoisie had produced.[15]

The law that equilibrates the relative surplus-population or industrial reserve army rivets the laborer to capital more firmly than the wedges of Vulcan did Prometheus to the rock. Accumulation of wealth is at the same time accumulation of misery, agony of toil slavery, ignorance, brutality, and mental degradation.[16] The monopoly of capital has become a fetter placed upon the mode of production by the centralization of the means of production and the socialization of labor. Unconditional development of the productive forces of society came into conflict with the self-expansion of the existing capital. The capitalist mode of production is a historical means of developing the material forces of production and creating an appropriate world-market.[17]

Through the materialist conception of history and the revelation of capitalist production through surplus value, socialism for Marx became a science, a "scientific" socialism. Furthermore, Engels distinguished his and Marx's view from economic reductionism. According to the materialist conception of history, production and reproduction are the ultimately determining elements in history. If one twists this conception by saying that the economic element is the only determining factor, one transforms such a materialist conception into a meaningless, abstract, senseless phrase. The various elements of the superstructure—political forms, juridical forms, philosophical theories, and religious views among others—exercise their influence upon the course of the historical struggles. In many cases, they preponderate in determining their form. At issue here is consideration of the interaction of all these elements, although the economic movement

14. McLellan, *Karl Marx*, 73,

15. Ibid., 237, 231.

16. Marx, *Capital, I* 1604.

17. Marx, *Capital* 3, 1250.

asserts itself as necessary. Nevertheless, a concept of "scientific" socialism proves to be unscientific and illusionary because of its unqualified integration of highly advanced social order within the fixed consciousness of the working class.

Labor and Alienation: Hegel and Marx

Philosophically, no doubt, Marx was inseparably connected with Hegel. This connection can be seen in their notion of labor, alienation, and fetishism. Marx asserted that Hegel's *Phenomenology of Mind* retained a hidden and mystifying critique. The separate sections such as the unhappy consciousness, the struggle of the noble and base consciousness, etc., in the *Phenomenology of Mind* contained the critical elements of whole spheres such as religion, the state, civil life, etc. The following division of the *Phenomenology* is feasible:

> Subjective spirit: Consciousness, Self-consciousness, Reason
>
> Objective spirit: Spirit—customary morality, culture, morality
>
> Absolute spirit: Religion (natural religion, the region of art, revealed religion), Absolute Knowledge.

Hegel had been profoundly affected in his youth by economic studies, particularly by the work of Adam Smith. In his important work the *Young Hegel*, Lukacs investigates, in detail, the economic ideas of the young Hegel.

Marx saw in the Hegelian system a veritable philosophy of labor. Hegel's philosophy of labor provided Marx with the conceptual tools with which to undertake his first struggle with political economy. *The Economic and Philosophical Manuscripts* presents us with a fascinating encounter between philosophy and political economy in Marx's thought. Marx's Manuscript entails Marx's critical engagement with Hegel's *Phenomenology of Mind*.

Hegel developed a real dialectic of needs and labor and thus arrived at a twofold definition of labor as alienating and alienated; alienating because labor is, by its nature, the externalizing of a human capacity; alienated because needs always run ahead of production and the latter can never fully satisfy the former. Hegel's remarks about the social contradictions produced by bourgeois society in the *Philosophy of Right* read like an anticipation of the famous passage in *Capital* tied to the general tendencies of capitalist accumulation.

... [large] profits are derived ... The other side is the subdivi-
sion and restriction of particular jobs. This results in the dependence and distress of the class tied to work of that sort ... [18]

For Hegel human being was a historical animal, while for Aristotle human being was a political animal. Hegel's dialectical approach was
to see the particular individual in light of the universal individual (self-
conscious spirit). The particular individual has to go through the stage
through which the general mind has passed. The individual gradually
comes to perceive that the real character of society and history is something created by people. With this realization the conscious individual en-
ters the second cycle. He now recognizes history as real; it is the product of
activity, of human praxis. Having achieved an understanding of what history really is, the individual has arrived at the stage of absolute knowledge.
The basic structure of this phenomenology corresponds in all essentials
to the arrangements Marx proposed in the *Economic and Philosophical
Manuscripts*.

In the course of development, the term externalization (*Entäusser-
ung*) and alienation (*Entfremdung*) came to occupy a central position in
the Hegelian system. There are three stages in the Hegelian concept of
externalization: 1) the complex subject-object relation bound up with all
human activity of an economic or social kind; 2) the specifically capitalist
form of externalization—what Marx later would call fetishism. However,
Hegel had an intimation of the problems arising from the fetishization of
objects in capitalist society. He regarded many things as the products of
social work, of human praxis in general, which are only the fetish-forms of
objectivity specific to capitalism in Marx's view. 3) A broad philosophical
extension of the concept externalization, which then comes to be synony-
mous with thinghood or objectivity.[19]

For Hegel, the transforming process of consciousness is a cycle that
reaches out to the other and then returns into itself.. The peak of the
process is absolute spirit, absolute knowledge, as philosophy. The goal of
the process is the revelation of the depth of spiritual life that is absolute
concept. The goal finds its pathway in the recollection of spiritual forms.

According to Marx, in Hegel's system the absolute spirit becomes
conscious of itself as the creative world-spirit only in the philosopher and
in the wake of historical process and realization. Its making of history

---

18. *Hegel's Philosophy of Right*, para.243.

19. Lukacs, *Hegel*, 539–41.

exists only in the consciousness, in the opinion and conception of the philosopher—in the speculative imagination.[20]

In the *Economic and Philosophical Manuscripts* of 1844 Marx provided a comprehensive and systematic critique of the Hegelian dialectics. Herein Marx contended that Hegel's standpoint was that of the modern political economy. Conceptualizing labor as the essence of humanity, Hegel saw only the positive side of labor and very little of its negative side. According to Marx, Hegel's greatness was his comprehension of the self-generation of human being as a process; this refers to objectification as the process of confronting objects, namely, externalization and the critical integration (*Aufhebung*) of this externalization. Thus, Hegel comprehended the essence of labor.[21]

Marx emphasized externalization as the central concept of the *Phenomenology of Mind*, while criticizing it in light of economic realities associated with alienated labor. Marx's salient definition of labor in the capitalist society is alienation. In the sphere of political economy the realization of labor appears as loss of realization for the workers. This implies objectification as loss of the object and bondage to it. So, appropriation appears as alienation, as externalization. The worker is related to the product of his labor as to an alien object. Alienation is a consequence of the social division of labor under capitalism. Alienated labor does not freely develop one's physical and mental energies, but mortifies one's body and ruins one's mind. Objectively, the product of labor appears as an alien thing ruling over the human being. Subjectively, the process of labor is a self-alienation. Thus, Marx argues that in the capitalist society a human being is necessarily alienated from a human being and nature.

For Marx, Hegel had no insight into the negative aspects of work in capitalist society, since he considered only its positive sides. The contradictions in the basic categories of capitalist economics and surplus value that Marx unveiled had never become apparent to Hegel. For Hegel all alienation of human essence was nothing but alienation of self-consciousness rather than expression of the real alienation of the human being. Real people and real nature become mere predicates of absolute self-consciousness, absolute spirit, and the self-knowing and self-manifesting idea.

Thus, Marx discovered the connection between labor and interaction in the dialectic of the productive forces and the relations of production. For the sake of social praxis Marx did not explore the interrelationship

20. Ibid., 547.
21. McLellan, *Karl Marx*, 101.

of interaction and labor; rather the communicative action is reduced to the instrumental reason. For Marx, instrumental action, the productive activity, regulates the material interchange of the human species with the natural environment. Everything is resolved into human self-production in which the dialectical relationship between the forces of production and the relations of production would be vulnerable to misinterpretation in a mechanistic manner.[22]

Beyond Marx's critique, it is certain that Hegel did not sidestep the dehumanization of the workers that the progress of capitalism entailed. For Hegel the division of labor in capitalism and the increase in the forces of production led necessarily to the pauperization of great masses of people.

> The individual's skill is his method of preserving his own existence. The latter is subject to the web of chance which enmeshes the whole. Thus a vast number of people are condemned to utterly brutalizing, unhealthy and unreliable labor in workshops, factories and mines, labor which narrows and reduces their skill. [23]

Despite the limitations of Marx's critique of Hegel, the transition from Hegel to Marx is a transition to an essentially different stage and direction. Marx's staring point is his practical observation of the misery of the workers. Marx discovered that subjecting political economy to systematic critique tended to conceal the social contradiction and the misery of the workers.

> We proceeded from an economic fact of the present . . . The worker becomes an ever cheaper commodity the more commodities he creates. The devaluation of the world of men proceeds in direct proportion to the increasing value of the world of things [commodities]. Labor produces not only commodities; it produces itself and the worker as a commodity—and this in the same general proportion in which it produces commodities.[24]

HEGEL: NEO-LIBERAL INTERPRETATION IN THE U.S CONTEXT

Proponents of the end of history such as Fukuyama take seriously Hegel's dialectic of recognition for prestige in the context of the U.S.

22. Habermas, *Theory and Practice*, 169.

23. Lukacs, *Hegel*, 331.

24. McLellan, *Karl Marx*, 107.

For Fukuyama, the unequal recognition of the master and the slave was replaced by universal and reciprocal recognition in the modern state.[25] Driven by the historical process of revolutions, the struggle for recognition culminated in the modern state by truly satisfying human being through universal and reciprocal recognition. According to Fukuyama, there is no further progressive historical change. Liberal democracy has achieved the universal principle of recognizing the legitimacy of all nations, providing much less incentive for war. Since liberal democracy definitely solved the question of recognition by overcoming the relationship between lordship and bondage, humanity was completely satisfied with the modern state.[26]

Fukuyama misunderstands and misuses Alexandre Kojève as the representative who championed Hegel as a proponent of liberal democracy and economy. For Hegel, liberal society consisted of reciprocal and equal agreement among citizens for mutual recognition. If Hobbes or Locke grounded liberalism in the pursuit of rational self-interest, Hegel saw liberalism as the pursuit of rational recognition. This means that recognition is undertaken on a universal basis. In it the dignity of each person as a free and autonomous human being is recognized by all. The liberal democratic state values us by our own self-esteem and self-worth, showing us to the end of the recognition of our freedom. The universal and homogeneous state appears at the end of history and it can be seen as resting on the twin pillars of economics and recognition. The desire for recognition is the missing link between liberal economics and liberal politics.

According to Fukuyama, Kojève interpreted Hegel by maintaining that the universal and homogeneous state would be the last stage in human history since it satisfied completely the human desire for recognition. The recognition provided by the contemporary liberal democratic state adequately satisfied the human desire for recognition.[27]

Kojève worked in France and held his lectures on Hegel's *Real Philosophy* from 1933 –1939 at Ecole des Hautes-Etudes, Paris.[28] His class lectures on the *Phenomenology of Mind* were translated and published under the title, *Introduction to the Reading of Hegel*. According to Allan Bloom, an American editor of Kojève, an impression occurs from Kojève's

---

25. Fukuyama, *End of History*, xviii.

26. Ibid., xx.

27. Fukuyama, *End of History*, 207.

28. Kojève, *Hegel*, 7.

portrayal of Hegel that the citizen of the universal homogeneous state is identical with Nietzsche's Last Man.[29]

Fukuyama upholds Bloom's model of Kojève's interpretation of Hegel. According to Bloom's model of the end of history and the last man, Kojève is interpreted as the one who maintains that the universal and homogeneous state would be the last stage in human history; it completely satisfied the human being. The desire for recognition became, for Kojève, a trans-historical standard by which to measure the adequacy of human institutions. This claim is taken to suggest that the recognition provided by the contemporary liberal democratic state adequately satisfied the human desire for recognition.

In contrast to the neo-liberal interpretation of Hegel, Kojève's own reading strategy was interested in the actualization of Hegel for our time. Driven by a left-wing Hegelian orientation, Kojève emphasized the role of death-consciousness and the significance of prestige struggle in the process of humanization. The moment of dominion in Hegel's dialectic between lordship and bondage became a condition for the humanizing effect of labor. Oftentimes, Marxists fail to conceptualize the important role of political dominion because of their economic reductionism. Conversely, Fascists sidestepped the place of economy and reduced the human-social reality merely to the struggle.[30]

Kojève portrayed Hegel as an atheist who had accepted the finitude of humanity. To overcome the insufficiency of the Christian ideology, to realize freedom, and to live in the world as a human being, all this was possible only on the condition of atheism. Thus Kojève removed the difference between absolute knowledge and absolute Mind in Hegel, further insisting that Hegel replaced God with absolute knowledge.[31] Only by overcoming Christian theology will a human being cease to be a slave and realize the ideal of freedom. The French Revolution completed the evolution of the Christian world and inaugurated the third historical world. Freedom realized in this world will finally be conceived by German philosophy, especially by Hegel.[32]

According to Kojève, the end of history must be seen in a different way from the universal and homogeneous world state that Hegel assumed.

29. Ibid, xi–xii.

30. Kojève, *Hegel*, 9.

31. For the critique of Kojève's atheistic interpretation of Hegel, see Theunissen, *Hegel*, 108. Footnote 12.

32. Kojève, *Introduction*, 57.

Consequently, Kojève, contrary to Fukuyama, insisted that Hegel's concept of the state did not necessarily mean the end of history, and the bourgeoisie was not the last man in the fashion of Nietzsche. Kojéve argued that the end of history would be an egalitarian society equipped with the recognition of individual rights.[33] By what right can we assert that this state will not engender a new desire other than the desire for recognition? Will not the state consequently be negated someday by a negating or creative action?[34]

According to Iring Fetscher, one of the most important German interpreters of Hegel, Kojève's mistake lay in his grounding on Hegel's bourgeois optimism which stands for the emancipated bourgeois class. Thus, Kojève subsumed the future society without class and dominion under Hegel's state of *Citoyen* with equality of rights.[35]

Fetscher is right because Hegel insisted that a human being can be truly satisfied in perfect freedom and independence, in the form of the "We," a plurality of Egos.[36] The associated "We" first appeared as the result of the struggle between the master and the slave. The slave without a master, the master without a slave is what Hegel calls the bourgeois, the private property-owner. The capital enslaves the bourgeois just as the master enslaved the slave. The central phenomenon of the bourgeois world is not the enslavement of the working people by the rich, but the enslavement of both by capital.[37]

At any rate, Kojève's Hegel is a progressive Hegel whose spirit is still alive for our time. The dialectic between lordship and bondage that is based on struggle for recognition—labor, struggle, and recognition –finds its validity in the sphere of politics, economics, and culture. This portrayal of Hegel, which is different from Fukuyama's neo-liberal Hegel, is more relevant to a post-colonial portrayal of Hegel.

HEGEL IN A LIBERATIVE-POSTCOLONIAL CONTEXT

Hegel's master-slave dialectic paves the way to a post-colonial logic of the white master's dominion over against black slaves in Africa and Europe. Aristotle established a notion that from the beginning the human

33. Kojève, *Hegel*, 12.
34. Kojève, *Introduction*, 192–93.
35. Kojève, *Hegel*, 19.
36. Hegel, *Phenomenology*, 104.
37. Kojève, *Introduction*, 65.

being was necessarily master or slave. However, for Hegel, only the slave overcomes his/her nature and finally becomes citizen. The final fight that transformed the slave into citizen overcomes mastery.

Hegel's dialectic finds its echo in liberating struggle in Latin America, especially in Freire's pedagogical analysis. In reference to Husserl, Freire attempts to articulate how objects in our environment become the object of our cognition. According to Freire, "I" cannot exist without a "not-I": the world brings consciousness into existence and becomes the world of that consciousness. Human beings begin to choose elements from their background awareness and to reflect upon them. These elements are objects of human consideration, and objects of their action and cognition.[38] For the sake of the critical consciousness of education, Freire's method in *Pedagogy of the Oppressed* is under the influence of Hegel's *Phenomenology.* Freire examines each person-center of consciousness in reference to the relationship between the consciousness of the master and the oppressed.

According to Freire, the individual who does not risk life can neither be recognized as a person, nor attain the truth of recognition as an independent self-consciousness. The difference between Hegel and Freire is that the latter's pedagogy of the oppressed is rooted in concrete situations including the reactions of laborers—peasant or urban—and middle-class persons.[39]

However, Freire presents the relationship of the oppressor and the oppressed in typical Hegelian dialectics. Freire reminds us that the status, power, and domination of the oppressor are not possible without the existence of the oppressed. He further conceptualizes his notion of both the oppressor and the oppressed through manifestations of dehumanization.[40] The oppressor is dehumanized by the act of oppression while the oppressed are dehumanized by the existential reality of oppression and the internalization of the image of the oppressor. Consequently, the oppressed sustain an existential dual identity being ". . . at one and the same time themselves and the oppressor whose consciousness they have internalized."[41]

Thus, the goal of a pedagogy of the oppressed is to restore lost humanity and thereby liberate both the oppressed and the oppressor. This liberation is a painful one in which the oppressor-oppressed contradiction is replaced by the humanization of both. For the attainment of liberation

38. Freire, *Pedagogy,* 70.
39. Ibid., 20, 34.
40. Ibid., 30.
41. Ibid., 30.

the oppressed must perceive the reality of oppression as a limiting situation to be transformed. This critical consciousness must become the motivation for liberating action. Hegel's insight operates thusly: the oppressed discover that they exist in dialectical relationship to the oppressor. This is antithesis. Consequently, the oppressor could not exist with the oppressed—this is the constitutive principle of liberation.[42]

Furthermore, Freire integrates Lukacs' notion of critical intervention of the revolutionary leader into the consciousness of the oppressed in order to explain their actions to the masses. This intervention is undertaken for Freire's own method of dialoguing with the people about their actions. Freire's pedagogy of the oppressed is in accordance with the intervention of the revolutionary party, which is in need of the critical intervention of the people in social reality through praxis.[43]

In contrast to Freire's critical intervention outside, however, Hegel's notion of the dialectic gains weight in the laborer's consciousness of emancipation shaped internally in the process of struggle, labor, and self-articulation. Freire neglected the place of freedom and language in Hegel's dialectical movement.

Hegel considered in the *Phenomenology of the Mind* a communication process distorted by the dialectical relation of self-consciousness in terms of state power and economic wealth. The role of language is seen as the mediating role in its positive and negative side in the history of suppression, distortion, rebellion, and reconstruction.

In becoming conscious of transformation of the thing through the work, the slave becomes conscious of his freedom, and his autonomy in articulation of his transformed status. The realization of freedom comes through the conscious and voluntary transformation of given existence by the active abolition of slavery. Discourse operates implicitly in the process of liberation, because the language of the slave is that of revolt, rather than that of flattery. This perspective contradicts the intervention from outside directing the consciousness of the working class through the elitism of the revolutionary party.

According to Hegel, the slave's dialectical or revolutionary overcoming of the world can free the slave and should be expressed in his or her own discourse. This dialectical-revolutionary transformation of the world presupposes the negation, the non-accepting of the given world in its totality. In the transformation of the universal will through work in the

42. Ibid., 34.
43. Ibid., 39.

public sphere, the slave assumes the role of representing the emancipating ideas of liberty, equality, and fraternity, not the politics of terror. In the final analysis, the originally dependent, serving, and slavish consciousness realizes and reveals the idea of autonomous self-consciousness through their cultural manifestation: labor, discourse of freedom and emancipation, and cultural recognition.

For the sake of a postcolonial reading of Hegel, Fanon develops his theory of master and slave. In a title "The Negro and Hegel," Hegel's sentence remains central to Fanon: self-consciousness exists in itself and for itself in relation to another self-consciousness for being acknowledged and recognized.[44] Fanon's focus is on the situation of the Black African in the French (post) colonial context; this situation has little to do with Black community in North America. In the French context there is not an open conflict between white and black. The guiding principle in Hegel's dialectic is absolute reciprocity: "they recognize themselves as mutually recognizing each other."[45] But Fanon wants to overcome the limitation of Hegel's dialectic of recognition.

In a fierce struggle with the master the slave is risking life and freedom is obtained. For Fanon, Hegel's view of the struggle of life and death can be achieved by life-risking conflict and combat. Historically, the Negro in the French colonial context did not fight for freedom. Rather, the white master set the inessentiality of servitude free. It is the white who has allowed the slaves to eat at the table. Fanon argues that now it is important to battle for the creation of a human world, a world of reciprocal recognition.[46] The other for the slave is the white, the colonizer, and Western culture. In the (post) colonial context Hegel's dialectic is to be renewed and radicalized in a direction toward alterity of rupture, conflict, and battle.[47]

Fanon argues that the master in a colonialist context differs basically from the master in Hegel's sense. For Hegel there is reciprocity with emphasis on the liberating role of the consciousness of the slave. However, for Fanon the colonizer only sees the laborer's production without recognition of the laborer as a human being; the colonized recognize themselves in and through the image of the master. The colonized do not have enough self-consciousness to have the desire for recognition as an independent and autonomous consciousness. The lack of dialectical tension and its

44. Fanon, *Black Skin*, 216.

45. Ibid., 217.

46. Ibid., 218–19.

47. Ibid., 222.

result in the absence of a desire for full recognition make the colonized non-existent, a feeling of nonexistence. Disalienation of the black indicates the liberation of the colored for helping them to recognize themselves as human beings. The effective disalienation of the black entails social and economic realities in addition to the psychological factor. An inferiority complex is the outcome of this economic reality and this inferiority is internalized. This is "the epidermalization of this inferiority." [48]

For Hegel and Fanon, humanity depends on being with and for others. Hegel's thought was grounded in the world of German idealism tied to the emerging civil society while Fanon's theory is embedded within the anti-colonial struggle for the sake of liberation or disalienation of the colored. Fanon's starting point is anchored in the specific situation of the colored and colonial consciousness; he writes of his experience as a colored person. Hegel's ontology does not allow the colored to understand the existence and otherness of the colored with respect to language and cultural formation. One who has a language consequently possesses the world that is expressed and implied by that language. Language is "the god gone astray in the flesh" (Paul Valéry).[49] Every colonized population was created by the death and burial of its local cultural originality and finds itself in the face of the civilizing language of the white.

Hegel, in the *Phenomenology*, developed his reflection on language within the framework of culture in regard to the political dominion and economic property.[50] Even Diogenes in his tub—with his pretense of withdrawal from the cultural world—was still under the sway of that perversion of the culture.[51] In his dialectical view of the power of the state and wealth, Hegel related self-consciousness to dominion and wealth.

Wealth tends to the general enjoyment, becoming universal beneficence; it is continuously created as a result of labor. Thus, enjoyment is the result of universal action just as wealth reciprocally calls forth universal labor.[52]

The attributes of nobility in the conscious life find themselves in accord with the public authority of the state, rendering obedient service to the interest of the state and inner reverence toward it. However, the attribute of baseness is in discord with dominion and wealth. It looks upon

48. Ibid., 13.
49. Ibid., 18.
50. Hegel, *Phenomenology*, 288.
51. Ibid., 308.
52. Ibid., 293, 291.

political dominion as a chain. It hates the ruler, obeying only with secret malice; it stands ready to burst out in rebellion. It sees in wealth something discordant, standing in disagreement with its permanent nature.

In the case of the base type of consciousness individual self-existence is not yet surrendered to the state and "is the inner secretly reserved spiritual principle of the various classes and stations."[53] Discordance is in its relation to the state, arriving at the point of breaking out into rebellion.[54]

We must find an anti-colonial aspect in Hegel's concept of the liberating discourse of the slave, which complements Fanon's reading. Language exists to be its content, possessing authority through spoken word (written legal documents); it is the power of utterance through speaking (discourse). In speech the self-existent consciousness comes as such into existence. The particular individuality is something for others. Speech alone expresses "I" itself. Ego becomes intersubjective ego in its particular and universal form. "Its otherness is taken back into itself."[55]

The noble consciousness assumes the role of producing language; "the heroism of dumb service passes into the heroism of flattery."[56] Through this language, the state power of an unlimited monarch comes into existence; the language of flattery elevates this power into universality. Flattering language puts individuals on its pinnacle, by giving the monarch his proper name. The spirit of its gratitude turns into the condition of humiliation; it feels the deepest revolt.[57] "Wealth shares repudiation with its clientele; but in place of revolt appears arrogance."[58]

In the pure disintegration the self, identity becomes sheer internal discordance, all oneness and concord is taken asunder; the repute and respect for the benefactor are the first to be shattered; it stands in front of the abyss, cleaving the bottomless pit in which every solid base and stay have vanished.[59] Self-consciousness had a mode of speech in dealing with state power as well as with wealth. In revolt and disintegration it adopts a language of its own, which is the perfect form of utterance for the entire realm of spiritual culture and development and of the formative process

53. Ibid., 297.
54. Ibid.
55. Ibid., 298.
56. Ibid., 300.
57. Ibid., 303.
58. Ibid., 304.
59. Ibid.

of shaping self-consciousness. This self-consciousness finds befitting the rebellion, which is the absolute self-identity in absolute disintegration.[60]

Nevertheless, Hegel was not capable of developing his master-slave dialectic for the struggle of recognition in historical reference to the Spanish colonialism in the new world, as previously shown in the case of Las Casas in chapter one. Despite the limitations of Hegel, his legacy is be reinterpreted in solidarity with the marginal, the voiceless, and the vulnerable. For this purpose it is another task to refurbish Hegel's concepts such as labor, service, cultural recognition, and discourse of freedom and emancipation to challenge our era of Empire as a pseudo reality of the end of history.

60. Ibid., 305.

6

The Dynamism and Limitations of the Capitalist System

MARX APPLIED THE SOCIOHISTORICAL method of the materialist dialectic to the study of economic problems. The use of the dialectical method is the *differentia specifica* of *Capital,* distinguishing Marx from all other economic theories. Economic phenomena are seen in their inner connection as an integrated totality which is structured by a basic mode of production. This totality is analyzed in all its aspects and manifestations in terms of the unfolding of the inner contradictions of that economic structure. The object of Marx's investigation is the capitalist mode of production and the relations of production and forms of intercourse corresponding to it. Every historical period possesses its own laws in different times and places. Economic life is analogous to the history of evolution. For his inquiry Marx investigated the special laws that regulated the origin, existence, development, and death of a given social organization and its replacement by another, higher one.[1]

Within Marx's dialectical analysis and method, fetishism and reification of commodity undergird capitalist society. Analysis of capital logic in accumulation and expansion is tied to the internal crises of capitalism. Commodity society is seen as crisis-ridden society in connection with a problem of overproduction, and world market. These complex issues are the object of our study in this chapter in which our interest is in analyzing Marx's critique of fetishism and mammon. His sociocritical dialectical

1. Marx, *Capital I,* 101–2.

method entails a theological implication for a kingdom of freedom in contrast to the kingdom of mammon. For Marx the Protestant ethos is the driving force for capital accumulation. Such an aspect, despite its limitation, can facilitate our understanding of the reality of capital accumulation, expansion, crisis, and world-economy in the context of late capitalism. This study helps us to investigate the reality of late capitalism in terms of monopoly capital and colonialism in the subsequent chapter. Through that study we will be in a better position to examine the responsibility of the church as it regards global capitalism and economic globalization.

DIALECTICAL METHOD AND THE REALM OF FREEDOM

Marx's own dialectical method of investigation and knowledge (or inquiry and presentation) is opposed to that of Hegel. Marx's materialist dialectic is a form of turning Hegel upside down, by applying Hegel's method to the field of economic phenomena. For Marx the dialectical method in Hegel stands on its head.[2]

Marx argues that empirical facts have to be gathered first, and the given state of knowledge has to be fully grasped. Based on this empirical investigation, a dialectical reorganization of the material can be undertaken in order to understand the given totality of society. As for the method of political economy, Marx attempted to move analytically toward ever more simple concepts until he had arrived at the simplest determination. This is a way of going deeper to the social material life. He retraced from the simplest determination until he had finally arrived at the real and the concrete. In this dialectical and interpretive circulation the real and concrete is grasped as a rich totality of many determinations and relations. A dialectical method ascending from the simple relations (such as labor, division of labor, need, and exchange value) to the level of the state, exchange between nations and the world market are the scientifically correct method. For Marx "the concrete is concrete because it is the concentration of many determinations, hence unity of the diverse."[3] This is a reproduction of the concrete by way of theory.

According to Marx, the method rises from the abstract to the concrete (dialectical movement). This is the only way in which human thought can appropriate the concrete, by reproducing it as the concrete in mind.

2. Marx, *Capital I*, 103.
3. Marx, *Grundrisse*, 101.

Insofar as "human anatomy contains a key to the anatomy of the ape,"[4] Marx endeavored to write the present history of capitalism. Theoretical, epistemological conceptualization of the totality appropriates the world in the only way it can; this scientific and dialectical understanding of the world is different from the artistic, religious, practical and mental understanding of the world.[5]

Starting from the commodity toward the theoretical abstract (labor power, value, and instruments of labor), Marx set out to reproduce the concrete reality of capitalism in its theoretical analysis. Historical and logical analysis of commodity and capital accumulation can be seen in the interpretive circle for reproduction and reconstruction in understanding the capitalist social system.

For Marx, the commodity is understood as including both a unity and a contradiction between use value and exchange value. The social character of the labor embedded within the commodity can only appear as a thing outside the commodity, money. Social relations between human beings under capitalism appear as relations between things: the fetishism of the commodity.[6]

Commodity relationships are the realms of necessity as opposed to the realm of freedom. This mystical character of the commodity comes from its exchange value.[7] If the fetishism in the world of commodities arises from the peculiar social character of the human labor built on the exchange value, this world is in the realm of socioeconomic necessity; it is not in the realm of freedom grounded on the use value.

As one of the civilizing aspects of capital, capital extorts the surplus labor in a higher form of society, more advantageous to social relations and to the creation of elements in a new and higher formation than under the earlier forms of slavery, serfdom, and so on. The realm of freedom begins only where labor determined by necessity and external expediency come to an end. It is beyond the sphere of material production proper. Freedom consists in the socialized person, the associated producers, governing the human metabolism with nature in a rational way, bringing it under their collective control. The true realm of freedom begins beyond the realm of

4. Ibid., 105.
5. Ibid., 101.
6. Marx, *Capital I*, 163–77.
7. Marx, *Capital I*, 163–64.

necessity, although it can flourish within this realm of necessity as its basis. The reduction of the working day is the basic prerequisite.[8]

Given this fact, Marx discounts the possibility of fully achieving the realm of freedom, something beyond the production process. Socialist society is conceived as approaching, not achieving the Beyond. The realm of necessity must be organized in a way that we bring it under their collective control and with the least expenditure of energy and in conditions most worthy and appropriate for their human nature. The realm of freedom flourishes on the foundation of this realm of necessity. Marx's mature view contradicts his earlier optimism about the classless society established on earth as the realm of freedom.

In the prologue to *A Contribution to the Critique of Political Economy* (1859), Marx was optimistic because humankind was able to solve the problem of the capitalist society. In the *Economic and Philosophical Manuscripts* of 1844, Marx was convinced of communism as the positive abolition of private property. Communism as the restoration of the human being as social being is a completed naturalism which is humanism. Communism as completed humanism is naturalism. It is the genuine resolution of the antagonism between person and nature and between person and person. It is the true resolution of the conflict between existence and essence, between objectification and self-affirmation, between freedom and necessity, and between individual and species. In fact, "it is the solution to the riddle of history and knows itself to be this solution."[9]

In the context of *Capital*, however, the realm of freedom can only be approached rather than being a definitive solution to the antagonism. Freedom which can consist only in the associated producers brings the sphere of production under the collective control. But this collective control always remains a realm of necessity, because the true realm of freedom begins beyond it, although it only flourishes within the realm of necessity as the basis of freedom.[10]

A socialist society is heading and approaching the reality of freedom—an association of free human beings. This later perspective stands in tension with his dominant view that communism can be achieved by replacing capitalism with a classless society of associated producers.[11]

8. Marx, *Capital III*, 958–59.

9. Mclellan, *Karl Marx*, 89.

10. Marx, *Capital III*, 959.

11. Hinkelammert, *Ideological Weapons*, 58.

A Myth of Fetishism

In *Grundrisse*, Marx turned to the concept of alienation. Capital thus appears as social wealth which confronts human labor in more powerful portions as an alien and dominant power. The monstrous objective power belongs to capital, not to the worker. This process appears as an alienated quality, as a process of dispossession, whether from the standpoint of labor or from that of capital. This twisting and inversion is a real phenomenon and obviously a historical reality.

The economic alienation which is the result of the social division of labor, of commodity production, and of the division of society into classes is added to social, religious, and ideological alienation. It produces political and cultural alienation associated with the state and the phenomena of violence and oppression. Under the capitalist mode of production, the multiple alienations reach their climax. The transformation of all objects into commodities, their quantification in fetishistic exchange values becomes an intense process which affects every objective form of life. All other alienated categories of the economy can be seen in light of the fetish character of the commodity under the capitalist mode of production.[12]

Marx's analysis of alienated labor in the *Manuscripts* of 1844, through refining its concept in *Grundrisse*, finds its place in his analysis on fetishism of commodity in *Capital I*. The fetish is the personification of commodities (and money and capital) and the reification (or commoditization) of persons. This process of fetishism in the course of capitalist production follows the sequence: commodity fetishism, money fetishism, and capital fetishism. The specific term "fetishism" analyses a form of the coordination of the division of labor that tends to make invisible the effect of the division of labor over human life and death: commodity relationships.

According to Hinkelammert, Marx's theory of fetishism is a transformation of Plato's myth of the cave. In the cave myth reality is an approximation of the idea. The cave myth describes a transcendence that is outside real life. In the theory of fetishism the idea is an approximation of the reality of life, revealing how this ideal transcendence is the reversed reflection of another to be found with real life itself.[13] However, in my view, the Platonic myth of the cave implies a dialectical movement of the human soul approaching the illuminating truth (sun) existing outside the cave, without connection to actual historical, social life. Marx's theory of

12. Lukacs, *History and Consciousness*, 83–110.
13. Hinkelammert, *Ideological Weapon*, 4, 60–61.

fetishism demonstrates a dialectical movement revealing the actual social life of humanity controlled and dominated under the guise of a fetish-cave, a capitalist mode of production.

For Marx it is easier to discover the earthly kernel of the misty creations of religion by analysis than to do the opposite. The latter is to develop from the actual, giving relations of life the forms in which these have been apotheosized. The latter method is the only materialist, and the only scientific one.[14] The commodity question arises only when, in the context of a division of labor based on private property, the shoe becomes a means of acquiring wheat through exchange. In this context Marx cites Aristotle for the sake of the use value of every product.[15] Insofar as the table emerges as a commodity in the context of the market, it changes into a physical-metaphysical object. The mystical character of the commodity does not emerge from the use-value, but exchange-value.[16] According to Marx, the mystical character of the commodity-form reflects on the social characteristics of human labor as the socio-natural properties of these things. Human labor becomes equal, taking on a physical form in the equal objectivity of exchange value. This implies a social relation which exists apart from and outside the producers. "Through this substitution, the products of labor become commodities, sensuous things which are at the same time supra-sensible or social."[17]

ANALYSIS OF COMMODITY FETISHISM

The commodity–form and the value–relation of the products of labor are "nothing but the definite social relation between men themselves which assumes here, for them, the fantastic form of a relation between things."[18] This social phenomenon Marx calls "the fetishism which attaches itself to the products of labor as soon as they are produced as commodities."[19]

Exchange value in the exchange of products equates the different products to each other, transforming each product of labor into a social hieroglyphic. People attempt to decipher the hieroglyphic, getting behind the secret of their own social products. Social products become their

14. Marx, *Capital I*, 494, n.4.
15. Marx, *Capital I*, 179, n. 3.
16. Ibid., 164.
17. Ibid., 165.
18. Ibid.
19. Ibid.

language (or ideology) which is, in turn, of socioeconomic implication.[20] It has little to do with describing the value branded on its forehead. The social relations between their private labors appear as material relations between persons and social relations of things in the market.[21] Beneath the sum of commodities there is a unifying principle which is ultimately the collective labor of society, or the basic system of the social division of labor through the intermediary role of capital. The market becomes a sacrosanct sphere. The relations of production belong to the historically determined mode of social production which is commodity production.

Marx's concept of fetishism, called the economic mystification, is further developed in his notion of the trinity formula in *Capital* III: Capital-profit (capital-interest), land-ground-rent, labor-wages. This economic trinity completes the mystification of the capitalist mode of production, that is the reification of social relations. The trinity formula corresponds to the self-interest of the dominant classes; "it preaches the natural necessity and perpetual justification of their sources of income and erects this into a dogma."[22] *Monsieur le Capital* and *Madame la Terre* haunted the bewitched, distorted and upside-down world. The personification of things and reification of the relations of production is a religion of everyday life which reduces interest to a part of profit and rent to the surplus above the average profit. It presents the circulation process as simply a metamorphosis of forms.[23]

In earlier forms of society, the economic mystification transpires in connection with money and interest-bearing capital. However, in Antiquity and the Middle Ages, slavery or serfdom formed the broad basis of social production. The dominant condition of production over producers was concealed by the relations of domination and servitude.[24] In the ancient Asiatic, Classical-antique, and other such modes of production, the transformation of the product into a commodity played a subordinate role. In these societies, social organisms of production were very simple and transparent like the gods of Epicures (c. 341-c.270 BCE) in the *intermundia*: here the gods are portrayed to exist only in the *intermundia*, or spaces between different worlds, so that they had no influence on the course of human affairs.[25]

20. Marx, *Capital I*, 166–67.

21. Ibid., 166.

22. Marx, *Capital III*, 969.

23. Ibid.

24. Marx, *Capital I*, 172; *Capital, III*, 970.

25. Marx, *Capital I*, 172, note.

Marx transformed the Robinson Crusoe model into the social Robinson Crusoe model, which implies:

> an association of free men, working with the means of production held in common, and expending their many different forms of labor-power in full self-awareness as one single social labor force. [26]

The social relations of the individual producers (all Robinson's products) are here transparent in their simplicity, in production as well as in distribution. The association of free human beings is what leads to the end of commodity fetishism. The religious veil vanishes to the extent that social production is performed by freely associated people and it stands under their conscious and planned control.[27]

To highlight his concept of money fetishism, Marx quotes a letter of Christopher Columbus from Jamaica, 1503. "Gold is a wonderful thing! Its owner is master of all he desires. Gold can even enable souls to enter Paradise."[28] Our intercourse as commodity makes us relate to each other as exchange-value. The value of commodities may be expressed under the fetishist appearance of arbitrary exchange-values. The creation of money is a social act. Society determines that a particular commodity will be money. Only the action of society can turn a particular commodity into money as the universal equivalent. Through the agency of the social process, money is set apart to be the universal equivalent, that is, the specific social function of the commodity. In money every qualitative difference between commodities is extinguished. "The bones of the saints cannot withstand it."[29] "Modern society . . . greets gold as its Holy Grail, as the glittering incarnation of its innermost principle of life."[30]

THE THEOLOGICAL LOGIC OF MAMMON

Quoting Rev 17:13, 17, Marx argues that money is the beast causing humankind to lose its freedom. The prologue of John's Gospel is changed as in Goethe's Faust: "In the beginning was the deed." This is, according to Marx, what exactly happens in the world of commodities. The reference

26. Ibid., 171.
27. Ibid., 173.
28. Marx, *Capital I*, 229.
29. Ibid.
30. Ibid., 230.

to the brand on the forehead appears at all the crucial points in the analysis of commodities: value, money, capital. In the analysis of money, Marx connects this allusion directly with the beast of Revelation, the Antichrist. Money keeps driving the hoarder back to his Sisyphean task: accumulation. The hoarder sacrifices the lusts of his flesh to the fetish of gold, taking the gospel of abstinence very seriously.[31] Human beings become representatives of commodities. Commodity relationships are the crucial factor for determining the property system, the legal and state system, and the system of behavioral norms. The religious system could also be added.

In money every qualitative difference between commodities is extinguished. "Circulation becomes the great social retort into which everything is thrown, to come out again as the money crystal."[32] Driving the hoarder to accumulation, money as wealth takes on the nature of autonomous embodiments and expressions of the social character of wealth. Nothing escapes from this alchemy, since the saints were not able to resist it.[33] Wealth as a fetish must be crystallized in a particular substance, and gold and silver are its appropriate embodiment. Insofar as the hoarder of money combines asceticism with assiduous diligence, he/she is intrinsically a Protestant by religion and still more a Puritan.

According to Marx's description of the Capitalist system, faith in money brings salvation. Faith in money value as the immanent spirit of commodities is faith in the mode of production and its predestined disposition. It is faith in the individual agents of production as mere personifications of self-valorizing capital. The monetary system is essentially Catholic while the credit system is essentially Protestant.[34] Marx made a distinction between mercantile capitalism and industrial capitalism. After Catholic hoarding came Protestant asceticism, basing itself on the faith that saves. Accumulation of capital was the first duty of every citizen.

Insofar as the capitalist is the personification of capital, consumption should be minimized and accumulation maximized. The capitalist retains the motivating force in the acquisition and augmentation of exchange values, not in the acquisition and enjoyment of use values. Fanatically intent on the valorization of exchange value, the capitalist ruthlessly forces the human race to produce for production's sake. Capitalist production develops itself, making it necessary constantly to increase the amount of capital

31. Ibid., 231.
32. Marx, *Capital, III*, 707.
33. Marx, *Capital I*, 229.
34. Marx, *Capital, III*, 727.

invested in a given industrial undertaking; competition subordinates every individual capitalist to the immanent laws of capitalist production. The capitalist can only extend it by means of progressive accumulation.[35]

ACCUMULATION AND THE PROTESTANT ETHOS

Accumulation is service to the Beyond personified in capital. It is the conquest of social wealth. This is Marx's analysis of the abstinence theory related to Puritan entrepreneurship (Max Weber).

> While the capitalist of the classical type brands individual consumption as a sin against his function, as 'abstinence' from accumulating, the modernized capitalist is capable of viewing accumulation as 'renunciation' of pleasure.[36]

All the conditions for the labor process are converted into acts of abstinence on the part of the capitalist. Avarice and the drive for self-enrichment are the passions. Creating a world of delight, the progress of capitalist production lays open a thousand sources of sudden enrichment in the form of speculation and the credit system.[37]

At a certain stage of development, a conventional degree of prodigality becomes a business necessity to the 'unfortunate' capitalist. The degree of prodigality is also an exhibition of wealth and consequently a source of credit. The capitalist gets rich and compels the worker to renounce all the enjoyments of life. The expenditure of the capitalist is always restrained by the sordid avarice and anxious calculation lurking in the background. This expenditure grows with the accumulation. However, in the breast of the capitalist, a Faustian conflict takes place between the passion for accumulation and the desire for enjoyment.[38] As Marx poignantly asserts, "Accumulate, accumulate! That is Moses and the prophets! 'Industry furnishes the material which saving accumulates.'"[39]

With the possibility of keeping hold of the commodity as exchange-value, the lust for gold awakens. The hoarder sacrifices the lusts of his flesh for gold, taking the gospel of abstinence very seriously.[40] Usury seems

35. Marx, *Capital I*, 739.

36. Ibid., 740–41.

37. Ibid., 741.

38. Marx, *Capital, I*, 741.

39. Ibid., 742.

40. Ibid., 231.

to live like the gods in Epicurus's *Intermundia*.[41] Usury, just like trade, exploits a given mode of production and both relate to the mode of production from the outside, simply making the mode of production more wretched.[42]

HERMENEUTIC OF REVEALING AND REIFICATION

The starting point for capital is money. Labor becomes wage labor and the ownership of the means of production becomes capital. Capital fetishism has two faces: the face seen by workers and the face seen by the commodity owner. It is now the machinery that exercises the right to decide the worker's life or death. The machinery is an automation, powered by the pulsations of the common prime mover;[43] it has its principle of life or death over against the life of the worker. Capital threatens the workers with death, while guaranteeing the life only of those workers necessary for its own life process.

> The capitalist transformation of the process of production also appears as a martyrology for the producer; the instrument of labor appears as a means of enslaving, exploiting and impoverishing the worker; the social combination of labor processes appears as an organized suppression of his individual vitality, freedom and autonomy.[44]

Capital appears as a mysterious and self-creating source of interest, of its own increase. The thing (money, commodity, value) is capital simply as a thing. In interest-bearing capital, the automatic fetish is elaborated into self-valorizing value, money breeding money. Money is potentially self-valorizing value as the property to create value. Money becomes the true source of value. The fetish character of capital and the representation of this capital fetish is now complete. This is capital mystification in its most flagrant form.[45]

All capital is money capital in its value expression. Value differentiates itself as original value from itself as surplus value. Marx's trinitarian formulation reads: Capital-profit (capital-interest), land-ground-rent,

41. Marx, *Capital, III,* 733.

42. Ibid., 745.

43. Marx, *Capital I,* 500.

44. Ibid., 638.

45. Marx, *Capital III,* 516.

labor-wages. This economic trinity, as the driving force, underlines and propels the mystification of the capitalist mode of production.[46] Interest-bearing capital displays the conception of the capitalist fetish in its consummate form. Capital fetishism further projects and upholds the process of technology. The infinite technological progress and horizon relate to the infinite horizon of capital. In fact, Capitalist production as the process of destruction undermines the original source of all wealth—the soil and the worker—by developing the technique and social process of production.[47] Capital sows death on the earth, and takes lives of human beings and the earth. It radiates itself as the light in a pitch-black infinite: "By its own inherent laws, all surplus labor that the human race can supply belongs to it. Moloch."[48]

Marx's theory of the fetish character of commodities can be appropriated as a hermeneutical analysis of reification laying bare the extent to which the basic relation between people assumes the fantastic form of a relation between humanity, things, and earth. The reification of social relations that is the heart and core of Marx's doctrine of fetishism insists that the fetish character of the commodity world has its origin in the peculiar social character of the labor producing commodities. Native natural attitude (the first naiveté) toward the social relation built on commodity is corrected and renewed in terms of an analytical understanding of what lies behind the social relation (the second naiveté). This analytical understanding of social relation leads to a practical engagement with improving and transforming which functions as an obstacle to the human life and environment.

The practical moment provides us with a renewed epistemological attitude toward the social reality. Such a dialectical interplay between appearance and essence aims at debunking the hidden and mysterious principle of mammon which shapes and rules social life and relation. Capital becomes a very mystical being. Profit on alienation depends on cheating, cunning, expertise, talent and a thousand and one market conjunctures.[49] There occurs the indiscriminate amalgamation of the material conditions of production with their historical and social forms. The capitalist society is an enchanted, perverted, topsy-turvy world haunted by *Monsieur*

---

46. Ibid., 969.

47. Marx, *Capital, I*, 638.

48. Marx, *Capital III*, 521.

49. Ibid., 966.

le Capital and *Madame la Terre* carrying on their goblin tricks as social characters and as mere things.

THE LOGIC OF CAPITAL: EXPANSION AND CIRCULATION

The historical condition of capitalism can spring into life only when the owner of the means of production and subsistence finds the free worker in the market available with the condition that the free laborer sells his/her labor power. The capitalist epoch is characterized by the fact that labor power takes on the form of a commodity while taking the form of wage labor. Thus, the commodity form of the products of labor becomes universal.[50]

As the commodity circulation extends, there is an increase in the power of money. When everything becomes saleable and purchasable, circulation becomes the great social network and retort. Nothing can escape from this alchemy. In this sense, Marx quotes Columbus's letter from Jamaica, 1503. According to Columbus, gold is a wonderful thing, even enabling souls to enter Paradise.[51]

World trade and the world market dated from the sixteenth century, and since then the modern history of capital started to unfold. Under capitalism the capitalist went to the market with money, purchased commodities (labor power and means of production), and then returned to the market with a product which he/she again converts into money. Marx designates this process as M (money) $\rightarrow$ C (commodity) $\rightarrow$ M* (money with increment), where M* is larger than M. This is the general formula for capital.

The qualitative transformation of use value is here replaced by the quantitative expansion of exchange value. The difference between M* and M is called surplus value. The circulation of money as capital is an end in itself. The circulation has no limits. The expansion of value which is the main spring of the circulation (M $\rightarrow$ C $\rightarrow$ M*) becomes the subjective aim. The restless never-ending process of profit-making alone is what the capitalists aim at gaining. Capital, K, is made up of two components, c (money laid out on means of production: constant capital) and v (money expended on labor power: variable capital): K = c + v. Under the conditions of capitalist production the product of necessary labor accrues to the laborer in the form of wages. The product of surplus labor is appropriated

50. Marx, *Capital I*, 274.
51. Ibid., 229.

by the capitalist in the form of surplus value: c (constant capital) + v (variable capital) + s (surplus value) = total value. Or $K^* = (c + v) + s$.

This formula constitutes the analytic backbone of Marx's economic theory of organic composition. The capitalist has to divide capital into two different parts: constant capital (for acquiring machinery, buildings, raw material, auxiliary products, etc) and variable capital (for purchasing labor power; increased by the surplus value). The rate of surplus value is defined as the ratio of surplus value to variable capital ($s/v = s^*$). The organic composition of capital is the ratio between constant and variable capital. The rate of surplus value is the ratio between surplus value and wages. Organic composition of capital is formulated by constant capital / constant capital + variable: $c/(c + v)$. In the process of production, all capital is divided into means of production and living labor power. The former is called the value composition while the latter is called the technical composition of capital. This technical composition is determined by the relation between the mass of the means of production and the mass of labor necessary for the employment. The combination of the value composition of capital with its technical composition means the organic composition of capital.[52]

In the course of the circulation process, Marx introduces the reproduction and circulation (turnover) of the total social capital. Insofar as capitalist production is production for profit, growth always entails accumulation of capital. Capitalization of surplus value for profit and expanded reproduction become fundamental. The accumulation of capital is the capitalization of surplus value in terms of the transformation of profit into additional capital. Through his analysis of the process of circulation, Marx insists that capital in the capitalist mode of production appears as money capital, productive capital, and commodity capital. Marx's metaphor of metamorphosis of capital is analogous to a butterfly which passes through the successive stages of larva, chrysalis, and moth; so, capital takes on the forms of money capital, productive capital, and commodity capital.

Marx distinguishes between circulating capital and fixed capital based on the amount of time. Circulating capital which is spent on raw materials and wages is recovered to its original form after each production cycle and circulation cycle of commodities. Fixed capital is recovered after

52. Marx, *Capital I*, 762. Rate of profit is the ratio of surplus value to total capital outlay: surplus value/constant capital + variable capital. Under mathematical manipulation we come to the formula: p (rate of profit) = $s^*(1 - q)$. Here q denotes the organic composition of capital. The rate of profit is dependent upon the rate of surplus value and the organic composition of capital. Even as the surplus value increases the rate of profit decreases.

cycles of production and circulation. A part of the capital advanced in a form of constant capital (means of production) is fixed and determined by the function of the means of labor in the process of production (fixed capital). All other material components of the capital advanced in the production process form circulating or fluid capital.[53] Productive capital can be divided up into fixed and fluid capital. There is the circulation of money capital in its most general form: $M \to C \to M^*$, where M^* equals M plus increment (m). In the process of circulation, C (commodities bought by the capitalist) is replaced with the purchase of means of production (mp) and labor power (L): $M \to C \to$ (mp and L) . . . production . . . $C^* \to M^*$.[54]

The Theory of the Law in the Dynamism of Cycle and Crises

In view of the process of production and circulation, we observe that the rate of profit is affected by the ratio between the rate of surplus value and the organic composition of capital. The rate of profit is lowest in the sector with the highest organic composition of capital, because only variable capital produces surplus value. Increase in the organic composition of capital means a fall in the rate of profit. The organic composition of capital displays a steadily rising trend in terms of the constant revolutionizing of the means of production. It steadily increases with the development of the capitalist mode of production. The cycle of related turnover–because the value and durability of the fixed capital has an average of ten years–becomes one of the material foundations for the periodic cycle; in this cycle business passes through successive periods of stagnation, moderate activity, over-excitement, and crisis. But Marx adds that a crisis is always the starting point of a large volume of new investment, a new material basis for the next turnover cycle.[55]

---

53. Marx, *Capital II*, 238.

54. Marx, *Capital II*, 110–13, 133. C* and M* denote an increase in C and M as the result of surplus-value. The money, M, divides into one for the purchase of labor power (in the labor market) and into the other for means of production (in the commodity market). Money capital is transformed into productive form. Within the circulation stages capital undergoes a series of metamorphoses: money capital and commodity capital in circulation and productive capital in the sphere of production. Industrial capital encompasses every branch of production. The circuit of productive capital on an expanded scale has the general movement: $P \ldots C^* \to M^* \to C^*$ (L + mp) . . . P^*.

55. Ibid., 264.

Furthermore, the world market becomes an important factor in the progress of capitalist production which consequently develops the means of transport and communication; this technological advancement shortens the circulation time and introduces the necessity of working for the world market. The variations in turnover brought about one of the material bases for differing periods of credit, just as overseas trade in general, for instance, in the case of Venice and Genoa. Foreign trade formed one of the original sources of the credit system.[56]

Considering the development of the capitalist mode of production in the domestic context in relation to the world market, Marx deduced his famous law of the falling tendency of the rate of profit in the absence of countervailing tendencies. This is the substance of what Marx calls the theory of the Law itself.[57] It also demonstrates that capitalist production had certain internal barriers to its own indefinite expansion. Although there is an inbuilt tendency for the average rate of profit to decline, it implies a tendency, not an uninterrupted linear development. It is certain that Marx enumerates several counteracting causes which can thwart and annul the general law of the falling rate of profit. 1) Cheapening of the elements of constant capital –a given increase in the organic composition of capital, through lowering the value of constant capital, acts as its own corrective. 2) Raising the intensity of exploitation of labor, 3) relative surplus overpopulation (the reserve army), 4) foreign trade–it cheapens partly the elements of constant capital, partly the necessities of life for which the variable capital is exchanged, finally 5) the increase in share capital.[58] These are powerful countervailing forces at work in the capitalist system. The capitalist system entails a possibility to increase the rate of surplus-value. According to Mandel, it is hard to increase the rate of surplus-value substantially without seriously lowering real wages. This provokes a sharp social and political crisis and creates a tremendous problem of overproduction. However, we know the long waves of capitalist development which refer to the successive periods of growth of the capitalist economy as a whole.[59]

Marx's notion of the downfall of the rate of profit originates from Adam Smith according to whom the expansion of trade and production is inseparable from a continual increase in competition among its

56. Marx, *Capital II*, 329.
57. Marx, *Capital III*, ch. XIII.
58. Ibid., 339–48.
59. Mandel, *Late Capitalism*, ch. 4.

agencies. If there is an increase in real wages and rents, it drives down the rate of profit. Following in the footsteps of Smith, Marx saw the increase in competition associated with an increase in the concentration of capital in regard to the revival capitalist and technological innovation; this increase restrains the growth of real wages and opens up new opportunities for commercial, agro-industrial expansion; thus a new and international division of labor springs up; it is suited to the requirements of the main industrial countries. According to Arrighi, if Smith's version is more useful in explaining the inner dynamic of systemic cycles of accumulation, Marx's version is more useful in explaining the transition from one cycle to another.[60]

THE CENTRALIZATION OF CAPITAL AND THE CYCLE OF CRISES

Marx's dictum—"Accumulate, accumulate! That is Moses and the prophets"—indicates that the progress of capitalist production reveals a thousand sources of sudden enrichment in speculation and the credit system. The composition of capital affects the course of the process of accumulation. A part of the surplus value must always be re-transformed into variable capital, or additional labor funds. Reproduction on an expanded scale, accumulation, reproduces the capital relation on an expanded scale. Accumulation of capital multiplies the proletariat because it does not abolish the exploitation of the wage-laborer and the situation of dependence.[61]

All methods for raising the social productivity of labor and for the increased production of surplus value are the formative element of accumulation which means methods for the production of capital by capital, or methods for its accelerated accumulation. This formative accumulation causes an accelerated accumulation of capital. Through the formative and accelerated accumulation of capital, a capitalist mode of production develops. These two economic factors bring about change in the technical composition of capital. Here the variable component becomes smaller and smaller in comparison with the constant component.[62]

The credit system concentrates all the potential capital in the hands of banks, making it into disposable capital (loanable capital). Here money

---

60. Marx, *Capital I*, 580. See Arrighi, *Long Twentieth Century*, 222.

61. Marx, *Capital*, I. 764, 769, 770.

62. Marx, *Capital I*, 776.

capital becomes active, usurious, proliferating capital.[63] Accumulation presents itself as increasing concentration of the means of production and of the command over labor, while showing itself as the repulsion of many individual pools of capital from one another. This accumulation associated with concentration is counteracted by their attraction which is centralization proper. Distinct from accumulation and concentration, centralization is

> concentration of capital already formed, destruction of their individual independence, expropriation of capitalist by capitalist, transformation of many small into few large capitals.[64]

The most powerful levers of centralization are competition and the credit system. The entire social capital is united in the hands of either a single capitalist or a single capitalist company. Centralization supplements the work of accumulation, enabling capitalists to extend the scale of their operation; the fusion of a number of sources of capital takes place by the process of organizing joint-stock companies.

Centralization accomplished this construction of a railway in the twinkling of an eye by means of joint-stock companies. It also brings about a revolution in the technical composition of capital, raising its constant portion at the cost of its variable portion. Speaking of the progress of social accumulation includes the effects of centralization.[65]

At a certain stage of capitalist development, prodigality and a source of credit become a business necessity to the "unfortunate" capitalist. Capital reaps profits by investing its stock of money in trade and production or in speculation and the credit system. It endows the stock with the greatest power of breeding. The accumulation and expansion of capitalist production leads to the profitable investment of money in speculation and in the credit system.[66]

Marx regards depression as more than just hard times. A depression is rather the specific method of remedying the evils of prosperity. An accelerated rate of accumulation brings on a reaction in the form of a crisis; the crisis turns into depression; the depression, through filling up the reserve army and depreciating capital values, restores the profitability of production and thereby sets the stage for a resumption of accumulation.

---

63. Marx, *Capital II*, 569.
64. Marx, *Capital I*, 777.
65. Marx, *Capital I*, 780.
66. Arrighi, *Long Twentieth Century*, 229–30.

The chain of causation runs from the rate of accumulation to the volume of employment, from the volume of employment to the level of wages, and from the level of wages to the rate of profit. A fall in the rate of profit chokes off accumulation and precipitates a crisis. The crisis turns into depression, and finally the depression recreates the conditions favorable to an acceleration in the rate of accumulation. A repetition refers to the business cycle rather than a theory of crisis. Marx regards the business cycle as the specific form of capitalist development and the crisis as one phase of the cycle. Having considered this, Sweezy argues that in the business cycle there is no threat to the permanence of the capitalist system itself. Crisis and depression are looked upon as restorative forces rather than *memento mori* (moment of death).[67]

CRITIQUE AND EVALUATION

Marx's theory of crises comes from the standpoint of disproportionality and under-consumption which is associated with Marx's analysis of two departments in the reproduction scheme. The process $M \to C \ldots P \ldots C^* \to M^*$ and $P \ldots C^* \to M^* \to C \ldots P$ indicates that the movement of capital is both the starting point and the concluding point.[68]

According to Marx, the capitalists or workers of department I (means of production) must prove themselves to have sufficient purchasing power to buy the consumer product from department II (consumer goods) at their value. Marx does not say that the proportions are automatically guaranteed by the "invisible hand" of market forces in his reproduction scheme. On the contrary, these proportions are difficult to realize. The reproduction schemas show that equilibrium is the exception under capitalism. Disproportions are more frequent than proportions.

The sum total of output of both departments must be equal to the total demand generated by expanded reproduction. This is in no way assured under capitalism.[69] Marx utilizes the simple production $v_1 + s_1 = c_2$

---

67. Sweezy, *Theory of Development*, 155.

68. Marx, *Capital II*, 468.

69. Marx, *Capital II*, 478, 502. For Marx, the following takes place under simple reproduction:

> Department 1 (production of means of production):
> Capital 4,000c + 1,000v = 5,000
> Commodity product 4,000c + 1,000v + 1,000s = 6,000 means of production

as a conceptual tool by way of simplification in order to bring out the underlying assumptions of equilibrium (proportionate growth) under conditions of commodity production. If conditions (methods of production, wants of consumers, productivity of labor, etc) never changed, eventually the correct proportions would be discovered by trial and error, and all selling prices would correspond to values. In practice, however, conditions continually change, so that conformity of selling prices to values is at best but approximate and temporary. Such a crisis is easily traceable to what we have called the disproportionality between the various branches of production, and this disproportionality in turn has its roots in the planless, anarchic character of capitalist production. It is certain that the theory of disportionality originated in Marx himself.[70]

However, the dynamic nature of expanded reproduction involves regular revolutions in technology and the struggle of competition among industrialists. Regular increases take place in the average labor productivity of production, so a tendency runs for the value of each commodity to decline. The adjustment of market prices declines commodity value and it explains over-production. Unlimited growth of department one leads to faster growth of the productive capacity of department two. The basic causes of periodic crises of over-production are the inevitable periodic decline of the rate of profit, the capitalist anarchy of production, and the impossibility of mass consumption in correlation with the growth of productive forces.[71] This is because Marx makes a number of crucial points about capitalist crises of over-production.[72] Crises of over production are inevitable under capitalism.

Nevertheless, against the Marxist theory of the inevitable collapse of capitalism, or capitalist breakdown, a reproduction formula indicates that the conditions of capitalist production continue as a whole in a cycle: birth in a non-capitalist setting, transfers of capital from one sector to another, the role played by credit, fluctuation of money prices, etc. The reproduction formula indicates that the continuity of production is maintained in the long run despite periodic interruptions. Increasing organic composition of capital is the basic tendency of the capitalist mode of production.

Department 2 (production of means of consumption)

Capital 2,000c + 500v = 2500

Commodity product 2,000c + 500v + 500s = 3,000 means of consumption

70. Marx, *Capital II*, 545.

71. Marx, *Capital II*, introduction, 73.

72. Marx, *Capital II*, 391, note.

Capitalism shows corrective forces capable of avoiding and reforming the crises. The circulation time of commodities related to phases of the trade cycle results in periodic expansions and contractions of money capital as compared to productive capital. There is a parallel with Keynes who discarded the assumption of the full employment of manpower and capital through the operation of market forces. Hoarded capital is an important source of disequilibrium and under-employment in generalized commodity production.[73]

The formulae cannot explain concretely either capitalist expansion or the reason why crises break out.[74] The overall development of the capitalist mode of production cannot be subsumed under the notion of equilibrium. It is rather a dialectical unity of periods of equilibrium and periods of disequilibrium. Marx's reproduction scheme constitutes a special case of the tendency, just as economic equilibrium is only a special case of the tendency. Prosperity leads to over-production. The inherent susceptibility of capitalism to crises is ascribed not only to the anarchy of production, but also to the discrepancy between the development of the forces of production and the development of mass consumption.

Marx's expanded formula is a methodological abstraction to fulfill the purpose of the schemes, which is to prove that periodic equilibrium in the economy is possible. It does not take into account the following central themes: the organic composition of capital; distribution of constant capital between fixed and circulating capital; the development of the rate of surplus value; the development of the rate of accumulation; the relations of exchange between the two departments. Marx's model of the increasing organic composition of capital, the increasing rate of surplus value, and the falling rate of profit must be corrected within the framework of the inner logic of the specific mode of production and its general long-term tendencies of capitalist development.

As we have already seen a cyclical dimension, a theory of the capitalist mode of production becomes effective only through periodic adjustments and increases in a cyclical movement: economic recovery—boom and prosperity––overproduction and slump—crisis and depression. The cyclical movement of capital is nothing but the mechanism through which the tendency of the average rate of profit to fall is realized. In a theory of cycles and crises the upswing and acceleration of capital accumulation underlines extended reproduction. A crisis always forms the starting point

73. Marx, *Capital II*, Introduction, 76.
74. Mandel, *Marxist Theory*, vol.1. 328–29.

for large new investments. The problem of the increase in the organic composition of capital, i.e., the process of extended reproduction at a higher technical level includes not only the problem of the value composition of capital out of constant and variable capital but also a technological element or composition. This is the technological condition of the process of production.[75]

If the overproduction of the laborer is production for others, then the production of the industrial capitalist is production for the sake of production. Production lacks an objective unless it is directed toward a definite goal in consumption. On the one hand, unfettered productive power and increase of wealth, which consists of commodities, must be turned into money. On the other hand, it causes the limitation of the consumption of the mass of producers to the necessary means of subsistence.

The sale of commodities, the realization of the commodity capital and also of the surplus value are limited by the consumption requirement of a society in which the great majority are poor and must always remain poor.[76] The poverty and restricted consumption of the masses remain the last cause of all real crises when it is compared to the tendency of capitalist production. The role of under-consumption is seen as secondary to that of the falling tendency of the rate of profit.[77]

Under-consumption and over-production are opposite sides of the same coin. Under-consumption which is a special case of disproportionality arises from the inner nature of capitalism. There is undoubtedly a contradiction between the limitless striving for expansion of production and the restricted consumption of the masses. This contradiction testifies to its historical-transhistorical character.[78] Nevertheless, in the dynamism of the business cycle, the social condition of the proletariat is not worsened, but ameliorated in an advanced country. This perspective calls Marx's theory of crises into question.

CAPITAL ACCUMULATION, COLONIALISM, AND THE WORLD MARKET

The drive to accumulate capital characterizes the basic drive of the capitalist mode of production. This driving force is inseparably connected with

75. Marx, *Capital I*, 693–94.
76. Marx, *Capital, II*, 363, note.
77. Sweezy, *Theory of Development*, 179.
78. Ibid., 185.

competition among various forms of capital. Capital accumulation under capitalism is the compulsion to accumulate, enlarged reproduction. Capital accumulation in the historical sense was the result of large scale piracy, robbery, violence, theft, enslavement of people and trade in slaves. The dynamics of capital accumulation on a world scale are seen in the operation of the world market which transfers value from the colonies to the mother countries.

For Marx the discovery of America and the rounding of the Cape opened up fresh ground for the rising bourgeoisie. The East Indian and Chinese markets, the colonization of America, trade with the colonies, the increase in the means of exchange and in commodities –all these gave an impulse never before known to the revolutionary element in the tottering feudal society; steam and machinery revolutionized industrial production. The rapid improvement of all instruments of production, the immensely facilitated means of communication drew all nations into the civilization of capitalism. The cheap prices of the commodities battered down all Chinese walls. The capitalist expansion on a global scale compelled all nations to adopt its mode of production, introducing civilization into their midst. In fact, it created a world according to its own image.[79]

However, Marx's limitation is that this colonial exploitative system is seen and evaluated only in light of industrialized capitalism. In contrast to Marx, Rosa Luxemburg argued that the realization of surplus value is possible, only to the extent that non-capitalist markets are open to the capitalist mode of production. Her work *Accumulation of Capital* entails serious critique of Marx's theory and also a contribution to an explanation of imperialism.[80] The road she took was to grasp the economic roots of imperialism in view of colonialism. She took issue with Marx's theory of expanded reproduction in volume 2 of *Capital*. Marx's premise was a closed society which was capitalistic, dominated by the law of value which was the law of the world market.

Luxemburg's critique began with Marx's theory of accumulation, because it was tied to a closed capitalist society. According to her, expanded reproduction is possible only in a closed society. Marx did not conceptualize the rule of capitalism in the entire world. For Luxemburg, accumulation occurs in the real process of accumulation through the conquest of the colonies. Accumulation is first of all a relation between capitalist and non-capitalist environments. As Luxemburg contends, Marx's analysis of

79. McLellan, *Karl Marx*, 225.

80. Luxemburg, *Accumulation of Capital*. See Tarbuk, *Anti-Critique*.

accumulation was undertaken at a time when imperialism had not yet begun on a world scale. It entailed the a priori exclusion of the process of imperialism.[81]

However, for Luxemburg capital has been driven from its inception to expand into non-capitalist strata and nations and proletarianized the intermediate strata, the politics of colonialism. The development of capitalism undergirds the drive to globalism through constant expansion into new domains of production and non-capitalist countries; it results in violence, war, revolution; in short, it is catastrophic from start to finish which is the vital element of capitalism.[82]

According to Luxemburg, the discovery of America and the sea route to India were not just Promethean achievements of the human mind and civilization. They were also a series of mass murders of primitive peoples in the New World and entailed large-scale slave trading with the peoples of Africa and Asia. Likewise, the economic expansion of capital in its imperialist final phase is not separated from the series of colonial conquests and World Wars.[83]

According to Luxemburg, accumulation of capital in the Marxian sense and its formulae presupposes ad infinitum a vicious circle in such a way that production is consumed internally; the coal industry is expanded for the sake of expansion of the iron industry; the iron industry is expanded for the sake of expansion of the machine-construction industry, etc.[84]

However, the capitalists do not produce for production's sake. The market is something expendable outside of the production relationship. She contends that the non-capitalist societies are the reservoir of labor power, denying Marx's theory of an unemployed workers army. Marx's principal standpoint lies in conflict between capital and labor, and it is aggravated and exacerbated with the expansion of production and expansion of credit; this conflict can be reflected in the declining rate of profit or in the reserve army of labor.

However, Luxemburg held that capitalism is not collapsed automatically through a decline in the rate of profit. The cause of capitalism's downfall is brought when the real source of capital accumulation ceases. Capitalism's downfall comes from an outside force, non-capitalist strata and societies rather than from the internal organism of capitalism.

81. Tarbuk, *Anti-Critique*,145.

82. Ibid.

83. Ibid., 147.

84. Luxemburg, *Accumulation of Capital*, 229.

Luxemburg is correct because capitalism was born essentially in a non-capitalist milieu. It was enriched immensely by plundering that milieu. Pure capitalism has never existed. Capitalism sucks wealth and value from pre-capitalist communities and classes. However, Luxemburg's mistake lies in treating the world capitalist class as a whole, by leaving out competition. It is competition that determines the whole dynamic, all the laws of development, of capitalism. It is the uneveneness of the rate of development between different countries, different sectors and different enterprises that is the driving force of the expansion of the capitalist market. In practice, exchange with non-capitalist surroundings is one aspect of the uneven development of capitalism.

In fact, Marx himself observed capitalist accumulation and development in the context of colonialism, though his view remains limited. In the actual history of colonialism, force, in the form of conquest, enslavement, robbery, and murder, played a great part. The different moments of primitive accumulation embrace the colonies, the national debt, the modern mode of taxation, and the protectionist system. Military force is the midwife of every transition from an old society to a new one. Capital came into the world dripping from head to foot, from every pore, with blood and dirt. However, Marx did not see all the great powers of successive epochs through the interplay between state formation and capital accumulation. According to Arrighi, the political structures and powers were formed and endowed with ever-more extensive and complex organizational capabilities which controlled the social and political environment of capital accumulation on a world scale.[85]

In the sixteenth and seventeenth centuries, the great revolutions transpiring in commerce with geographical discoveries overwhelmingly contributed to the rise of capitalist production. The world-market formed the basis for the capitalist mode of production. Industry revolutionized commerce. Unequal exchange or colonial underdevelopment must be brought to light because it corrects the limitations of Marx's economic theory.

What preoccupied Marx was the affirmation of the universal and exclusive domination of capitalist production based on wage labor. Marx handled the primitive accumulation merely as signaling the rosy dawn of the era of capitalist production, not as the constant epiphenomenon of accumulation.[86]

---

85. Arrighi, *Long Twentieth Century*, 14.

86. Luxemburg, *Accumulation of Capital*, 364–65.

An international trade under actual conditions was essentially an exchange between capitalistic and non-capitalistic modes of production. There was a need to recruit labor for core areas from the periphery.[87] Luxemburg had experienced the shift in global politics, that is, imperialism, in the Chinese-Japanese war in 1895. Her analysis of the economic roots of imperialism led to anti-imperialist politics. The real process of accumulation was undertaken through the conquest of Algeria and India. We add more: the opium wars against China; the Anglo-Boer war and the carving up of the African Empire; and the extermination of the American Indians. Under the impact of capitalist economy, the American farmer had driven the Red Indian West. The Boer drove the Negro to the North. Free Republics between the Orange River and the Limpopo protested against the designs of the English bourgeoisie on the sacred right of slavery. The battle between the Boers and the English government was fought on the backs of the Negroes.[88]

The typical phenomena of imperialism must be taken into account:

> competition among capitalist countries to win colonies and spheres of interest, opportunities for investment, the international loan system, militarism, tariff barriers, the dominant role of finance capital and truths in world politics.[89]

Not production, but the market that effectively demands and determines production. Each new colonial expansion is accompanied by a relentless battle of capital against the social and economic ties of the natives. The accumulation of capital, seen as a historical process, employs force as a permanent weapon. Permanent occupation of the colonies by the military, native risings, and punitive expeditions are the order of the day for the colonial regime. In the final analysis the imperialist phase of capitalist accumulation implies lending abroad, railroad constructions, revolutions, and wars. The achievement of capitalist autonomy in the hinterland and backward colonies is attained amidst wars and revolutions. The revolutions in Turkey, Russia, and China fall under this heading. The process of world capitalist development and the colonial capitalist phenomenon of underdevelopment are interconnected. Imperialism brings catastrophe back from the periphery of capitalist development to its point of departure. The stage of capitalist expansion is related to monopoly capital and

---

87. Ibid., 359–61.

88. Ibid., 412.

89. Tarbuk, *Anti-Critique*, 60.

late capitalism, which is the object of our study in the next chapter. In the political-economic reality of late capitalism, world politics and its tendency toward crisis become an acute reality.

7

The Reality of Late Capitalism
and Its Challenge

SINCE THE DAYS OF Marx, the shift to monopoly capitalism in the phase of imperialism has made Marx's theory questionable and even obsolete. The unemployed army as capitalism's gravediggers turned into labor aristocrats. Not competition in industrial capitalism, but monopoly played a decisive role in changed economic life. Bank capital has merged with industrial capital and this merger created finance capital. The export of capital became greatly important. Through international monopoly the territorial division of unoccupied parts of the world was established among the major capitalist powers and their satellites.[1]

In our study of the relationship between monopoly capitalism and late capitalism, our focus is on three different perspectives; 1) a theory of monopoly capital (proposed by Paul Baran and Paul Sweezy in the U.S), 2) a theory of late capitalism by Ernest Mandel based on the relation between labor and capital, and 3) Habermas' sociological approach to late capitalism based on the relation between lifeworld and system. In the discussion of late capitalism we shall attend to the perspective of the Third World which runs counter to a unilateral Eurocentric view of worldwide expansion of capitalism. Kondratieff cycles and the long wave of capitalism become instrumental in the debate of late capitalism and world-economy system. Although the role of the church may not be obvious in this chapter, the study of the relationship between monopoly capitalism and

---

1. Lenin, *Imperialism*, 81.

late capitalism will be of significance in analyzing the church's endeavors to support alternatives to global capitalism and economic globalization in subsequent chapters.

Monopoly Capitalism: Competition or Monopoly

Sweezy added the progressive replacement of competition by monopolistic or semi-monopolistic control.[2] Sweezy accepted Hilferding's theory, according to which banks strove to eliminate competition among firms and took interest in the highest possible profit. The banks pursued the elimination of competition and the erection of monopolies.[3] The dominance of bank capital, not industrial capital, marked a passing phase of capitalist development; it was roughly in coincidence with the transition from competitive capitalism to monopoly capitalism.[4]

Sweezy furthered his work on his theory of monopoly capitalism in tandem with Baran. Baran and Sweezy in their common project of *Monopoly Capital* defined monopoly capitalism as a rational and progressive system made up of giant corporations; its prime mover was big business organized in giant corporations. For the sake of the tendency of surplus to rise in the stage of monopoly capitalism, they followed in the footsteps of Schumpeter. The largest scale-unit of control (Schumpeter), which was emergent giant corporations, eliminated the foundations under their smaller competitors and expanded output, bringing down prices in the process. In this process "the new commodity, the new technology, and the new type of organization" tend to be monopolized by a handful of giant corporations. Schumpeter characterized it as co-respective. The giants can buy out and absorb the smaller companies.[5]

For the elaboration of monopoly capitalism, Baran and Sweezy argue,

> If it were necessary to give the briefest definition of imperialism we should have to say that imperialism is the monopoly stage of capitalism.[6]

The political reality of imperialism is to be seen in light of the monopoly stage of capitalism. In this train of thought, they critiqued Marx because

2. Sweezy, *Theory of Development*, 257.
3. Ibid., 266.
4. Ibid., 268.
5. Baran and Sweezy, *Monopoly Capital*, 73–74.
6. Ibid., 4.

he treated monopolies not as essential elements of capitalism but only as remnants of the feudal and mercantilist past.

For Baran and Sweezy, competition was the predominant form of market relations in nineteenth century Britain; it has ceased to occupy an important position in the stage of monopoly capitalism. Unlike the nineteenth century, a large scale enterprise produces a significant share of the output of an industry on a global scale. In the analysis of monopoly capitalism they focused on the central theme: the generation and absorption of the surplus under the conditions of monopoly capitalism.[7] The modes of utilization of surplus constituted the indispensable mechanism by linking the economic foundation of society with its political, cultural, and ideological superstructure. In the fundamental change of competitive capitalism to monopoly capitalism, Marx's law of the falling tendency of the rate of profit must be replaced by the law of rising surplus.[8]

According to the basic argument of Baran and Sweezy,

> under monopoly capitalism there is no necessary correlation, as there is in a competitive system, between the rate of technological progress and the volume of investment outlets.[9]

Unlike Sweezy and Baran, however, the industrial capitalism of free competition was born directly of that commercial capitalism which found its chief source of profit in monopolies. The state in the age of free competitive capitalism came along with the political and military use of coercion and violence to capture international markets. The relation between the national and international expansion of capital was an expression of the law of uneven and combined development inherent in the capitalist mode of production. World-wide capitalist relations of exchange bound together capitalist, semi-capitalist, and pre-capitalist relations of production in an organic unity. Thus the aspect of competition must not necessarily be replaced by the reality of monopoly.[10]

MONOPOLY CAPITAL AND IMPERIALISM

The contradiction of capitalist competition on the domestic market led to inter-imperialist rivalry and the world market tended to be redistributed

---

7. Ibid., 8.
8. Ibid., 72.
9. Ibid., 97.
10. Mandel, *Late Capitalism*, 311.

periodically by imperialist wars. Competition caused the immanent laws of capitalist production to be felt by each individual capitalist as external coercive laws. The battle of competition was fought by the cheapening of commodities. The larger sources of capital beat the smaller. Centralization via the credit system in its developed form did not imply the expropriation of smaller capitalists by the larger. In the process of centralization, competition among the capitalists is not reduced, but hastened and intensified at the international level and also in colonial contexts.

The industrial revolution at the end of the nineteenth century proved a powerful stimulant to the centralization and concentration of industrial capital. However, the real capitalist today is not the individual businessman, but the corporation, which is different from the stereotype out of a nineteenth-century novel. The corporation itself has to maintain a high standard of living.[11] The prime mover of monopoly capitalism is Big Business organized in giant corporations.

The empires of the financial groups emerge, becoming masters of banks, insurance companies, industrial, commercial and transport companies. The term oligopoly describes the situation in a sector of industry which is dominated by a small number of firms–with absolute power in a single firm. In the form of monopoly, the cartels, trusts, and monopolies do not suppress capitalist competition.

Monopoly capitalism becomes more and more a fetter on the development of the productive forces. If the monopoly comes out of the growth of the concentration of production and centralization of capital, finance capital is established though the merging of banks with industry. Thus finance capital coupled with monopoly capitalism precipitated competition, rivalry, and monopoly both on the national and international scale.

In *State and Revolution,* Lenin defines the epoch of the development of monopoly capitalism as "state monopoly capitalism." Imperialism is the era of bank capital, which paved the way to gigantic capitalist monopolies and developed monopoly capitalism into state-monopoly capitalism. State machines in this phase of imperialism demonstrate extraordinary strength with an unprecedented growth in the bureaucratic and military apparatus in connection with the intensification of repressive measures against the working class.[12]

In the epoch of state monopoly capitalism, the state assumed the function of accumulation or extended reproduction. The state actually

11. Baran and Sweezy, *Monopoly Capital,* 43, 45.

12. *On Historical Materialism,* 546.

performed the principal function of capital accumulation. The advanced capitalist countries have passed through this transitional stage and entered into the epoch of state monopoly capitalism.[13]

However, Baran and Sweezy take issue with Lenin's emphasis on the role of the state in state monopoly capitalism. According to them, state intervention is undertaken in service of the interests of the capitalist class. Their perspective underscores the use of the state as an economic instrument within the framework of capitalism; furthermore they bring it to an interrelated world economy which consists of numerous capitalist, semi-capitalist, and non-capitalist nations; here varying degrees of monopoly are a common phenomenon.[14] Baran and Sweezy favor the term "monopoly capital."

According to Baran and Sweezy, terms like state capitalism or state monopoly capitalism cause a misunderstanding that the state coordinates with private business, and the functioning of the system is determined by the cooperation of these forces between state and capitalists as well as by their antagonisms and conflicts. Conflicts between business and government are reflections of conflict within the ruling class—thereby, it causes a serious misleading view.[15] For the sake of monopoly capitalism, they also advocate for the law of rising surplus over against the classical-Marxian law of the falling tendency of the rate of profit. Here their theory of monopoly capitalism, under the influence of Schumpeter, emphasizes the absorption of surplus into the metropolis in terms of militarism and imperialism.

For Baran and Sweezy, capitalism had always been an international system, with a hierarchical structure of metropolis at the top and dependent colonies at the bottom. There were many degrees of superordination and subordination between metropolis and colonies. Emphasizing metropolis and peripheral relation as the center of analytic focus, they critique Marx, because the international character of the capitalist system remained secondary to Marx. This critique is not alterable, although Marx understood the crucial importance of the international structure of capitalism.[16]

Concerning the international use of armed forces, they distinguish the top of the hierarchy (metropolises) from those at or near the bottom

13. Mandel, *Late Capitalism*, 517. Cf. Baran and Sweezy, *Monopoly Capital*, 66.

14. Sweezy, *Theory of Development*, 249, 252.

15. Baran and Sweezy, *Monopoly Capital*, 66–67.

16. Ibid., 178.

(colonies). The sphere of exploitation of a given metropolis is its empire. Some in the intermediate layers may become incorporated into an empire (for example, Portugal and the Portuguese empire as subordinate units within the larger British empire). During the period from 1914 to 1945, the relative strength of the United States grew more or less continuously at the expense of both allies and enemies. At the end of the Second World War, the United States emerged as the undisputed leader nation, its position in the capitalist world was just as commanding as that of Britain had been after 1815. The undisputed leader must have maintained a clear military superiority either through its own armed forces or through the manipulation of alliances, or both. The United States chose both. The United States used its military and financial power to attract large segments of the old colonial empires into its own neo-colonial empire. In this fashion, a vast world-wide American empire has come into being.[17]

LATE CAPITALISM: ITS LEGITIMACY AND LIMITATIONS

Proponents of late capitalism such as Mandel configure the relation between monopoly capitalism and late capitalism in distinction from Baran and Sweezy. Mandel attempts to develop a theory of late capitalism by refining Marx's notion of concentration and centralization. Monopoly capitalism is confronted with the increase in the organic composition of capital and with the growing risks of depreciation of fixed capital during periodic crises. It aims to safeguard and increase the rate of profit of the trusts.[18] Monopoly capital does not need to be understood or localized separately from competition as seen in Baran and Sweezy. Competition is still an important arbiter in the shape of monopoly capitalism. Monopoly super-profits result from restricting competition. Monopoly capitalism develops a series of restrictive techniques which amount to a regular negation of the way the capitalists behaved in the age of free competition.[19] Thus monopoly capitalism is to be understood as a deepening continuity of capital concentration and centralization.

In the era of late capitalism there is a further development of the imperialist, monopoly-capitalist epoch. Competitive capitalism in industrial society has become monopoly capitalism in which competition between capitalists was subsumed under the monopoly of a few capitalists. Mandel

---

17. Ibid., 181–83.

18. Mandel, *Marxist Economy II*, 419.

19. Ibid., 428.

further applies this model of imperial capitalism to the analysis of the long post-war wave of rapid growth in the international capitalist economy. In this framework of late capitalism, Mandel runs counter to Lenin's theory of state monopoly capitalism which failed to understand the dynamic of late capitalism as a whole and overemphasizes the contradiction between the world camps of capitalism and socialism.[20]

For Mandel, capital investments in colonial and semi-colonial countries became an important factor of the accumulation process; a steady growth took place in the contribution undertaken by colonial surplus-profits. State intervention is used increasingly to ensure the surplus-profits of the monopolies. In this line of thought, Mandel defines the era of late capitalism as a further development of the imperialistic, monopoly-capitalist epoch. Late capitalism is not fixed independently as a new epoch of capitalist development. The third technological revolution (nuclear energy) and the formation of late capitalism underscores that the international concentration of capital began to develop into international centralization. The multinational company became the determinant organizational form of big capital in the phase of late capitalism.[21] The surplus-profits take the form of technological surplus-profits.

In dealing with the crises of late capitalism, Mandel envisages an intensification in the age of late capitalism of all the contradictions inherent in imperialism: the antagonism between capital and labor in the metropolitan countries and the semi-colonies; the antagonism between imperialist metropolitan states and colonial or semi-colonial nations; the intensification of inter-imperialist contradictions will necessarily bring in its wake a tendency for certain imperialist powers to amalgamate. Mandel includes greater emphasis on the independent revolutionary tasks of the proletariat in the metropolitan countries.[22]

The crises of late capitalism must be understood as a combination of all the contradictions based on the capitalist mode of production. Thus the cyclical movement of capitalist production is related to the cyclical movement of the average rate of profit; this perspective explains the contradictory development in the process of production and reproduction. The cyclical movement of the rate of profit is linked to the uneven development in the process of production and reproduction. Furthermore, the resultant increase in the accumulation of capital is coupled with an

20. Mandel, *Late Capitalism*, 9–10.

21. Ibid., 316.

22. Mandel, *Late Capitalism*, 334.

accelerated rhythm of technological innovation and a reduced turnover-time of the fixed capital; it led to the third technological revolution, to a long term expansion of the market on an international scale. This economic reality explains Mandel's view of a long wave with an undertone of expansion from 1940(45)–66.[23]

Every period of radical technical innovation appears as a period of sudden acceleration of capital accumulation. Only a sudden increase in the rate of profit can explain the massive investment of surplus capital—just as a prolonged fall in the rate of profit can explain the idleness of the same capital over many years. In the early 90's of the nineteenth century, the triggering factors of the new long wave of expansion were the momentous drive of capital exports to the colonies and semi-colonies, and resultant cheapening of raw materials and foodstuffs, which similarly led to a sharp increase in the rate of profit in the imperialist countries. The long wave with an undertone of expansion from 1940 onwards transitions to a long wave with an undertone of stagnation, intensifying social antagonism and the international class struggle.[24]

LIFEWORLD AND SYSTEM

Mandel's economic interpretation of the crises of late capitalism implies a creative development, but his overemphasis on the economic factor of the capitalist mode of production undervalues the complex reality of late capitalism in regard to cultural hegemony, discourse, the system's colonization of the lifeworld, and people's resistance in civil society.

Habermas deals with the reality of late capitalism in terms of system and life-world. The expression 'late capitalism' implies for him the hypothesis that social developments involve contradictions or crises even in state-regulated capitalism. Habermas distinguishes social integration and system integration from the standpoint of a social scientific conflict of crisis; social integration is undertaken in relation to the systems of institutions, here social systems are seen as symbolically structured life-worlds. From the life-world perspective, Habermas thematizes the normative structures of a society (values and institutions) in reference to social integration. On the other hand, Habermas speaks of system integration in regard to the specific steering performances of a self-regulated system (politics, economy, and mass media).

23. Ibid., 442.
24. Ibid., 472.

In an illustration of the social principles of organization, Habermas distinguishes four social formations: primitive, traditional, capitalist (liberal capitalist/organized or advanced capitalist), and post-capitalist. In the examination of crisis tendencies in late and post-capitalist societies, Habermas explores the possibilities of a postmodern society which implies a principle of organization of aged, advanced, late capitalism in a current, historical phase. Postmodern society is a historically new principle of organization; it is not a different name for the vigor of an aged capitalism.[25] The expressions organized, late or state-regulated capitalism refer to the advanced stage of the accumulation process in terms of the process of economic concentration (the rise of national and multinational corporations) and in terms of the organization of markets for goods, capital, and labor. This structure of late capitalism means the end of competitive capitalism due to regulation.[26]

What is specific to the crisis tendencies of the system of late capitalism is the economic crisis (from the economic system), rationality and legitimation crisis (from the political system), and motivation crisis (from the socio-cultural system).[27] Habermas' view of late capitalism corrects Mandel's theory of late capitalism which is unilaterally built on the dialectical logic of capital and labor.

For the sake of a social scientific concept of system and life-world, Habermas utilizes the Marxian concept of social formation within the framework of social evolution.[28] Although the spread of an oligopolistic market structure put an end to competitive capitalism, many companies broaden their temporal perspectives, expanding control over their environments. State intervention marked the end of liberal capitalism. Nonetheless, the society as a whole is developed in an unplanned manner free of state regulation. In advanced-capitalist societies the economic sphere is characterized by the articulation of the competitive sectors and the monopolistic and public sectors. At the administrative level, the state performs numerous imperatives of the economic system. By means of global planning, the state regulates the economic cycle as a whole, creating and improving. The state demands measures for guiding the flow of capital, improving chances for capital investment in the international market.[29]

25. Ibid., 17.
26. Ibid., 33.
27. Ibid., 45.
28. Habermas, *Legitimation*, 7.
29. Ibid., 35.

As the functional weakness in the market appears, the basic ideology of fair exchange collapses. An attempt to re-couple the economic system to the political creates an increased need for legitimization. The need for legitimization is reduced to civic privatism (political abstinence coupled with an orientation to career, leisure, and consumption). Or, it requires justification either by democratic elite theories or by technocratic system theories. To the degree that the relations of production are repoliticized in organized capitalism, the political anonymity of class domination is superseded by social anonymity. In the process of capitalist development in the decades since World War II, the social identity of the classes broke down and class consciousness was fragmented. The class compromise has become a part of the structure of advanced capitalism. Here everyone can become both a participant and a victim. It is certain that with the unequal distribution of wealth and power, a distinction is made between the privileged and underprivileged. In this regard, the self-transformation of advanced capitalism remains dubious. Economic crisis can be permanently averted, and the disturbance of capitalist growth can be administratively processed and transferred through the political and into the socio-cultural system.[30]

Based on his perspective on the legitimization problem of late capitalism, Habermas takes issue with the theory of state monopoly capitalism; this theory is based on the assumption that the unplanned development of the capitalist process of reproduction has been replaced by state monopolistic planning and the centralized steering of the production apparatus. The united monopolies pursue a collective capitalist interest with the help of the state apparatus. The alleged union of the power of the monopolies with that of the state apparatus is described in terms of an agency theory. The societal control center is allegedly subordinated to the collective-capitalist interest. Against the theory of state monopoly capitalism, Habermas argues that the assumption that the state apparatus can actively plan and carry through a central economic strategy cannot be empirically proven and verified. The theory of state monopoly capitalism failed to appreciate the limits of administrative planning in advanced late capitalism.

Habermas argues that the theory of state monopoly capitalism overestimates the significance of the state apparatus in direct regulation of transactions. It fails to distinguish between the structure of an

30. Ibid., 39–40.

administrative system, the process of conflict resolution and consensus formation, and of decision and implementation.[31]

According to Habermas, Marx analyzes the tendency toward a falling rate of profit and the weakening impulse in continuing the process of accumulation. Economic crisis is transformed into social crisis. The economic crisis results from a contradictory system of imperatives and threatens social integration. The theory of value is intended to fulfill the task of a critique of commodity fetishism and of the derivate cultural phenomena of bourgeois society. Nevertheless, Marx's theory remains considerably limited and unqualified given the administrative system and social integration in the context of late capitalism.

In contrast to Marx's economy system, Habermas takes into account the administrative system, the legitimization system, and class structure.[32] He emphasizes an issue of disturbance of ecological balance, violation of the consistency requirements of the personality system (alienation), and potentially explosive strains on international relations. Ecological balance designates an absolute limit to growth. Growth imperatives originally followed by capitalism have meanwhile achieved global validity through system competition and worldwide diffusion (notwithstanding stagnation or even retrogressive tendencies in Third World countries). The economic needs for a growing population and increasingly productive exploitation of nature are faced with two important material limitations: on the one hand, the supply of finite resources—the area of cultivable and inhabitable land, fresh water, foodstuffs, non-regenerating raw materials (minerals, fuels, etc); on the other hand, the capacities of irreplaceable ecological systems to absorb pollutants such as radioactive byproducts, carbon dioxide, or waste heat.[33]

In parallel to the process of socializing outer nature,—disturbance to ecological balance indicates the degree of exploitation of natural resources—there is the danger of the self-destruction of the world system through the use of thermonuclear means. In late capitalism, according to Habermas, possible crisis tendencies can be classified into economic system, political system, and socio-cultural system. Economic crisis comes from the economic system, rationality crisis and legitimation crisis come from the political system; finally motivation crisis comes from the socio-cultural system.

31. Ibid., 60.

32. Habermas, *Legitimation*, 34–40.

33. Ibid., 41.

The output consists in executed administrative decisions. Output crises have the form of a rationality crisis, in which the administrative system does not succeed in reconciling and fulfilling the imperatives from the economic system. Input crises have the form of a legitimization crisis. A rationality deficit in public administration means that the state apparatus cannot, under given boundary conditions, adequately steer the economic system.

During the course of capitalist development, the political system shifts its boundaries not only into the economic system but also into the socio-cultural system. While organizational rationality spreads, cultural traditions are undermined and weakened. The socio-cultural system receives its input from the economic and political systems. Output crises in both of the other systems are also input disturbances in the socio-cultural system and translate into withdrawal of legitimization. Motivation crises are a result of changes in the socio-cultural system itself. In late capitalism such tendencies are becoming apparent at the level of cultural tradition (moral system, and worldview) as well as at the level of structural change in the system of childrearing (school, family, and mass media). In this way, the residue of tradition off which the state and the system of social labor lived in liberal capitalism is eaten away.[34]

COMMUNICATIVE ACTION AND CIVIL SOCIETY

To overcome the limitation of late capitalism Habermas further develops his theory of communicative action for the lifeworld within which communicative actions are moving. Here civil society is differentiated from a system (political society or the state) and conceived as a lifeworld. Lifeworld is represented by a culturally transmitted and linguistically organized stock of interpretive patterns. Language and culture, assuming a certain transcendental status in relation to everything, are constitutive for the lifeworld itself.[35] Communicative action, or discourse is moving already and always within the horizon of their lifeworlds which refers to the totality of sociocultural facts; it provides a jumping-off point for social theory.

From the internal perspective of the lifeworld, civil society is understood as a network of communicatively mediated cooperation, a web of communicative actions. The lifeworld, which we cannot go behind, makes

34. Ibid., 48.
35. Habermas, *Theory of Action II*, 124.

a universal claim in a horizon of unrestricted possibilities of mutual understanding.[36]

However, in capitalist societies the integration of society within system integration presents society according to the model of a self-regulating system of money and power. In modern societies autonomous organizations are increasingly connected with one another through media of communication. These systematic mechanisms, for instance, money, steer social intercourse; the systematic mechanisms are to be institutionalized and anchored in the lifeworld. At higher levels of integration, new social structures take shape as the state and media-steered subsystem.[37] In the uncoupling of system and lifeworld, structural violence and distortion are exercised through systematic restrictions on the public sphere of communication.[38] The mediatization of the lifeworld takes the form of a colonization; lifeworld is reified and colonized. For Habermas, the communicative rationality gives an inner logic to resistance against the colonization of the lifeworld by the mechanism of system.

According to Habermas, Marx's concept of alienation remains ambiguous, because Marx was unable to distinguish between the aspect of reification and that of structural differentiation of the lifeworld.[39] System and lifeworld appeared in Marx only under the rubric of the realm of necessity and the realm of freedom. However, for Habermas, the process of reification does not merely appear in the sphere of social labor. Rather it is manifested in public and in private domains, by absorbing communicative contexts of life through media—money and power.

From the perspective of democratic constitutions, Habermas argues that modern societies must assert the primacy of a lifeworld in relation to the subsystems of money and political power. Social welfare policy considers external effects in the ecologically sensitive areas (town planning, highway construction, energy and water policy, protection of the countryside, or in the areas of health, culture, and education).[40] Insofar as the political system in developed capitalist societies manages to overcome the structural dilemmas through government interventionism, mass democracy, and the welfare state, structures of late capitalism take shape. Late capitalism strengthens itself by uncoupling system and lifeworld. It alters

36. Ibid., 149.
37. Ibid., 154.
38. Ibid., 187.
39. Ibid., 341.
40. Ibid., 347.

the conditions of the relations between system (economy and state) and lifeworld (private and public spheres).

As an alternative to late capitalism, Habermas proposes civil society associated with deliberate democracy. The communicative rationalization of the lifeworld heightens the systematic complexity of economy and state, bursting the capacity of the lifeworld to be instrumentalized by the system. Against the structural violence of systems of money, power, and mass media on the sphere of lifeworld, Habermas attempts to erect a democratic dam against the colonizing encroachment of system on the areas of lifeworld.[41]

The communicative theory of deliberate democracy is composed of the political public sphere and civil society. The political public sphere is characterized by open and shifting horizons and presented as a communication structure which is rooted in the lifeworld through the association network of civil society.[42] Civil society is attuned to the political public sphere, comprising a network of associations. It institutionalizes problem-solving discourses in matters pertaining to general interest with the public sphere.

Habermas' perspective could facilitate the church's understanding of the public sphere in terms of lifeworld and civil society. Public theology which is interested in promoting the church's ethical responsibility may appreciate Habermas' insight. The church must stand for the lifeworld, against the system; the church struggles against the colonization of the lifeworld in light of the liberating message of the gospel.[43]

Nevertheless, Habermas's project of civil society and deliberate democracy needs to refine a concept of civil society in critical regard to the tradition of possessive individualism represented by Hobbes and Locke. A theory of lifeworld built on communicative rationality and action is to be deepened by analyzing the institutionalized dimension of the discourse embedded within sociocultural hegemony and epistemological knowledge. A communicative rationality can be sharpened in solidarity with those whose discourses are marginalized and victimized. It is also to be widened in connection with global capitalism.

41. Calhoun, ed. *Habermas*, 444.

42. Habermas, *Facts and Norms*, 359. See Simpson, *Critical Social Theory*.

43. Chung, *Cave and Butterfly*, 101.

CAPITALIST WORLD EXPANSION AND WORLD POLITICS

All the contradictions inherent in the system of monopoly capitalism imply that the effective socialization of production is accomplished on the world scale, and leads to effective control by a few monopolies over whole peoples. Despite a high rate of surplus transfer from the developing countries, both the falling tendency of the rate of profit and the tendency toward underconsumption (or overproduction) stand in the way of the path of ongoing accumulation.[44] Capital export to underdeveloped countries paved the way for an active colonial and imperialist policy.

At the beginning of the twentieth century, many socialists greeted the establishment of international cartels as the coming of a new phase of capitalism, that of organized capitalism. They were convinced that capitalism would overcome competition and economic nationalism. It would constitute a period of transition to socialism through world-wide planning in the sphere of production.[45] The cartels, trusts, and monopolies did not suppress capitalist competition. State intervention was used increasingly to guarantee the surplus-profits of the monopolies.

The rivalry between the great capitalist nations hardened. Crises widened. But capitalism was adapting itself, transforming itself, opening new prospects. In a related development, there was an extraordinary proliferation of scientific and technical advances, and innovations. The armaments industries experienced a renewal with the development of steel, engines, and new explosives.

A study of imperialism is heavily indebted to two scholars' studies: J. A. Hobson's book *Imperialism* and Hilferding's *Finance Capital*. Hobson, an English liberal, did groundbreaking work on imperialism which exercised a profound impact on Lenin. Hobson argued that one of the causes of imperialism in search of surplus capital was the concentration of capital into cartels and monopolies. As Hobson stated,

> Imperialism is the endeavor of the great controllers of industry to broaden the channels for the flow of their surplus wealth by seeking foreign markets and foreign investments to take off the goods and capital they cannot sell or use at home.[46]

Capitalism had grown into a world system of colonial expansion and of the financial strangulation of the majority of the people of the world

44. Sweezy, *Theory of Development*, 289, 304.

45. Mandel, *Marxist Theory, II*, 434.

46. Hobson, *Imperialism*, 85.

by a handful of advanced countries. Finance capital as the latest phase of capitalist development (Hilferding) altered imperialism as the highest stage of capitalism. The transformation of competition into monopoly was one of the most important and characteristic features of modern capitalist economy. Here capitalism has been transformed into imperialism.

According to Hilferding,

> "Finance capital signifies the unification of capital. The previously separate spheres of industrial, commercial and bank capital are now brought under the common direction of high finance, in which the masters of industry and the banks are united in a close personal association.[47]

The finance capital intensified and accelerated the process of capital in the formation of monopolies. However, Lenin held that Hilferding's definition of finance capital lacked the increase of concentration of production and capital which led to monopoly.[48] In Lenin's view,

> "The concentration of production; the monopoly arising therefrom; the merging or coalescence of banking with industry—this is the history of the rise of finance capital and what gives the term 'finance capital' its content.[49]

Here, Lenin reiterates Marx's limited view of monopoly capital.

Hilferding furthers,

> the policy of finance capital has three objectives (1) to establish the largest possible economic territory; (2) to close this territory to foreign competition by a wall of protective tariffs, and consequently (3) to reserve it as an area of exploitation for the national monopolistic combinations.[50]

Consequently, imperialism, which implies the domination of finance capital, is the highest stage of capitalism. As exports increased from capitalist countries, international competition became still more severe; capital was exported and overseas holdings and affiliates were created. Within the same movement there was a second, powerful wave of colonization, accompanied by rivalries, conflicts, and wars. Colonization is the people's expansion and multiplication, submitting the foreign countries to this

---

47. Hilferding, *Finance*, 301.

48. Lenin, *Imperialism*, 47.

49. Ibid.

50. Hilferding, *Finance*, 326.

people's language, ideas, and laws. People who colonized cast the foundations of their greatness and supremacy into the future.

Here economic realism and racism support each other. Hilferding maintained that a scientifically-cloaked foundation for the lust for power of finance capital emerged in racial ideology. The theory of racial superiority underscored the oligarchical ideal of mastery in place of the democratic ideal of equality.[51] The civilization or religion blessed this movement. Racism and certitude removed the last scruples. When necessary, whole populations were massacred. The mad scramble was on.

Accordingly, Hobson wrote in 1902.

> The new imperialism differs from the older, first, in substituting for the ambition of a single growing empire the theory and the practice of competing empires, each motivated by similar lusts of political aggrandizement and commercial gain, secondly, in the dominance of financial or investing over mercantile interests.[52]

Along with rivalries, competition, confrontation, industrial and financial interests, as well as patriotic spirit, the imperialist expansion of national capitalism was a fundamental cause of the Great War of 1914–18. The specious myth of proletarian internationalism was shattered to the core.[53] This perspective on imperialism and colonialism finds an acute analysis in those representing the standpoint of the third world reality.

THE RELATION BETWEEN METROPOLIS AND PERIPHERY

Metropolitan economists have assumed "a white man's burden" attitude that increased contact, closer integration, diffusion of capital, technology, and institutions, and so on. Anthropologists who specialized in the study of natives abroad have assumed that the societies they studied have been traditionally at rest as they found them unchanging. Many intellectuals in the colonized and neo-colonial countries themselves have been so culturally colonized and brainwashed by the metropolis that they study their own societies only following the metropolitan image-civilization.

51. Sweezy, *Theory of Development*, 310.

52. Lenin, *Imperialism*, 92.

53. According to Arrighi, Hilferding's notion of finance capital as a new stage of capitalist development refers to the state monopoly capitalism in analysis of the late nineteenth-century. Financial expansion was the closing phase of the third British systematic cycle of accumulation. Lenin failed to distinguish these two different forms of finance capitalism. Arrighi, *Long Twentieth Century*, 162.

Against intellectual-colonial imposition during the last decade Asians and Africans have begun to rewrite their own history. Scholars in the Third World perspective point out that Marxists in the former socialist countries devoted their attention to this problem only from the perspective of metropolis capitalism.[54] This perspective remains insufficient and questionable in analysis of the reality of underdevelopment in the Third World.

Capitalism's entrance to the country under the conditions of imperialist domination must be considered in connection with ethnological, demographic, geographical, or religious (ideological) conditions. The colonial countries especially in Africa and Asia, or the semi-colonial countries became transformed into economic dependents of the imperialist countries. This phenomenon is today known by the term 'underdevelopment.' The unlimited industrial advance of the Western world has been possible only at the expense of the so-called underdeveloped world, which has been doomed to stagnation and regression.

In the final analysis, this situation constituted the main root of the whole 'development ideology' which has been fostered in the Third World by the ruling classes of the metropolitan countries. This new turn in the structure of the world economy simply meant a change in the forms of juxtaposition of development and underdevelopment. Unequal exchange on the world market was always the result of a difference in the average productivity of labor between two nations. Foreign capital invested almost nothing in the development of the manufacturing industry.

The colonial countries were transformed into semi-colonial countries. They attained political independence. The system of indirect domination—neo-colonialism or neo-imperialism—corresponds to an economic interest among the imperialist metropolis. They see the industrialization of the underdeveloped countries as the emergence of potential clients. In trade as visible in propaganda, aid to the underdeveloped countries amounted to a redistribution of profits within the metropolis. This world became characteristic of the development of underdevelopment, or the development of dependence.

Frank distinguishes between *colonialisation* and *colonization*; the first refers to mode of production, low wage level, and colonial unequal exchange as underlying factors of a subordinate dependence and development of underdevelopment within the process of world capital accumulation. The second refers to a mode of production on the part of transplanted

---

54. Frank, *Dependent Accumulation*, 140–71.

settlers equipped with relatively high wage level and partial protection against external unequal exchange. With this different mode of production, implanted settlers were allowed to achieve economic development. The external relations of exchange (colonialisation) and the internal ones (colonization) are interconnected with each other in the New World.[55]

In accordance with the third World perspective, Samir Amin, in his 1989 work *Eurocentrism*,[56] denounced the ideology of Orientalism with which the Palestinian-American Edward Said took issue in his 1978 book *Orientalism*. Amin attempts to analyze capitalism in an age of globalization in terms of unequal development and the historical forms of capitalism. According to him, the logic of capitalist expansion should not be identified in terms of development. He distinguishes the market and capitalism, emphasizing that they are not identical. The truth is that capitalism requires the intervention of the state as the collective authority which represents capital as a whole. The policies of capital and the state as representative of capital have their own logic which is not merely the expression of abstract market laws. There is the logic of world polarization immanent in the capitalist system itself; it gradually erodes national systems of production generated by the previous historical period and adapts to the methodical industrialization of the peripheries.[57]

In the analysis of the domination of the center over the peripheries on the scale of world-economy, Amin examines the present world-system through the five monopolies of the center: technological monopoly, control of worldwide financial markets, monopolistic access to natural resources, media and communication monopolies, and monopolies over weapons of mass destruction.[58]

The Third World perspective on world economy helps the churches in the context of anti-colonialism develop a liberation-oriented postcolonial theology especially committed to those on the underside of the universal history of capitalism. Their strategies can be seen in their creative but controversial utilization of Marxist theory to overcome the gap between metropolis and periphery. However, the current reality of economic globalization has deeply challenged these Marxist interpretations, making it more clear that the reality of world economy must be analyzed on a global scale. A notion of Empire appears and we shall have occasion

55. Ibid., 24
56. Amin, *Eurocentrism*.
57. Amin, *Capitalism*, 15–16.
58. Ibid., 4–5.

to deal with it in more detail later. Our interest in the following excursus is in investigating the long wave of capitalism and its sustainability in terms of the Kondratieff Cycles.

EXCURSUS: KONDRATIEFF CYCLES AND THE LONG WAVE OF CAPITALISM

Kondratieff waves—also called long waves or K-waves—are described as regular, sinusoidal-like cycles in the modern (capitalist) world economy. The Russian economist Nikolai Kondratieff brought these observations to international attention in his book *The Major Economic Cycles* (1925). Kondratieff attempted to set up the concept of a major cycle (embracing approx. fifty years) along with the minor cycle (covering a period of ten years).

Later, in *Business Cycles* (1939), Joseph Schumpeter suggested this theory by naming the cycles "Kondratieff waves." Schumpeter elevated the theory to the explanation of long periods of the capitalist development. Schumpeter contended that Kondratieff cycles could be traced to the sixteenth century. Understanding Kondratieff cycles is crucial in the study of capitalistic accumulation, development, and crisis. Knowledge of this theory will be helpful for the church in developing understandings of economic justice in the reality of global capitalism.

Based on reliable and empirical data, Kondratieff identified three phases in the cycle: expansion, stagnation, and recession. The world economy over time is drawn according to the Kondratieff theory. Wallerstein uses the Kondratieff theory in his two-phase explanation of expansion and stagnation (or recession) in the capitalist world-economy. This accounts for the cyclical rhythms and curves of the world-economy. We speak of expansion of the world-economy when there are quasi-monopolistic leading industries; we also speak of contraction in the world-economy when there is a lowering of the intensity of quasi-monopoly. The process of expansion and contraction can be drawn as an up-and-down curve of A-phase (expansion) and B-phase (recession).

Phase A (Expansion)

Phase B (Recession)

Rate of Growth

Time

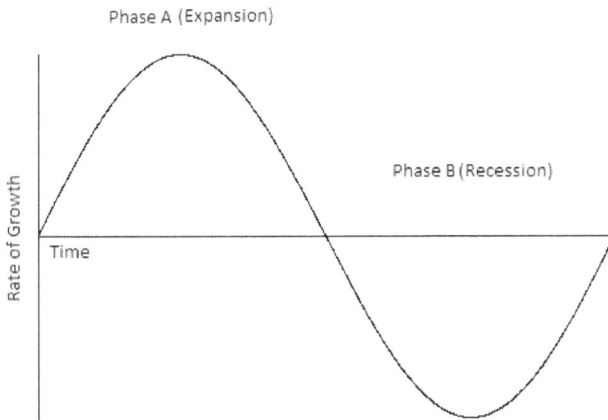

A cycle, consisting of A-phase and B-phase, generally lasts fifty to sixty years. It is certain that there is much debate about what explains the cycles and especially what explains the upturn from a B-phase to an A-phase. The exact length between expansion and recession depends on the political measure which can be taken by the state to avert a B-phase. A Kondratieff cycle never returns to the situation where it was at its beginning stage. The parameters of the world-system are changed by the cycle from A-phase to B-phase.[59]

Kondratieff himself called the cycles long waves. Ernst Mandel revived interest in long wave theory. According to Mandel, the cyclical course of the capitalist mode of production takes the form of the successive expansion and contraction of commodity production. A further cyclical movement of expansion and contraction can be seen in the realization of surplus-value and the accumulation of capital. In a period of upswing, there is an increase in the mass and the rate of profit. It gives a rise in the volume and the rhythm of accumulation. In a crisis and subsequent period of depression, both the mass and the rate of profit will decline. In this industrial cycle, we observe the successive acceleration and deceleration of accumulation. We understand the entire capitalist cycle in terms of the consequence of accelerated capital accumulation, over-accumulation, decelerated capital accumulation, and under-investment.[60]

However, in Mandel's theory, Kondratieff's theory of long waves is modified and critiqued in light of Marx's theory of cycles and crises according to which the renewal of fixed capital explains not only the length

59. Wallerstein, *Essential Wallerstein*, 207–20.
60. Mandel, *Late Capitalism*, 109–10.

of the business cycle but also the upswing and acceleration of capital accumulation. The notion of the organic composition of capital includes a technological element, so that the value-composition is determined by the technological composition. Furthermore, a revolution in technology affects the whole apparatus of social production by leading to a fundamental renewal of productive technology or fixed capital and a qualitative change in the productivity of labor.[61] Against Kondratieff, Mandel defines the long waves of accelerated and decelerated accumulation as ones determined by long waves in the rise and decline of the rate of profit; then the theory of long waves must be explained by a series of social changes. Mandel's reconstruction emphasizes the fluctuation in the rate of profit.

At any rate, we have experienced the history of capitalism on the international scale, not only based on a succession of cyclical movements every seven or ten years, but also a succession of longer periods (approximately fifty years). Kondratieff designated a major cycle by the contingent, external conditions and events of the capitalist development (for instance, the integration of new countries into the world economy, the discovery of new natural resources, fluctuations in the extraction of gold, change in technology, wars and revolutions). However, he did not consider the cycles in terms of the internal interplay of capitalist forces. The external factors determined the character and the replacement of ascending, stagnation, or declining epochs of capitalist development.[62]

Kondratieff did not manage to develop his theory of long waves because he excluded two crucial factors: long term fluctuation in the average rate of profit and the influence of technological revolution. For the solution of the problem of long waves, diverse combinations of factors need to be considered affecting the rate of profit: a radical fall in the cost of raw materials, a sudden expansion of the world market, or new fields for investment for capital, a rapid increase or decline in the rate of surplus-value, wars and revolutions in reference to the inner logic of the process of long term accumulation and valorization of capital, and radical renewal in productive technology.[63]

Wallerstein utilizes Kondratieff cycles to explain the rise and development of the modern world-system. He describes the origin of the European world-economy in the expansive long sixteenth century from 1450 to 1640 (in the first volume of the Modern World-System), consolidation

61. Ibid., 112.
62. Ibid., 129.
63. Ibid., 145.

from 1600 to 1750 (in its second volume), and the second era of great expansion from 1730 to the 1840s (in its third volume). In this light Wallerstein applies the explanations for the post-1800 Kondratieffs to the 1500–1800 situation. One of his basic arguments is that the capitalist world-economy has both cyclical rhythms and secular trends. One of the most important cyclical rhythms is the Kondratieff cycles, having more or less 50 years in length (45–60 years). Quantitative indicators of social life in the modern world fluctuate, going up and down. Cycles suggest some element of regularity, some pattern in these fluctuations.

Wallerstein follows Schumpeter's definition of capitalism as one process both in the economic and sociological sense, along with the whole world as its stage. Given this fact, Wallerstein argues that Kondratieff cycles must first of all be phenomena of the world-economy as a whole.[64] What needs to be measured is the world-economy as a whole. If Kondratieff cycles are a phenomenon of capitalism, the key issue must be found in profit rates. As we have already seen, Mandel attempted to ground a Marxist theory of the long waves of capitalist development on a theory of the accumulation of capital, in other words, a rate of profit theory. However, Wallerstein runs counter to Mandel who proposed interest rates as a barometer of profit.[65] Following the advice of Schumpeter, Wallerstein maintains that the cycle is a process within which all elements of the economic system interact with each other. Thus no one element can be singled out as the role of prime mover.[66] Wallerstein embraces three different emphases on the explanation of Kondratieff's theory: 1) exhaustion of technology, 2) capital overexpansion, and 3) overexpansion of primary production.[67]

A long A-phase (expansion) came to an end and was supplanted by a B-phase (stagnation). If Kondratieff's theory integrates political processes, it is important for Wallerstein to view the consequence of major political struggles in the various parts of the world-economy; cyclical rhythm is connected with secular trends. From the perspective of the capitalist world-economy as a historical system, the B-phases are an essential element of its existence. The A-phases and B-phases are likened to the relationship between inhaling and exhaling in breathing.[68] Kondratieff cycles are a construct of the analyst based on empirical data, thus it is an

---

64. Wallerstein, *Essential Wallerstein,* 210.

65. Ibid., 211.

66. Ibid., 212.

67. Ibid., 214.

68. Ibid., 218.

interpretive argument. The theory's justification lies in its defensibility, its heuristic value, and its utility.[69]

Some scholars find Kondratieff's theory limited because it fails to provide a coherent theoretical foundation for the interpretation of long cycles. For instance, Arrighi utilizes Marx's formula of capital (MCM*) for the sake of a recurrent pattern of historical capitalism as world system and constructs his systemic cycle of accumulation. In this sense, he investigates a comparative analysis of successive systemic cycles of accumulation in terms of: a Genoese cycle (from the fifteenth to the early seventeenth centuries), a Dutch cycle (from the late sixteenth century through most of the eighteenth century), a British cycle (from the latter half of the eighteenth century through the early twentieth century), and a U.S. cycle (beginning in the late nineteenth century and continuing into the current phase of financial expansion). Consecutive systemic cycles of accumulation last longer than a century. Arrighi's criticism is that Kondratieff cycles are not reliable indicators of the contractions and expansions which are specifically capitalist in the modern world system.[70]

69. Ibid., 209.

70. Arrighi, *Long Twentieth Century*, 7.

8

Capitalism and World-Systems Analysis

WE HAVE EXAMINED THE development and expansion of capitalism in terms of a critical study of Marx's idea and theory of monopoly capital and late capitalism. However, those committed to economic study from the standpoint of the world-system take issue with monopoly capitalism as a rational and progressive system which retains big business organized in giant corporations as its prime mover. Smaller business was treated as a part of the environment around the operation of big business.[1] A state under monopoly capitalism has a responsibility to insure that prices and profit margins in the deviant industries are brought within the general run of giant corporations.[2] The law of monopoly capitalism is articulated: the surplus tends to rise as the system of monopoly capitalism develops.

The Marxian law of falling profit lost its validity in this context. The absorption of surplus by the military machine in the advanced capitalist countries is a significant factor. An international relation between metropolis and colonies is connected with the notion of metropolis-empire. At the end of the Second World War the United States emerged as the leader nation or neo-colonial empire; a vast world-wide American empire has come into existence coupled with its military needs and forces.[3]

1. Baran and Sweezy, *Monopoly Capital*, 52–53.
2. Ibid., 65.
3. Ibid., 182–83.

The U.S., like Great Britain in the nineteenth century, needs a global military machine to police a global empire. The Third World countries are characterized by: (a) domination by a traditional oligarchy supported by the army, (b) a military dictatorship, (c) domination by a techno-bourgeoisie of the state supported by the army, (d) an alliance of techno-bourgeoisie of the state with the petty bourgeoisie, and (e) a populist regime of a progressive or regional character.

However, Capitalist development in peripheral countries has demonstrated more underdevelopment (destructive side) than development (creative side). Paul A. Baran (1910–1964) attempted to propose the political economy of growth in this context.[4] It was important for him to consider the famous socialist law of uneven development; this theory suggests not only that the historical process is different in different societies, but also that the stage reached at any given time differs from country to country.[5] Baran, together with Sweezy, formed a bridge with the theory of dependency in Latin America (Frank). The economic theory of dependency is renewed and critically developed within the framework of world-systems analysis and Capitalist world-economy (Wallerstein). The study of economic theory from the standpoint of dependency and the world-system facilitates our understanding of the political economy of the Third World and the reality of unequal exchange in the context of global capitalism. Understanding this theory of dependency is crucial for us in examining the church's responsibility and solidarity with those who are economically weaker, especially in the context of liberation theology in Latin America.

THE POLITICAL ECONOMY OF SURPLUS

Baran's most significant analytical innovation in economics is his critical use of the concept of the economic surplus. For him, profits are not identical with economic surplus, but constitute the visible part of the iceberg with the rest of it. Monopoly capitalism generates not only profits, rent, and interest as elements of the economic surplus, but conceals an important share of the surplus under the rubric of costs.[6]

Baran was influenced by Keynes, and introduced a concept of economic surplus which was not tied to Marx's labor theory. For Baran, the

4. Baran, *Political Economy*.

5. Ibid., xxvii.

6. Ibid., xix–xx.

actual economic surplus is the part of surplus value that is being accumulated. This is tantamount to the "current saving or accumulation."[7] It does not include the consumption of the capitalist class, the government's spending on administration, military establishment, and the like.[8]

Baran used the surplus concept to analyze underdeveloped economies in his *The Political Economy of Growth*. In the functioning of the economic system, large-scale enterprise became the basis of monopoly and oligopoly which were the characteristic features of modern capitalism.

> Western penetration of backward and colonial areas established
> ruthless oppression and exploitation of the subjugated nations
> instead of spreading the blessings of Western civilization in the
> globe.[9]

Competition among business people has continuously forced them to improve their methods of production, to promote technological progress, and to make full use of its results, as well as to increase and to diversify their output. Competition among workers would prevent wages from rising above the subsistence minimum. In a society dedicated to the maximization and rational utilization of the economic surplus value the state was to abstain from interfering with the formation of capital; it refrains from collecting excessive taxes, foregoes meddling in social affairs; and it subsidizes the poor and reduces the number of unproductive workers.[10]

Weber and Sombart stressed the development of rational calculation and accountancy as an important factor in the growth of bourgeois culture. For Marx, the bourgeoisie was too enlightened; they calculated too well. The conditions of existence of the bourgeoisie compelled them to calculate.[11] This spirit was accompanied by the prevalence of Puritan ethics and established a system of social values in which thriftiness and the drive to accumulate was elevated to the position of supreme merit and paramount virtue.

Similarly to Weber, Marx asserted the intimate relation between the rise of Protestantism and Puritanism as well as the genesis and development of capitalism in its Christian character. "The money cult implies its own asceticism, its own self-denial, its own self-sacrifice—parsimony and

7. Ibid., 23.
8. Ibid., 22, note 1.
9. Ibid., 6.
10. Ibid., 47.
11. Ibid., 48.

frugality, a contempt for worldly, temporal, and transient satisfactions: it implies the striving for everlasting treasure. Hence the connection of English Puritanism, but also of Dutch Protestantism, with money making."[12]

Integrating Weber with Marx, Baran further emphasizes that the principal vehicle of expanding productivity led to the evolution of monopoly and oligopoly and the dominant forms of economic organization in today's capitalism. Monopoly was ubiquitous. The basis and nature of monopoly in the seventeenth and eighteenth centuries was distinct from the monopoly capital in the age of imperialism.

The economic surplus value under monopolistic capitalism is much larger than under competitive capitalism. The transition from competitive to monopolistic capitalism has resulted in a tremendous increase of the absolute volume of the economic surplus. It also resulted in the shift of control from the relatively small capitalist to a few giant corporations.

In the monopolistic phase of capitalist development the rates of profit are low and the mass of profits available for investment are relatively small. Consequently, there is a tendency toward underemployment and stagnation, a tendency toward overproduction. General overproduction occurs because there is too much produced both for consumption and too much for accumulation.[13] The competition among oligopolists in the world arena becomes a power contest among imperialist countries.

Keynesian economic policy only knows that government has both the power and the will to remedy the major defects of the capitalist system. However, it does not know that government has the will and the power to abolish it altogether.

On the roots of backwardness in certain areas, according to Baran, western Europe's penetration into slave traffic and slavery plays a major role in the primary accumulation. The requirements of navigation gave a strong stimulus to scientific discovery and technological progress. Shipbuilding, outfitting overseas expeditions, manufacturing arms and other supplies were required for protection as well as conducting negotiations with their overseas trading partners. The resulting far-reaching trade, combined with piracy, outright plunder, slave traffic, and discovery of gold led to a rapid formation of vast fortunes in the hands of western European merchants. Capital formation stemmed from merchant and usurer

12. Ibid., 49. Cf. Marx, *Capital I*, 738–46.
13. Ibid., 85.

wealth. These all provided a mighty impulse to the development of capitalist enterprise.[14]

For Baran the primary accumulation of capital (Marx) became a key concept to solve the historical roots of underdevelopment. The contact with Western technology provided a powerful impetus to the development of capitalism, while this development distorted and crippled the "backward" country to suit the purposes of Western imperialism. The colonized and peripheral countries remained in a state of the darkest "backwardness."

According to Baran, capitalism breaking into the underdeveloped countries precluded the materialization of the classical conditions for growth. Far from serving as an engine of economic expansion of technological progress and social change, the capitalist order in these countries has represented a framework for economic stagnation. Foreign enterprise in the underdeveloped country's economic system plays an important role: (1) the significance of the investment undertaken by the foreign enterprise, (2) the direct effect of its current operations, and (3) its more general influence on the underdeveloped country as a whole. Their own economic surplus is removed by foreign capital or reinvested by foreign enterprise.[15]

Within the world system of imperialism equal rights are unequal for unequal labor.[16] In this inequality the majority of humankind has perished in continual misery while a tiny minority has built its advanced status upon this very misery. Paradoxically, the state of equal rights of all nations has given rise to the powerful popular movement against imperialism and colonialism and for national and social liberation.

POLITICAL ECONOMY OF DEPENDENCY AND UNDERDEVELOPMENT

Baran's economic position finds its voice in Frank's theory of dependency. Frank, in his *Capitalism and Underdevelopment in Latin America*,[17] concurs with Baran. Capitalism, both international and national, has produced underdevelopment in the past and it still generates underdevelopment in the present.[18]

14. Ibid.,139.

15. Baran, *Political Economy,* 251.

16. Ibid., 295.

17. Frank, *Capitalism and Underdevelopment.* .

18. Ibid., xi.

For Frank one particular feature of capitalist underdevelopment is connected with the loss and misappropriation of economic surplus in the process of capitalist underdevelopment. The economic structure of underdevelopment was caused by the rise of imperialism and its consolidation in the twentieth century. Imperialism is far from promoting industrial capitalism; rather it strengthened a form of mercantile capitalism in the underdeveloped countries.

The key concept for Baran's analysis of monopoly capitalism is the economic surplus which was not identical with profits.[19] As we have already seen, Baran and Sweezy, in *Monopoly Capital* (1968), accepted imperialism as the monopoly of capitalism. They attempted to analyze "the generation and absorption of the surplus under conditions of monopoly capitalism"[20] in order to explain underdevelopment in the Third World.

Accordingly, Frank argues that the problem is structural underdevelopment in regard to the contradiction of expropriation/appropriation of the economic surplus of the satellite by the metropolis. For the generation of structural underdevelopment the impregnation of the satellite's domestic economy with the same capitalistic structure and its fundamental contradictions is more important than the drain of economic surplus.[21] The contradictions are the expropriation of economic surplus from the many and its appropriation by the few, the polarization of the capitalist system into metropolitan center and peripheral satellites, and the continuity of the fundamental structure of the capitalist system throughout the history of its expansion and transformation; these are because of the persistence or recreation of these capitalist contradictions everywhere and at all times. The economic surplus of the peripheral satellites was appropriated, generating economic development in the metropolitan centers.[22]

In Frank's view, the first of the three contradictions within the structure of economic development and underdevelopment was the expropriation/appropriation of economic surplus. This was the exploitative relation, which has extended the capitalist link between the capitalist world and national metropolis to the regional centers in a chain-like fashion.[23]

The second capitalist contradiction was the imminent centralization of the capitalist system. This contradiction of capitalism took the form of

19. Baran, *Political Economy*, xviii–xix.

20. Baran and Sweezy, *Monopoly Capital*, 8.

21. Frank, *Capitalism and Underdevelopment*, 10.

22. Ibid., 3.

23. Ibid., 7.

polarization into metropolitan center and peripheral satellites. The rule of monopoly capitalism and imperialism in the advanced countries and socioeconomic backwardness in the underdeveloped countries were intimately related; they represent different aspects of what was a global problem. The satellites remained underdeveloped for lack of access to their own surplus. The historical process of the expansion and development of capitalism throughout the world has generated and continues to generate both economic development and structural underdevelopment.[24]

The third contradiction was the continuity and ubiquity of the structural essentials of economic development and underdevelopment throughout the expansion and development of the capitalist system at all times and places. In the case of Chile, the history of underdevelopment was punctuated by failures to eliminate or shorten the suffering created by underdevelopment.[25]

Based on the model of the metropolis-satellite colonial structure and on the development of capitalism, Frank explained that there were two underdevelopments: external and internal underdevelopment. The external structure was generated by the contradiction of expropriation and appropriation of the economic surplus of the satellite by the metropolis. The internal structure was created in a chain-like fashion in terms of the contradictions of expropriation/appropriation and the metropolis/satellite polarization that has penetrated the underdeveloped world as a whole.[26]

From the beginning the real flow of foreign finance has been heavily from Latin America to the metropolis.[27] The principal cause of inadequate domestic investment and of underdevelopment in Latin America was the domestic economic, political, and social structure of underdevelopment which was generated and maintained by foreign trade and finance.[28] In the colonial era of capitalist development, foreign finance was primarily an adjunct to stimulate the pillage of resources, the exploitation of labor, and the colonial trade.

Latin America's structural underdevelopment was deepened by the neo-imperialist drive of the metropolitan giant monopoly's investment finance to penetrate and take over Latin American manufacturing and service industries and to incorporate these as well into the monopoly's private

24. Ibid., 9.
25. Ibid., 14.
26. Ibid., xxi.
27. Frank, *Capitalism and Underdevelopment*, 282.
28. Ibid., 284.

empire. The principal impulse of these neo-imperialist forms of uneven world capitalist development and uneven Latin American underdevelopment are the increasing expansion and monopolization of the American-based international corporation and its new technological revolution.[29]

In *Dependent Accumulation and Underdevelopment*, Frank furthers an attempt to approach an explanation of underdevelopment through the analysis of the production and exchange relations of dependence within the world process of capital accumulation.[30] Frank distinguished three main stages or periods in the world of capital accumulation and capitalist development: mercantilist (1500–1770), industrial capitalist (1770–1870), and imperialist (1870–1930). He examined each of these periods in the historical development of the world process of capital accumulation, concentrating especially on the exchange relations between the metropolis and the periphery. And then he went on to analyze the associated transformation of the dependent internal relations of productions and the development of underdevelopment in each of the principal regions of Asia, Africa, and the Americas.

It is certain that in Frank's approach there is a tendency to overemphasize the 'external' of exchange relations to the virtual exclusion of internal modes of production. For a dialectical dynamic analysis of the worldwide historical process of capital accumulation, some scholars argue that Frank must analyze both metropolitan economic development and dependent peripheral underdevelopment as part of a single process. Analysis of the internal socio-economic relation and within the peripheral countries must be more incorporated.[31]

THE PERIPHERY AT THE SERVICE OF ACCUMULATION AT THE CENTER

The center-periphery relation of imperialism can be investigated with four typological concepts: a) the center in the center; b) the periphery in the center; c) the center in the periphery and d) the periphery in the periphery.

The exchanges between the center and periphery reveal the nature of dominance and dependency, at five levels: communication, culture, economy, military, and politics. Although the periphery in the center is

---

29. Ibid., 303.
30. Frank, *Dependent Accumulation*, xi.
31. Ibid., xiii.

poor and alienated, this group, like the rich, benefits from the dependence of the peripheral nations.

In the historical process of the origin and the appropriation of surplus value, a dialectical unity with three different moments is formed: unequal exchange on the basis of unequal values (mercantilist), equal exchange on the basis of equal value (capitalist), and unequal exchange on the basis of equal values (imperialism). The consideration of these three historical moments provides an answer to the question of origin, growth, and expansion of capitalism in connection with underdevelopment in peripheral countries.

According to Amin, three periods are distinguished: 1) mercantilist (the essential function of the periphery, principally American, supplementarily African, which supplied the former with slaves, was to permit the accumulation of monetary wealth by the Atlantic merchant bourgeoisie. Hence the system of plantations around which all of America turned from the seventeenth century to the eighteenth centuries was established after the pillage of the mines), 2) developed capitalist (post-industrial revolution, pre-monopolist; in this period capital has only one means at its disposal, commerce), and 3) imperialist (capital also has the very efficient means of the export of capital. Unequal exchange appeared in a true sense). To each of these periods there correspond specific functions of the periphery at the service of the essential needs of accumulation at the center. Unequal exchange is undertaken on the basis of equal values; this operation is to be seen in how exchange functions in the metropolitan process of accumulation and production.

According to Amin, autocentric accumulation played a part not only in the origin of the capitalist mode of production in the age of mercantilism, but also after the industrial revolution. External trade was subordinated to the requirements of autocentric accumulation. Autocentric economies imposed a type of unequal international specialization for their own benefit. However, in the periphery, which is subjected to the unequal specialization, a fundamentally different model of accumulation plays a central role. This is an extraverted accumulation tied to dependency. In the periphery the exporting sector plays a determining role in the shaping of the market. The products exported by the periphery bring interest to central capitalism, if the reward of labor is lower in the periphery than at the center. The reward of labor can be lower to the extent that the peripheral society is subjected to the new function of supplying cheap labor for the exporting sector. The periphery serves only a marginal, subordinate, and limited function which leads to an increasing polarization of wealth to the benefit of the center.[32]

In Frank's view, the deepening of underdevelopment took place in Latin America where the free trade and imperialist phases of world capitalist development again transformed the modes of production, class structure, and underdevelopment policy in order to serve the interests of metropolitan development.[33] The Latin American bourgeoisies came into ever greater dependence on and submission to the metropolis and the process of world capital accumulation in the classical imperialist period. This implies an essential factor of world capitalist uneven development, underlying the reality of the underdevelopment of Latin America which is also the basis for accumulation in the subsequent imperialist stage of capitalist development.[34]

WORLD-SYSTEMS ANALYSIS AND THE CAPITALIST WORLD-ECONOMY

World-systems analysis demonstrates a new perspective on the social reality beginning in the early 1970s. It is argued that the modern world-system as a capitalist world-economy had its origin in the sixteenth century. This world-system was located in a part of the globe, particularly in parts of Europe and the Americas.[35]

Wallerstein, the main figure of world-systems, argues that a world-economy is a large geographic zone; within it we observe a division of labor and significant internal exchange of basic goods as well as flows of capital and labor. Many political units existed inside the world-economy, containing many cultures and groups.[36] The endless accumulation of capital had generated a constant technological change and a constant expansion of frontiers (geographical, psychological, intellectual and scientific) on a global scale. Expanding over time to cover the whole globe, this modern world-system has become a capitalist world-economy.

Capitalism is not understood in terms of market and profit, or the wage-labor relationship. Only after the world-system in the sixteenth century gave priority to the endless accumulation of capital, can we talk

32. Amin, *Unequal Development*, 191–93.

33. Frank *Dependent Accumulation*, 146.

34. Ibid., 165–71.

35. Wallerstein, *Essential Wallerstein*, 129.

36. Ibid., 23.

about a capitalist system. Endless accumulation is the continual process of accumulating capital for the sake of accumulating capital. Thus a capitalist system cannot exist apart from a world-economy.

Contrary to Adam Smith and Karl Marx, world-systems analysis maintains that the capitalist world-economy is a particular historical system; it is to be examined within the framework of the *longue durée* (long period) of the historical system.

Core-periphery in the world-system is a relational concept which affects the degree of profitability of the production processes. Profitability is related to the degree of monopolization while peripheral process is competitive. This refers to the axial division of labor of a capitalist world-economy which divides production into core-like products and peripheral products.[37]

The concept of core-periphery (developed by the United Nations Economic Commission for Latin America) and the subsequent elaboration of dependency theory shaped one of the important contributions to the emergence of world systems analysis. As we already reviewed Frank's theory of underdevelopment, underdevelopment is taken as the consequence of historical capitalism, rather than as the original state of the colonies or their responsibility.

When it comes to the inequalities of core and periphery, Wallerstein appreciates the critical theory which appeals to the empirical evidence of historical reality. The thesis—the relations of production of every society form a whole—is the methodological point of departure and the key to the historical understanding of social relations. A mutual interaction takes place among the various elements as is the case with every organic body.

Wallerstein's historical social science calls for the construction of a historical social science without attachment to the idea of progress. In the historical systems there has been no linear trend: upward, downward or straight forward. The trend is rather uneven or indeterminate, implying a stochastic process.[38] In addition to the point of totality non-attached to the concept of progress, Wallerstein utilizes Braudel's concept of *longue durée*. This concept which embraces the multiplicity of social times and his emphasis on structural time became central to world-systems analysis. Insofar as the *longue durée* is the duration of a particular historical system, such systems had beginnings, lives, and terminal transitions. World-systems proponents analyze total social systems over the *longue durée*.

37. Wallerstein, *World-Systems Analysis*, 28.
38. Wallerstein, *Essential Wallerstein*, 148, 146.

Braudel seeks to find structural time or long lasting structure under-lying the historical system and the cyclical processes within the structures (for instance, the expansion and contractions of the world-economy). Thus the unit of analysis is emphasized, while he insists that the sixteenth-century Mediterranean constituted a world-economy.[39]

If we deal with social transformation over a long historical time (Braudel's 'the long term'), we must logically divide the long term into segments in order to observe the structural change from time A to time B. There are the cyclical rhythms of the world-economy from expansion to slow dissolution. Overproduction consequently increased price com-petition and thus lowered the rates of profit. Here we observe a reversal side of the cyclical curve of the world-economy (stagnation or recession in the world-economy). Rates of unemployment rise worldwide. An up and down curve of so-called A-phase (expansion) and B-phase (stagnation)—a Kondratieff cycle—becomes the parameter of the world-system. Given this fact, world-systems analysis seeks the framework (the cyclical rhythms of the system) and the patterns of internal transformation (the secular trends of the system).[40]

Historical systems have existed in three variants up to now: mini-systems and world-systems of two kinds (world-economies and world-empires). The world empires are vast political structures and encompass a wide variety of cultural patterns. The basic logic is the extraction of tribute developed from locally self-administered direct producers, moving up-ward to the centre and redistributed to crucial network of officials.

Wallerstein speaks of systems, economies, and empires as a world in the hyphenated sense (not in the sense of encompassing the entire globe). Wallerstein calls world-system (tied with a common political system) world-empire while world-system (without a political one) world-econ-omy. Examples of such world-empires emerging from world-economies are all the so-called great civilizations of premodern times, such as China, Egypt, and Rome. World-empires were basically redistributive in eco-nomic form.

Around 1500 a world-economy managed to escape the dominion of the world-empire which had destroyed or absorbed both minisystems in the pre-agricultural era and world-economies. The modern world-system was born out of the consolidation of a world-economy which had time to achieve its full development as a capitalist system. Its inner logic expanded

39. Wallerstein, *World-Systems Analysis*, 15.

40. Wallerstein, *Essential Wallerstein*, 136.

to cover the entire globe, absorbing all existing mini-systems and world-empires into capitalist development and expansion. By the late nineteenth century only one historical system existed on the globe.[41]

It was only with the emergence of the modern world-economy in sixteenth century Europe, Wallerstein contends, that we saw the full development and economic predominance of market trade. This was the system called capitalism. The modern world-system takes the form of a world-economy (in terms of the integration of Braudel's usage with the core-periphery analysis); the modern world-economy was a capitalist world-economy surviving over a long period and thriving. Capitalism and a world-economy (that is, a single division of labor but multiple polities and cultures) are obverse sides of the same coin. World-systems analysis views wage-labor only as one of the many forms of labor control within a capitalist system; it gives priority to the economic sphere over other spheres of human activity (for instance, the economic domain over against the political, cultural, and ideological domains of the superstructure).

For the sake of the circulationist base in the discussion of a core-peripheral axis of the division of labor, world-systems analysis seeks to eliminate the lines between the economic, political and sociocultural modes of analysis as units in light of the world-system, with insistence on the *longue durée* and a unidisciplinary approach.[42] In Wallerstein's view, Frank's concept of the development of underdevelopment articulates that the economic structures of contemporary underdeveloped countries are not an earlier stage in the transition to industrialization. It is rather the result of being involved in the world-economy as a peripheral, raw material producing area. "Underdevelopment . . . is the necessary product of four centuries of capitalism itself."[43]

THE WORLD-ECONOMY AND CAPITALIST PROGRESS OF THE MODE OF PRODUCTION

World-systems analysis remains skeptical about the inevitability of progress, thinking of it as a possibility, not as a certainty. According to Wallerstein, the essential feature of a capitalist world-economy is production for sale in a market in which the object is to realize the maximum profit. World-economy grew up with a single division of labor within which

41. Ibid., 140.

42. Wallerstein, *World-Systems Analysis*, 21.

43. Wallerstein, *Capitalist World-Economy*, 7.

there was a world market. Agricultural capitalism resolved the problems incurred by using the pervasiveness of wage labor as a defining characteristic of capitalism. Capitalism means that labor is identified as a commodity, but in the era of agricultural capitalism, wage labor was only one of the modes. Besides slavery, coerced cash-crop production ('second feudalism'), sharecropping, and tenancy were all alternative modes. For example, the Indians on a Spanish *encomienda* in New Spain in the sixteenth century world economy were working for landlords who paid them for cash crop production.

Northwest Europe was better situated in the sixteenth century to diversify its agricultural specialization than other parts of Europe. Northwest Europe emerged as the core area of this world-economy. Eastern Europe and the western hemisphere became peripheral areas. Mediterranean Europe emerged as the semi-peripheral area of this world-economy. The three structural positions in a world-economy—core, periphery, and semiperiphery—had become stabilized by about 1640. Capitalism was involved not only in appropriation of the surplus value, but also in an appropriation of surplus of the whole world-economy by core areas. Here we talk about the operation of unequal exchange. It was true in the stage of agricultural capitalism, as it is in the stage of industrial capitalism.[44]

In the beginning, capitalism was an affair of the world-economy rather than that of nation states. The Marxist thesis that capitalism has become world-wide only in the twentieth century is misleading. The tendency of the capitalist mode of production to become worldwide is manifested not only through an imperialist pole, but also through the constant transcending of national limits by big capital (the formation of international big capital, world firms, etc). However, an internationalization of *only advanced* national capital is misleading.

There have been three major mechanisms that have enabled the world-system to retain relative political stability. One is the concentration of military strength in the hands of the dominant forces. A second mechanism is the pervasiveness of an ideological commitment to the system as a whole. A third mechanism is the division of the majority into a larger lower stratum and a smaller middle stratum. Besides the upper stratum of core states and the lower stratum of peripheral states, there is a middle stratum of semi-peripheral states in a world-economy. The existence of the third category means that the upper stratum is not faced with the unified

44. Ibid., 18–19.

opposition of all the others because the middle stratum is both exploited and exploiter.[45]

The emergence of the European world-economy in the long sixteenth century (1450–1640) superimposed a more immediate cyclical crisis plus climatic changes, all of which created a dilemma that could only be resolved by a graphic expansion of the division of labor. The system-wide recession of 1650–1730 consolidated the European world-economy and opened stage two of the modern world-economy. Stage three of the capitalist world-economy began a stage of industrial rather than agricultural capitalism. The geographic expansion of the European world-economy meant the elimination of other world-systems as well as the absorption of the remaining minisystems. Colonial rule had been an inferior mode of relationship of core and periphery. In the peripheral areas of the world-economy, both the continued economic expansion of the core and the new strength of the semi-periphery have led to a further weakening of the political and hence the economic position of the peripheral areas.

Wallerstein designates this point of view as the world-system perspective based on the assumption that the modern world comprises a single capitalist world-economy (emerging historically since the sixteenth century and still existing today). The emergence of the world-system perspective is a consequence of the dramatic challenge to European political domination of the world, calling into question all Euro-centric constructions of social reality. The system functions by virtue of having unequal core and peripheral regions. The capitalist world-economy seems to go through long cycles of expansions and contraction. These cycles occurred within a secular trend that has involved the physical expansion and politico-structural consolidation of the capitalist world-economy as such.

WORLD-ECONOMY AND UNEQUAL EXCHANGE IN DEBATE

In the middle of the twentieth century the character of monopoly had made colonialism pointless under U.S. pressure to free trade. Direct plundering is excluded; the former imperialist states continue to perform the similar task by engaging the product of the indirect exploitation constituted by unequal exchange.[46]

Wages are low in the underdeveloped countries. High-priced products of the metropolis are exchanged for low-priced products of the

45. Ibid., 23.

46. Emmanuel, *Unequal Exchange*, 188.

195

underdeveloped countries. The underdeveloped countries are compelled to sell their goods at prices below their value and to purchase goods from the developed countries above their value. Here, exchange is unequal.

The progressive enlargement of the market attracts foreign capital and the influx of this capital constitutes a factor to increase wages. The increased investment generates an increase in the organic composition of capital; this forms the source of a second transfer of value from the poorer country to the richer country. Every increase in wages increases the inequality in external change and furthers enrichment to the richer country. The high-wage countries protect, if necessary, their high-wage levels by means of tariffs. This leads to a fresh increase in wages. By transferring a large part of its surplus to the rich countries, the poor country is deprived of the means of accumulation and growth. Unemployment puts an additional pressure on wages and restricts the trade-union struggle. The value of labor power in the poor country decreases further.[47]

For Emmanuel, unequal exchange is the elementary transfer mechanism, giving new impetus to the unevenness of development. This sets in motion all the other mechanisms of exploitation.[48] The structure of this inequality causes inequality in exchange and dictates an international division of labor inevitably unfavorable to the poor countries. Emmanuel's perspective contradicts the popular view, according to which the international division of labor through the capitalist world market makes advantageous exchange possible for the poor countries in relation to the rich countries.

From the perspective of world-system, a capitalist world-economy is marked by an axial division of labor between core-like production processes and peripheral production processes. When exchange occurs, competitive products are in a weak position while quasi-monopolized products are in a strong position. This core-peripheral relation of exchange resulted in an unequal exchange which stands in favor of those involved in core-like production. This world-system perspective articulates that production processes are based on the core-peripheral relationship. Given the unequal power between monopolized products and products in the free market, a constant flow of surplus-value from the producers of peripheral products to those states with a large number of core-like processes resulted from the unequal exchange between core and peripheral products.

47. Ibid., 130–31.
48. Ibid., 265.

For Wallerstein imperialism is a general, gradual extension of capital investment from the center to a periphery. Utilizing Hobson's theory of imperialism for explaining the role of over-accumulation in overseas economic and colonial expansionism, Wallerstein emphasizes the dynamic of inter-capitalist geopolitical competition. In the twenty-first century, some countries which have strong enterprises of export products to peripheral zones are labeled semi-peripheral; these countries relate to core zones as importers of more advanced products. Here, capitalism is defined in terms of the sphere of monopoly, not the free market. This model of world-economy implies a direct assault to the conflation of the market and capitalism.

Mandel found that the substantial difference in the average rate of profit between the colonies and the metropolitan countries resulted in the deceleration of capital accumulation in the colonies. The surplus value produced in the colonies was siphoned back to the metropolitan countries. In addition to the surplus profits, there is a further mechanism of exploitation of the colonies and semi-colonies by the metropolitan states; this refers to the general rule of unequal exchange. Colonial surplus-profits are the chief form of the metropolitan exploitation of the Third World, while unequal exchange becomes only a second form. However, in the late capitalist epoch unequal exchange becomes the main form of colonial exploitation while the direct production of colonial surplus profits takes a secondary role.[49]

In late capitalism, whose outcome is unequal exchange, multinational companies and the export of machines, equipment and vehicles reinforces this trend; this becomes one of the most important features in the late capitalist or neo-colonialist phase of imperialism. The main flow of capital exports is no longer from the metropolitan countries into the colonies but between the metropolitan states themselves. As the resource of unequal exchange, Mandel identifies more intensity on the part of the labor of the metropolis than that of the labor of the underdeveloped countries on the world market.[50]

Emmanuel states that the vast international differences in the value and the price of the commodity of labor power resulted from the uneven development of the capitalist mode of production. This is because inequality of exchange tends to increase, along with the worsening of the terms of trade. Consequently, the poor countries participating in the international

49. Mandel, *Late Capitalism,* 345–46.

50. Ibid., 351.

division of labor tend to become ever poorer in comparison to the ever increasing prosperity of the rich countries.

Prior to imperialist exploitation there was a commercial exploitation of the colonial or semi-colonial countries. Within the context of the capitalist world market, economic inequalities need to be explained by commercial exploitation as well as by imperialist exploitation. This perspective indicates that within the context of the capitalist world market economic inequalities cannot be explained only by imperialist exploitation.[51] The laws of the formation of international value and the possible transfers of wealth from one country to another may be hidden in the structure of the world economy.[52]

For Amin the extraverted origin of development in the periphery perpetuates itself in spite of the increasing diversification or industrialization of the economy; it is not external to the model of dependent peripheral accumulation. At the stage of diversification and the deepening of underdevelopment, new mechanisms of domination and dependence appear in the cultural, political, and economic spheres. Technological dependence and domination is established by the transnational firms. The big oligopolistic transnational firms can undertake capital investments, providing the material foundation for technological dependence. In an extraverted economy of the periphery, contradiction or an organic relation, in terms of social class, can be grasped only on the world scale rather than within the national framework.[53]

Given this fact, the existence of unequal exchange means simply the transfer of value. The bourgeois of the center which exists on the scale of the world system exploits the proletariat at the center and at the periphery; it exploits the proletariat of the periphery even more brutally. Amin's position contradicts Emmanuel's—the workers at the center exploit those at the periphery.[54]

The features of underdevelopment can be sought in the extreme unevenness typical of the distribution of productivities in the periphery. The center transmits the system of prices to the periphery. It dictates the structure of the distribution of income in these formations. The disarticulation occurs because production in the periphery is adjusted to the needs of the center. Economic domination by the center is expressed in the forms of

51. Emmanuel, *Unequal Exchange*, 276.

52. Ibid., 369, 383.

53. Amin, *Unequal Development*, 195.

54. Ibid., 196.

international specialization. In the structures of world trade, the center shapes the periphery in accordance with its own needs. In this light, a new path of development for capitalism in the underdeveloped countries expresses the future course of new relations organized between center and periphery instead of constituting a transition to socialism.[55]

However, Mandel strives to find the origin and nature of underdevelopment in a function of different organic compositions of capital.[56] Unequal exchange is the key to the underdevelopment, and the lower wages are a consequence rather than a cause of underemployment. The unequal exchange consists in the fact that on the world market the working hour of the developed country counts as more productive and intensive than that of the backward nation. The metropolitan countries and (semi) colonial countries represent two complementary movements of a single, worldwide process of capital accumulation. The thesis of the mutually determined development of the capitalist center and underdevelopment of the capitalist periphery is perfectly fit.[57]

According to Bettelheim the tendency of the capitalist mode of production to become worldwide includes the formation of international big capital, or world firms which constantly transcend national limits.[58] Bettelheim takes as the starting point relations of production and relative differences in productivity, when he deals with the unequal exchange in the semi-colonies and the metropolitan countries. Equivalence in capitalist production relations signifies the exchange of equal aggregates of factors (labor and use of capital), and non-equivalence (unequal exchange) can only signify the exchange of unequal aggregates of these same factors. The intensive exploitation of the workers in industrialized countries provides the chief explanation of the extreme concentration of international capital investments. The more the productive forces are developed, the more the proletariat in the advanced countries are exploited. This is one of the fundamental laws of the capitalist mode of production.[59]

At this point, Bettelheim challenges Emmanuel's stance by arguing that wage determination mainly based on capitalist production relations also includes the effects of the class struggle and the effects of the different instances (from the ideological and political levels as well as non-capitalist

---

55. Ibid., 202–3.

56. Mandel, *Late Capitalism*, 353.

57. Ibid., 363.

58. Ibid., 295.

59. Ibid., 302.

production relations) in a complex social formation. Instead of dealing with wages as an independent variable, Bettelheim insists that the specific combination of the productive forces and production relations in the poor country, under the system of worldwide capitalism, forms the objective basis of the poverty of certain countries; this perspective explains both the low wages and the unequal exchange anchored in this.[60] In contrast to Bettelheim, Emmanuel expresses an illusion of international workers' solidarity, because of the reality of labor aristocracy in the industrialized countries.

Given the debate about unequal exchange, the unevenness of the development of productive forces between the metropolis and periphery entails the expanded reproduction of economic inequalities which give rise to a certain division of labor unfavorable to the poor countries. This specific combination of internal production relations with production relations and political and ideological relations on the world scale engenders the blocking or hindering of the productive forces in the poor countries. The world capitalist system is not merely a market in which domination and exploitation take place by way of prices. On the world economic system, capitalism is transited to the imperialist stage played by the banks and financial organs as well as through the political and military. An issue of unequal exchange at the international trade level becomes more complex and intense.

In Backlash: Reverting to the Self-regulating Market

The development of capitalism generates the juxtaposition of overdevelopment in the metropolitan countries and underdevelopment in the colonies and semi-colonies. The uneven development of world capitalism rested on a fundamental imbalance of international trade between the metropolis and the under-developing, colonized countries. If the underdeveloped countries suffer from unequal exchange, their exchange is all the more unequal and their loss is greater. Hinkelammert, one of the important representatives of liberation theology, demonstrates an approach to a renewed dependency theory in Latin America. According to him "it is the policy of the total market itself which makes extensive growth impossible."[61] A

60. Ibid., 288.

61. Duchrow & Hinkelammert, *Property for People, not for Profit*, 145.

dynamic stagnation of productive investment takes place together with a stagnation of employment.

Trade imbalance and uneven economic development means that the export surplus of the underdeveloped countries supplies much of the excess merchandise consumption of the metropolis and helps finance the export surplus of the metropolis. This reality of trade imbalance accelerated the underdevelopment of the peripheral countries.

However, it is also important to see the dependency in terms of the specific combination of pre-capitalist, semi-capitalist and capitalist relations of production in the underdeveloped countries; this articulation of different relations of productions characterizes and determines their social structure. As the underdeveloped countries are increasingly integrated into the capitalist world market, this world-economic integration makes variant repercussions on the relations of production in the underdeveloped countries. The semi-colonies become capitalist countries because their relations of production are determined by their integration into the capitalist world market.

In the relations of production and social structure of the colonial and semi-colonial countries, the accumulation of capital consisted of 1) foreign capital and 2) money capital (in general unproductively invested). The distortion of capital accumulation takes place in the underdeveloped countries, because of their subordination to the capitalist world market and service to the interests of the metropolitan countries in the valorization of their capital.

In terms of integration of the underdeveloped countries into the world market, the sources of metropolitan, neo colonial exploitation of the semi-colonies flow more abundantly than ever in view of the exchange of light industrial goods for machines, equipment and vehicles; this can be compared with the classical notion of unequal exchange concerning foodstuffs and raw materials for industrial consumer goods.

The world market continues to function as a siphon, transferring from the semi-colonies to the metropolitan countries both ongoing surplus value and capitalized surplus value, i.e., capital. The fate of the underdeveloped countries assumes its most difficult form within the framework of world market.

In this light, the economic globalization of the capitalist system is nothing new. However, it has taken a quantitative and qualitative step forward in the most recent period. The advance of globalization affects trade, the productive system, technology, and financial markets (including many other important aspects of social cultural life). Unequal change becomes more complicated and intense within the framework of economic globalization. The capital logic of the total market is eroding the classic forms of the center/periphery polarization.

The economic background of globalization and its principle of neoliberalism advocate for the self-regulating market. An emphasis is on the subordination of the nation-states to economic interdependence and the transnationalization of the capital markets. This shift signals a decline of the social welfare principle advocated by Keynes toward laissez-faire economic globalization. Reverting to an economic principle of the self-regulating market appears to be the most viable, but the most questionable option in the stage of economic globalization. This perspective makes the church's responsibility for economic justice more acute regarding the dignity of the people and the environment.

9

Economic Globalization, Neo-Liberalism, and Empire

SHIFT TO ECONOMIC GLOBALIZATION

IN THE SHIFT TO economic globalization, we observe that the neo-liberalists begin to take initiative following the Bretton Woods conference in the United States (1944). The conference was intended to discuss a comprehensive set of new international regulations. It was designed to prevent a repeat of the mistakes that led to the collapse of the liberal international system in 1929. J. M. Keynes, the leader of the British delegation, submitted a plan to this effect. The core of the Keynes plan aims to further not only the short-term interests of creditors, but also the long-term economic balance. This plan attempts to achieve a balance between debtors and creditors. The welfare state was supported by the nation state. Development in the Third World was driven by the success of national liberation movements and benefited from the support of the former Eastern-bloc countries.[1]

The study of the historical development and the economic theory of neoliberalism shape the investigation of the reality of economic globalization and the theory of Empire in a postmodern or postcolonial fashion. A postcolonial theology that is based on the theory of Empire will be examined. This will facilitate our understanding of the church's endeavor

---

1. Amin, *Capitalism*, 35.

as an alternative to global capitalism and empire in an ecumenical and interreligious context, which will be explored in the subsequent chapter.

ECONOMIC INTERDEPENDENCE AND GLOBALIZATION

The end of the Bretton Woods mandate was marked by the adoption of the general system of floating currencies in 1973. In such a system, finance and economic policy are to be decided globally by the Bretton Woods institutions (IMF, World Bank, GATT). The practical tactics of the rich countries are aimed at strengthening the powers of the BW institutions and weakening or instrumentalizing the UN institutions, particularly the United Nations Conference on Trade and Development (UNCTAD) and the United Nations Development Programme (UNDP).

As the economy has begun to dictate government policy, market deregulation has become the great motto. A new mode of capital accumulation and de-regulation becomes an underlying principle of the power system of the global capitalist economy. The productive, trading, and monetary capital can be trans-nationalized (globalized). The political instruments of regulation remain either national or international. The capital market establishes itself transcending national regulation, that is, trans-nationally. Private foreign investment ("internalization of the world market") expands to a global scale, penetrating the other national economies. This inter-nationalization led to transnationalization.[2] The nation-state is subordinated to the economic power of international banks and multinational corporations.

Exchange rate stability was produced by the economic power of the United States. This power was reinforced by the dollar's gold convertibility and by administrative controls on capital movements. The choice of floating exchange rates in 1973 allowed the gigantic mass of floating capital to find an outlet in financial speculation.[3] The developing countries were left in the positions of helpless victims according to the logic of the international institutions involved in the global domination of finance.

The officials of the IMF declare that any nonparticipation in the world economy leads to poverty. The IMF intervenes in the economic, social and political structures of deficit countries, dictating social and political objectives to the deficit governments.[4]

2. Duchrow, *Alternatives*, 70–71.

3. Amin, *Capitalism*, 20.

4. Gorringe, *Capital and Kingdom*, 138.

The International Bank for Reconstruction and Development (IBRD) (normally called the World Bank) was set up; its chief function was to make funds available for economic recovery in Europe. The history of the World Bank was tied to the history of the expansion of the Third World's developmentalist project. However, the World Bank (IBRD: International Bank for Reconstruction and Development) has upheld its task to support capital's penetration of the Third World through the transnationals and has reinforced the dependent integration of Third World economies. The Bank's global strategy has not been concerned with the condition of the poor or the environment. This was true before 1980 and has been the case ever since.[5]

The aim of developing world trade and the Third World economy is to stimulate Third World countries to purchase the products of the First World market. People aided today will become the customers of tomorrow.[6] The reality of developing countries is transformed into the decomposing countries. In 1986 an article in *The World Economy* we read: "the breakdown in the GATT system is nowhere more evident than in trade relations between developed and developing countries. Here an undeclared trade war is in progress."[7]

The global economy of the early twenty-first century has removed or dramatically reduced barriers to world trade and has liberalized regulations in control of the flow of capital. Liberalization, stabilization, and privatization of the market have become a motto[8] of which the government is in service. The Trilateral Commission represents a systematic attempt to reformulate power relationships within the world capitalist system. The commission was to foster closer cooperation among the core democratic industrialized areas of the world with shared leadership responsibilities in the wider international system. The concept of interdependence is the central concept and the starting point. Through the advancement of technology, quantitative and qualitative change can be easily seen in the field of communication, mass media, and computers. At the scale of the international division of labor, interdependence, or mutual dependence has grown to an unparalleled degree through the rapid growth of international trade and finance.[9]

5. Amin, *Capitalism*, 24–25.

6. Goringe, *Capital and Kingdom*, 130–31.

7. Ibid., 132.

8. Rieger, *No Rising*, 14.

9. Hinkelammert, *Ideological Weapons*, 99–100.

Brzezinski was the main ideologue of the economic creed of the Trilateral Commission. According to Brzenzinski, international banks and multinational corporations act and plan far in advance of the political concepts of the nation-state.[10] National governments cannot intervene in the trans-national markets. Driven by the transnational finance market, the capitalist market economy has made significant progress toward its goal by making the world public into an appendage to self-regulating markets through the international banks and multinational corporations. The technetronic era has come under the impact of technology and electronics, especially in the field of computers and communications, thereby transcending industrial civilization.[11]

In the coming of the technetronic era, a religious creed of interdependence is linked with the search for the God of the world market.[12] The Trilateral countries seek to impose the multinational corporation to subordinate the nation-state to their operation and integration of economic interdependence. There has been a significant change from the internationalization to the trans-internationalization of the world market.

By this time the political climate was greatly influenced by monetarism, in other words, the transnational world market (monetarist Fordism). The outbreak of debt in 1979 introduced monetarism. In 1982 Mexico became the first country to reach the threshold of bankruptcy. This crisis refers to the Fordist development model and its method of regulation, which employs monetary relationships as a vehicle. The dollarization of national currency systems is undertaken for the sake of maintaining a hypertrophic international loan system.[13]

In the background of the new wave of globalization, we first observe that the dominance of the United States in trade and direct investment was weakened around the globe in competition with Japan and western European countries. Secondly, the boom that followed the Second World War ended, growth rates slumped, and overcapacity rose. The oil crisis in the early 1970s also pushed up the price of energy. Thirdly, disadvantaged industries and regions in the industrialized countries were threatened by the liberalization of the world market, and called for new protectionist measures.[14] The revolutionary impetus for the methods of accumulation and

10. Brzezinski, *Two Ages*, 56.

11. Ibid., 9.

12. Hinkelammert, *Ideological Weapons*, 102.

13. Duchrow, *Alternatives*, 79.

14. Ibid., 72–73.

regulation in the capitalist market economy was the transnationalization of the financial markets during this period.

The so-called flotation of the dollar, that is, the deregulation of the currency markets, led to more transnational money being used for currency speculation. Only 5 percent of the transnational currency markets are concerned with production of goods. The rest run into speculation.[15] The so-called financial innovations or derivatives (for instance, futures, options, and swaps) are undertaken for speculative profit-taking, causing more and more instability on the financial markets, to the point of threatened collapse. Financial speculation primarily draws the available money away from productive projects to the casino of the wealth-accumulating owners of financial assets—hence the name casino capitalism.[16]

In the neo-liberal monetarist system of the 1980s and 1990s the best-known example of white-collar crime in economics was the laundering of money from drugs or tax evasion. This is capitalist crime transcending the real distinction between what is legal and what is illegal.[17]

Capitalist globalization causes a gigantic surplus of capital, which finds no outlet in productive investment. It leads to a spiral of worldwide stagnation in which unemployment becomes a permanent feature and the development of many peripheral regions is blocked. The Fourth Worldization of Africa is the most extreme example. The countries of East Asia (Japan, Korea, China, and South-East Asia included) carry out two-thirds of their trade through internal exchange. This is because the Unites States pursues growth in this Asia-Pacific area.[18]

The goal of global capitalism is the accumulation of money via self-regulating markets. "Freedom" means "market freedom" in the sense of freedom for the accumulation of property and money. The social victims are led to believe that they are victims not of social and political decisions but of natural disasters, which "just happen". For a theoretical background of the current stage of economic globalization, Hayek and Friedman are two major figures.

15. Amin, *Capitalism*, 21.

16. Duchrow, *Alternatives*, 85.

17. Ibid., 90–91.

18. Amin, *Capitalism*, 39.

FREEDOM OR SERVITUDE

Friedrich Hayek, a teacher of Milton Friedman, was a staunch advocate of the individualism of the nineteenth century. He made the market into the principle for his argument. The market would be a kind of computer, "a true marvel," which was acclaimed as one of the greatest triumphs of the human mind.[19] What made possible the growth of civilization in the past was human submission to the impersonal forces of the market. Without the market a civilization could not have developed.[20]

Socialism was not only the gravest threat to market freedom but it also began as a reaction against the liberalism of the French revolution. It denounced claims of the individual as an outcome of the commercial spirit. Hayek argues that socialists typically regarded the ideas of the 1789 French Revolution—liberty, equality, and fraternity—as commercial ideas designed to secure certain advantages for individuals.[21] For Hayek, democracy is an essentially individualist institution that stands in an irreconcilable conflict with socialism. Democracy and socialism have nothing in common. The socialist view of freedom is seen in the transition from "the realm of necessity" to "the realm of freedom." This socialist demand for freedom, according to Hayek, implies another name denoting the demand for an equal distribution of wealth, that is, in the leap from the realm of necessity to the realm of freedom. However, such a claim is the road to servitude, having little to do with the road to freedom.[22]

Hayek's strategy is to denounce socialism or any form of community or collectivism without reservation; such a communal claim should end up with a non-economic society of unfreedom and inequality. Many of the Fascist leaders in Italy and Germany had begun their careers as socialists and ended up as Fascists or Nazis. Hayek argued that there were socialist roots in National Socialism. In the German concept of the people's community (*Volksgemeinschaft*) of National Socialism, the individual had no rights but only duties. In the case of the war economy of 1914, state and economic life formed a new unity. In the national development of Germany, conservative socialism or religious socialism prepared the atmosphere in which National Socialism took shape.[23]

19. Hayek, *Individualism and Order*, 87.
20. Hayek, *Road*, 204.
21. Ibid., 170.
22. Ibid., 27.
23. Ibid., 180.

According to Hayek, the masses of the totalitarian people were driven by moral fervor and passion, playing a significant role behind movements such as National Socialism or Communism. Such intensity of moral emotions can be compared to the great religious movements of history. The principle that the end justifies the means occupied its central place of moral fervor in socialistic collectivism. However, this principle denies all morals in the perspective of an individualist ethic.[24] From the collectivist standpoint, intolerance and brutal suppression of dissent, the complete disregard of the life and happiness of the individual were the essential and inevitable consequences of this principle.[25] The activity without ulterior purpose was abhorrent to the Nazis, the socialist intellectuals, and the communists. Every activity had to retain its justification from a conscious social purpose.[26]

Socialism as the abolition of private property created a system of planned economy. Such a system embodies collectivism, leading to dictatorship and counter-dictatorship, having nothing to do with freedom. According to Adam Smith, socialism obliged governments to be oppressive and tyrannical in order to support themselves.[27] The socialist's passion for the collective satisfaction of people's needs paved the way for totalitarianism grounded in a planned system.

Against socialist collectivism, Hayek argued for the liberal concept of laissez faire, which was in favor of making the best possible use of the forces of competition in connection with the market. Competition as a means of coordinating human efforts was regarded as superior because it was the only method of adjusting our activities to one another without any coercive or arbitrary intervention of authority. The law of corporations and patents has made competition work much less effectively, even leading to the destruction of competition in many spheres. The socialist propaganda for planning influences liberal-minded people who are opposed to competition.

Hayek's logic is black and white, because he contrasts state socialism with laissez faire capitalism. The democratic endeavor to reform the limitations of capitalism is denounced as representing the socialistic spirit of collectivism. For instance, in the United States, government interventions known as the New Deal (beginning in 1933) had features that were

24. Ibid., 146.
25. Ibid., 149.
26. Ibid., 162.
27. Ibid., 34.

suggestive of the corporate state. Furthermore, against fascism as well as state socialism, a democratic state is organized internally in a non-hierarchical, cooperative fashion, thereby undergirding economic democracy. However, for Hayek such an endeavor is suspicious because of its attachment to collectivism.

Hayek levels down the difference between fascism and state socialism. Fascism (deriving from the Roman symbol of collectivism and power) is normally described as a form of extreme right, although both the left and the right influenced fascism. Based on "blood and soil," Fascism represented the particularity of nationalism and racism over against the internationalism of both classical liberalism and Marxism. However, state socialism advocates control of the means of production by the state apparatus. State socialism is an economic system with few democratic characteristics, with an emphasis on a gradual process of developing socialism through state action.

Hayek advocates capitalism as a dynamic system fueled and driven by competition "without coercive or arbitrary intervention of authority."[28] Planning and competition can be combined only by planning for competition, not by planning against competition.[29] Planning is required to make competition effective and as beneficial as possible.

Hayek takes issue with Sombart who insists that the competitive system was inevitably developed into monopoly capitalism.[30] Against this trend, Hayek contends that the decline of competition and the growth of monopoly must not be accepted as the result of technological developments or an inevitable product of the evolution of capitalism.

Hayek defended liberalism and individualism. Within the social and economic spheres the individual's system of ends should be supreme. It should be recognized as the ultimate judge of the ends. The individual's own views should govern his/her actions. Such a principle constitutes the essence of the individualist position.[31]

Democratic institutions or parliaments may be regarded as ineffective "talking shops," because they are incompetent to carry out the tasks of a comprehensive economic plan. Taken out of politics, the direction of an economic plan is placed in the hands of experts, permanent officials, or

28. Hayek, *Constitution*, 27.
29. Hayek, *Road*, 42.
30. Ibid., 46.
31. Ibid., 59.

independent autonomous bodies.[32] However, such democracy will destroy itself within the system of planning or collective creed. Democracy, according to Hayek, only becomes possible within the system of capitalism. In fact, Hayek's view of society leads to Social Darwinism, which implies the denial of cooperation and compassion; here an idea of nature is constructed in the worst form of aggressive capitalism.[33]

Hayek endorses our submission to the impersonal forces of the market for the sake of individual market freedom. This is the only path to avoid serfdom. Following and submitting to the logic of the market becomes a religious creed or a force of nature for Hayek. An attempt to master the forces of the market brings us toward "the path to the destruction of our civilization and a certain way to block future progress."[34]

When the worker is opposed to the principle of market and capital—the spirit of this society—for the sake of collectivism, such rebellion is the sin against the "Holy Spirit." This option will take us on the road to serfdom. However, the policy of freedom for the individual that Hayek preaches is the only truly progressive policy. This remains as true today as it was in the nineteenth century.[35] However, flying in the face of Hayek, this progress becomes captive to the iron cage of economic privatization and faces the crisis of the self-regulating market in the world economy.

THE MARKET AND INDIVIDUAL FREEDOM

Friedman shared with Hayek the notion that government and state intervention toward social welfare and regulation of economic activity would pave the road to serfdom.[36] Friedman's political philosophy stresses the advantages of the marketplace and the disadvantages of government interventions and regulation.

In 1975, two years after the military coup that toppled the government of Salvador Allende, the economy of Chile experienced a crisis. Friedman accepted the invitation of a private foundation to visit Chile and lecture on principles of economic freedom. During his visit Friedman also met with the military dictator, President Augusto Pinochet. Friedman defended his role in Chile. He argued that the move towards open market

32. Ibid., 62.
33. Gorringe, *Capital and Kingdom*, 50.
34. Hayek, *Road*, 205–6.
35. Ibid., 240.
36. Friedman, *Capitalism and Freedom*, 11.

policies not only improved the economic situation in Chile but also contributed to the softening of Pinochet's rule and to the eventual transition to a democratic government in 1990. However, Friedman's self-defense remains controversial.

Milton and Rose Friedman in their book *Capitalism and Freedom* began their argument by taking issue with the inaugural address of President Kennedy; the paternalistic "what your country can do for you" implied that government was the patron while the citizen was the ward. This view is in contrast with the free individual belief in one's own responsibility for one's own destiny. On the other hand, the organismic "what you can do for your country" implied that government was the master or deity while the citizen was the servant or the votary. Friedmann's ambition is to keep the government from becoming a Frankenstein that will destroy the very freedom of the individual.[37]

The major theme in *Capitalism and Freedom* promotes

> the role of competitive capitalism–the organization of the bulk
> of economic activity through private enterprise operating in a
> free market–as a system of economic freedom and a necessary
> condition for political freedom.[38]

Individual liberalism associated with market freedom is Milton and Rose Friedman's slogan in which they emphasize freedom as the ultimate goal and the individual as the ultimate entity in the society. Laissez-faire at home is supported as a means of reducing the role of the state in economic affairs. Such a principle supports free trade abroad as a means of linking the nations of the world together peacefully and democratically. At issue here is political reduction of the arbitrary power of the state, while protecting the civil freedoms of individuals.[39]

According to Friedman's economic principle of freedom, one's freedom to murder one's neighbor must be sacrificed to preserve the freedom of the other to live.[40] The Friedmans do not seem to conceive of a conflict and its social cause between human freedom and murder. Relinquishment of the freedom to murder is simply enough to establish social relationships based on contracts of purchase and sale. The basic requisite is the maintenance of law and order to prevent physical coercion of one individual by

37. Ibid., 2.
38. Ibid., 4.
39. Ibid., 5.
40. Ibid., 26.

another and to enforce contracts into which people voluntarily enter. This gives substance to the term "private."[41]

The free exercise of the freedom to murder coexists alongside the exercise of the freedom to live. Here ethics and philosophy have nothing to do with the values relevant to relations among people; it is set up only by the relationships of production, that is, decisions about buying.[42]

For the nineteenth-century liberal, Friedman argues, an extension of freedom was regarded as the most effective way to promote welfare and equality. For the twentieth-century liberal, the thinking was different, because welfare and equality were regarded as either prerequisites of or alternatives to freedom. Here, the policies of state intervention and paternalism, which are reminiscent of seventeenth-century mercantilism against which classical liberalism fought, have come to the fore.

The Friedmans take their lead from Adam Smith, who extolled the market as benign and impartial providence. Economic freedom, which is provided by competitive capitalism, is an end in itself, becoming an indispensable means of achieving political freedom.[43] The market eliminated the source of coercive power, enabling economic strength to be a check to political power. The Friedmans follow Smith, who argued that a voluntary exchange between two parties will be mutually beneficial. All seek their own interest to make everyone better off.

The market system requires Smith's natural liberty, a concept that can be traced to Locke's idea of the equality of all in the state of nature. As Smith argued,

> every man, as long as he does not violate the laws of justice, is left perfectly free to pursue his own interest his own way, and to bring both his industry and capital into competition with those of any other man, or order of men.[44]

Self-interest produces the common good; our existence is a commercial animal. *Homo economicus* is led by an invisible hand to promote an end. Pursuing one's own interest, one promotes the common good of society more effectually than one really intends.[45]

41. Ibid., 14.
42. Ibid., 12.
43. Ibid., 8.
44. Smith, *Wealth of Nations*, IV, ch.9.
45. Ibid., 1., ch.2; 2, ch.2.

Milton and Rose Friedman argue that no one who buys bread knows whether the wheat of the bread was grown by a Communist, or a Republican, by a Fascist or by a Negro or a white. An impersonal market separates economic activities from political views, keeping people from racial discrimination.[46] Friedman finds the working model of a society of free private enterprise and exchange economy, which is called competitive capitalism, to be ideal.[47]

However, the Friedmans' projection of perfect freedom built on the idea of voluntary cooperation among freed individuals has always been a fiction.[48] Unlike the Friedmans, at least Smith kept Stoic notions of the common good in his earlier writing, *Theory of Moral Sentiments*. In this piece, Smith maintained that we must be prepared to sacrifice our interest for others.[49] It is hard to find Smith's moral pity concerning the disadvantage of the colonies exploited by Europe's trade system in the Friedmans.

According to the Friedmans, monopoly arose against the free market. When the technical conditions make a monopoly—due to market imperfections, which are the natural outcome of competitive market forces—three alternatives become possible: private monopoly, public monopoly, or public regulation. Private monopoly among others may be the least of the evils.[50] The neighborhood effects may justify a city park, not a national park like Yellowstone National Park or the Grand Canyon. The houses on all sides get the benefit of the open space from a park located in the middle of the city. It would be very expensive and difficult to maintain toll collectors. However, the entrances to a national park like Yellowstone are few. When admission to a national park like Yellowstone is free, things are bad. Visitors pay but things are still bad, because they pay too little. The charges do not cover the costs. If the public wants this kind of an activity enough to pay for it, private enterprises will have every incentive to provide such parks.[51]

When a fence is put up and visitors can enter only after paying, freedom is assured. Thus, the Friedmans reject important monopoly effects that would justify governmental activity in the public area.

46. Friedman, *Capitalism and Freedom*, 15, 21.

47. Ibid., 13.

48. Gorringe, *Capital and Kingdom*, 39.

49. Ibid., 35.

50. Friedman, *Capitalism and Freedom*, 28.

51. Ibid., 31.

CRITICAL REFLECTION

The Friedmans argue that state intervention is unnecessary in order to prove the unlimited scope and effectiveness of commodity relationships. The Friedman's happy fetishism upholds freedom as a privatization of erecting the fence.[52] In the framework of classical political economists, commodity relationships are conceived of as a fence around things. Neo-classical economic theory led to seeing freedom as a fence or a cage. The Friedmans see freedom as an endless number of cages around an endless number of goods. One cannot be both an egalitarian and a liberal.[53] In the Friedmans' view, all that is required is that the state does not grant recognition to any monopoly. Competition is an ideal type in political economy. Breaking up unions would be a decisive blow for industrial monopolies. A unilateral move to free trade is far better.[54]

What the Friedmans announce is the new police state. The police state means freedom and the socialized state means slavery. This is the Friedmans' new liberalism. Overarching and enclosing the many cages around individual commodities, they erect a larger cage. This whole new conception of the liberal state is aimed at justifying utter nonintervention on the part of the state. Hollywood's blacklist or McCarthy's blacklisting kept people from exercising their profession but at the same time it offered incentives for others to employ them.

> The commercial emphasis, the fact that people who are running enterprises have an incentive to make as much money as they can, protected the freedom of the individuals who were black-listed by providing them with an alternative form of employment, and by giving people an incentive to employ them.[55]

What the Friedmans picture is a noninterventionist police state that is utterly totalitarian. The police state employs repression against all who advocate intervention. Work done by a black person and a white person produce the same thing but their productivity is different, owing to purchasers' tastes. One who buys and employs the labor of blacks and whites pays the price of discrimination; first one pays less to one group because of its inferiority while paying the other group more because of its

---

52. Hinkelammert, *Ideological Weapons*, 74, 85–86.
53. Friedman, *Capitalism and Freedom*, 195.
54. Ibid., 73.
55. Ibid., 20.

superiority.[56] Discrimination has something to do with the taste of others.[57] All of these cases are matters of taste. Hitler had a taste for discriminating against Jews, and others have a taste for blocking discrimination.

In this light, Milton and Rose Friedman argue that fair employment practices, preventing discrimination in employment, involve interference with the freedom of individuals.[58] The widespread notion of monopoly associated with social responsibility would destroy a free society. But "competition is an ideal type, like a Euclidean line or point."[59]

With their radical anti-interventionism the Friedmans list all the forms of state intervention that should be ended.

> This is a defect of farm programs, general old-age benefits, minimum-wage laws, pro-union legislation, tariffs, licensing provisions of crafts or professions, and so on in seemingly endless profusion.[60]

The Friedmans attempt to keep the poor under the minimum. They consider the proposal of an income tax to support the unfortunate minority, the poor, to be quite dangerous.[61] So they hit on the idea of cancelling the voting rights of the poor. Although the Friedmans propose an idea of how to keep the government from becoming a Frankenstein state—one that will destroy the very freedom of the individual[62]—their proposal is similar to what they want to avoid: a Frankenstein police state without interventionism. There is a parallel between a Frankenstein police state and Empire emerging in the midst of economic globalization.

THEORY OF EMPIRE AND GLOBAL CAPITALISM

We have entered a new era characterized by a separation of the globalized space of economic management from the national space of social-political management. This logic calls for elimination of the state's social interventions, characterizing the reality of economic globalization. Like a conspiracy theory of economic globalization, a single center of rationality

56. Friedman, *Price Theory*, 225.

57. Friedman, *Capitalism and Freedom*, 111–12.

58. Ibid., 111.

59. Ibid., 120.

60. Ibid., 191.

61. Ibid., 194.

62. Ibid., 14.

guides the various phases of historical development in terms of the hidden hand of the world market. This refers to ideological meta-discourse in the era of Empire.[63] In this era, we observe that pre-emptive war against terrorism has become the global politics of Empire, and nature around the earth has undergone the process of devastation.

THE META DISCOURSE OF EMPIRE AND BIOPOLITICS

UN organizations along with the multi-transnational finance and trade agencies (The IMF, the World Bank, the GATT, etc) have become relevant in the supranational juridical constitution. What gives legitimacy to these organizations is their function in the symbology of the imperial order.[64] In the theory of Empire, Foucault's notion of bio-power remains central. The body is directly involved in a political field. Connected to the economic system, the body has become an important component in the operation of power relations in modern society. Power/knowledge is the process and struggle in their historical transformation of the human body that determines the forms and domains of knowledge.[65] Bio-power emerged as a political technology that implies a new type of political rationality. "Bio-power brought life and its mechanism into the realm of explicit calculations and made knowledge/power an agent of transformation of human life."[66]

The function of the police is broadened, concerned with people in their everyday activities, which is an essential component for the increase of the state's power. The police appear to be an administration heading the state, coupled with the judiciary, the army, and the exchequer, which is the department in the United Kingdom responsible for taxation and revenue.[67] The bio-power centered on the body as an object to be manipulated in terms of disciplinary power whose goal is to produce a human being as a docile body in workshops, barracks, prisons, and hospitals.

The proponents of the Empire continue to develop Foucault's biopolitical interest. The Fordist phase of development begins to structure global territories biopolitically, being transformed by the new reality of capitalism. They tend to make nation-states merely instruments to record

63. Hardt and Negri, *Empire*, 3.
64. Ibid., 31.
65. Foucault, *Discipline & Punish*, 27–28.
66. Foucault, *History of Sexuality*, I. 143.
67. Hardt and Negri, *Empire*, 22.

the flow of the commodities, monies, and populations. In the biopoliti-cal structuring of the world, a process of production and reproduction is dressed in monetary clothing. "Accumulate, accumulate! This is Moses and the Prophets!"[68] This view of accumulation is restructured in a bio-politcal framework of capital and discipline.

According to the model of Empire, the rupture or shift occurs in contemporary capitalist production and global relations of power.[69] This model contradicts the model of the world-system, which argues that capi-talism has always functioned as a world-economy.

EMPIRE VERSUS IMPERIALISM

For the sake of the biopolitical concept of world dominion and sovereign-ty, a model of Empire challenges the theory of imperialism. According to the theory of imperialism, there is an intrinsic relation between capitalism and expansion. The capitalist expansion inevitably assumes the political form of imperialism.

In the socialist framework of imperialism, capital constantly op-erates by transcending the boundaries of the inside and the outside. A creation of a world market is presupposed in the concept of capital. The need for a world market can be seen in the realization of surplus value in an adequate market.

However, Rosa Luxemburg critiques Marx's notion of capital accu-mulation and expansion, emphasizing capital's dependence on its outside market. In the process of capitalization, capital expansion meets the need for the realization of surplus value in the market outside and it also satisfies the subsequent moment of accumulation. Thus, capital ransacks the whole world by pillage and theft. Pursuing the domination and exploitation of the peripheries, the process of capitalization internalizes the outside.[70]

Seen within the expanding cycle of capitalist production and ac-cumulation, civilization and modernization mean capitalization. The eco-nomic relationship is also articulated in the historical and social context in terms of political relations of rule and domination. Here occurs an alliance between capitalism and imperialism. For Lenin, a logic of capital expan-sion of the world market is constructed in an imperialist stamp. Capital's entrance into a new phase of international development by monopoly led

68. Ibid., 32; cf. Marx, *Capital*, 1:742.

69. Hardt and Negri, *Empire*, 8–9.

70. Ibid., 226.

to an increase of contradiction and a crisis of equalization. It is the task of the revolutionary party to intervene in the contradiction of imperialist development for the sake of struggles, insurrection, and revolutions.

For a model of Empire, the imperialist state attempts to incorporate the multitude and its form of class struggle within its ideological structure; it also transforms the multitude into a people by undergirding a political articulation of the concept of hegemony. Later this political insight into hegemony finds its echo in Gramsci's philosophy of praxis.[71]

Imperialism and the monopoly phase as the expression of the global expansion of capital emphasize that competition declines necessarily in the imperialist phase as compared to the growth of monopolies. In this context Hardt and Negri discover the alternative in a direction toward either world communist revolution or Empire.[72] This perspective contradicts Luxemburg's critique of imperialism in terms of the outside market. There is no distinction between inside and outside.

According to the model of Empire, a view of subsumption of capitalist society toward the world market should be complemented by Foucault's biopolitical thesis of disciplinarity in regard to a global quasi-state of the disciplinary regime. The disciplinarity pushed the capitalist mode of production to its extreme. The globalization of markets is the consequence of Taylorist, Fordist, and disciplined labor power across the globe.[73]

The theoreticians of Empire specify the modern processes of primitive accumulation under two models: the relationship between wealth and command, as well as between inside and outside. The wealth for the primitive accumulation of capital comes from the colonial territories, while the command and discipline of the human body arises internally through the capitalist relations of production. In contrast to the model of Empire, however, in the model of dependency, the terms are reversed: the wealth arises from within through the capitalist mode of production. And the political, military command and discipline of the indigenous body comes from the outside of European capital. This is undertaken by central and peripheral capitalist formation.

At any rate, in the passage of modernity to postmodernity, the process of primitive accumulation continues in terms of the reproduction of

---

71. Rather Gramsci's theory of hegemony is culturally (in respect of the civil society) oriented rather than political-economically (in respect of political society).Cf. Sassoon, *Gramsci*.

72. Hardt and Negri, *Empire*, 234.

73. Ibid., 256.

capitalist relations of production and social classes. In postmodernity the social wealth accumulation is increasingly immaterial, involving social relations, communication systems, information, and effective networks. The proletariat in postmodernity is becoming the universal figure of labor, all those subordinated under the rule of capital. This has little to do with the hegemonic position of the industrial working class.[74] Informational accumulation integrates those previous productive processes in its own networks and generates the highest levels of productivity. Informational accumulation in the process of postmodern primitive and formative accumulation points beyond the era of capital toward a new social mode of production; it transforms the capitalist mode of accumulation and production.[75]

In the conceptualization of Empire, a qualitative passage takes place in modern history. Giovanni Arrighi provides a clue for this shift. In his analysis of the long twentieth century, Arrighi states that the crisis of United States hegemony and accumulation in the 1970s (the decoupling of the dollar from the gold standard in 1971 and the defeat in Vietnam) is a fundamental turning point in the history of the world economy. In Arrigh's construction of four great systematic cycles of capitalist accumulation, the United States is situated in line after the Genoese, the Dutch, and the British. The crisis indicates a passage, the turning point that transpires in every systemic cycle of accumulation from material expansion (investment in production) to financial expansion (including speculation). The passage toward financial expansion characterized the U.S. economy since the early 1980s, indicating the end of U.S. hegemony over the world capitalist system.[76]

In Arrighi's cyclical analysis, proponents of the Empire observe, nonetheless, that the history of capitalism becomes the eternal return of the same by assuming the changing role of capitalist accumulation. Arrigh's concept of the long century is not consonant with the Nietzschean concept of eternal recurrence. Against the cyclical argument the theoreticians of Empire insist that a rupture of the system occurred in the history of capitalism. In the transnational networks of production, the circuits of the world market, and the global structures of capitalist dominion, we have to recognize the potential for a paradigm shift or rupture.[77]

---

74. Hardt and Negri, *Empire*, 256.

75. Ibid., 258.

76. Arrighi, *Long Twentieth Century*.

77. Hardt and Negri, *Empire*, 239.

POST-IMPERIALISM AND BIOPOLITICAL DISCIPLINARITY

Utilizing Foucault's concept of bio-power, Hardt and Negri contend that the theory of imperialism is now replaced by the notion of a single power of Empire, which over-determines conflict or competitions among several imperialist powers. The logic of Empire considers imperialist powers through one common notion of right in a postcolonial or postimperialist framework.[78] The new paradigm of the Empire is defined by the decline of the sovereign nation-states and by the deregulation of international markets. Emerging Empire undergirds the globalization of productive networks and envelopes all power relations within the world order.[79]

In the postimperialist perspective, the model of Empire also takes issue with dependency theories in Latin America and Africa. The dependency theory has an illusion of economic development, because it argues that "real development" can be promoted by delinking an economy from its dependent relationship.

However, the system of world-economy should destroy any notion of delinking from the global networks of power. Even the dominant countries are now dependent on the global system. As the interactions of the world market have resulted in a generalized disarticulation of all economies, an attempt at isolation or separation from the world economy system will make nation-states increasingly vulnerable to powerlessness and poverty.[80]

In contrast to the theory of dependency, the first phase of capitalist accumulation was conducted under the paradigm of disciplinary power. Power is exercised through machines by organizing brains in communication systems and information networks as well as bodies in welfare systems and monitored activities. It leads to alienation from the sense of life and the desire for creativity. Intensifying and generalizing the normalizing apparatuses of disciplinarity, the society of control extends its scope and horizon outside the social institutions through flexible and fluctuating networks.

Nevertheless, it is mistaken for a model of Empire to marginalize the colonial reality of enslaved labor and world economic system of triangular trade in the study of biopolitical discipline of the human body.

78. Ibid., 9.
79. Ibid., 20.
80. Ibid., 284.

By sovereignty Foucault means the transcendence of the single point of command above the social field, while by governmentality he means the general economy of discipline running throughout society.[81] In modernity, the disciplinary processes put into practice by the administration manage to configure themselves as apparatuses. This process takes into consideration the collective biological dimension of the reproduction of the population. Insofar as modern sovereignty is realized, it gives birth to bio-power.

In the discussion of government disciplinarity, Hardt and Negri argue that the New Deal model produced the highest form of disciplinary government. A disciplinary society is a factory-society in which disciplinary production and disciplinary society are in coincidence. Civil society is absorbed into the state.[82] Under the hegemony of the U.S. the dominant imperialist countries were transformed in the postwar period in terms of three apparatuses: (1) the process of decolonization; (2) the gradual decentralization of production, and (3) the construction of a framework of international relations in terms of disciplinarity: disciplinary productive regime and disciplinary society. These three mechanisms characterize the imperial power of the New Deal, moving beyond the old notion of imperialism. The postcolonial transformation of the Third World was undertaken under the guise of modernization and development, which also defines the mass project of national liberation. A paradigm of modernization and modern sovereignty has replaced classical theories of imperialism and anti-imperialism paradoxically.[83]

The world market is constituted and organized along with a disciplinary model. The new transversal mobility of disciplined labor power indicates a nomadic desire not to be controlled within the disciplinary regime.[84] The First World is transferred to the Third in terms of stock exchanges and banks, transnational corporations and command. Workers of the Third World who go to the First World for work contribute to undermining the boundaries between the two worlds.[85]

81. Ibid., 88.
82. Ibid., 243.
83. Ibid., 251.
84. Ibid., 253.
85. Ibid., 253–54.

THE BIOPOLITICAL STRUCTURE OF PRODUCTION
AND THE IRON CAGE

Max Weber examined the administrative mechanisms involved in the formation of modern sovereignty in his socio-cultural analysis of Western
civilization. Weber has revealed the illusion of modernity in his analysis
of the disenchantment of the world: its final destination is an iron cage.

Foucault shares Weber's pessimism. Foucault's concern is to propose
a correspondence between discipline and an efficient machine in reference
to "permanent coercion, indefinitely progressive forms of training, and
automatic docility."[86] In his analysis of the Panopticon, Foucault suggests
that this architectural apparatus should be a marvelous machine that creates and sustains a power relation independent of the person exercising
it. "The Panopticon presents a cruel, ingenious cage."[87] Foucault's thesis of
disciplinary power seems to uphold Weber's analysis of Western civilization by expressing the disenchantment of the world that ends up with an
iron cage. Discipline is a technique for linking the economic growth of
power by increasing the docility, utility, and output of all the elements of
the system (educational, military, industrial or medical).[88]

The primary task of bio-power is to administer life in terms of the
production and reproduction of life. It is a control extending throughout
the depths of the consciousness and bodies of the population—across the
entirety of social relations. Foucault investigates the subsumption in terms
of the social bios itself, engaged in the modalities of disciplinarity or control. The concepts of the society of control and bio-power have a central
role in descriptions of the reality of Empire.

The society of control is expressed as a figure of power that is active
throughout the entire biopolitics of society. Transcending historical materialism, Foucault attempts to bring social production and all the elements
of the superstructure back within cultural, economic, corporeal, and subjective perspective.

In the grasping of the real dynamics of production in biopolitical
society, the constant functioning of social machines produces the world.
This is the productivity of social reproduction (creative production, production of values, social relations, affects, becoming). The labor power in

86. Ibid., 169, 173.
87. Ibid., 205.
88. Ibid., 218.

the production of surplus value is today filled by intellectual, immaterial, and communicative labor power.

A new political theory of value is demanded to correspond to the new capitalist accumulation of value at the center of the mechanism of exploitation. Along with this new theory of value, a new theory of subjectivity can be articulated, which operates through knowledge, communication, and language. For the task of a new political theory of value, the authors of the Empire take interest in elaborating the three aspects of immaterial labor: the communicative labor of industrial production (linked in informational networks), the interactive labor of symbolic analysis and problem solving, and the labor of the production and manipulation of affects.[89] The primum of the biopolitical world of Empire is generating and regenerating itself in order to exist. Bio-power includes a horizon of the hybridization of the natural and the artificial, needs and machines, desire and the collective organization of the economic and the social, becoming the basis and motor of production and reproduction.[90]

Communication organizes the movement of globalization by multiplying and structuring interconnections through networks. Language, as it communicates, produces commodities by creating subjectivities. The communication networks integrate the imagery and the symbolic within the biopolitical fabric. Communication and the biopolitical context are co-existent. Communicative production and the construction of imperial legitimization come along to the degree that the machine constructs social fabrics rendering ineffective any contradiction.

COMMUNICATION, LEGITIMIZATION, AND INTERVENTION

The deployments of the imperial machine are defined by interventions. Here, actions are internalized and universalized by the ruling structure of production and communication. We observe intervention in the threefold sense: intervention in the deployments of monetary mechanisms and financial maneuvers over the transnational field, interventions in the field of communication and their effects on the legitimization of the system, finally, intervention in the exercise of physical force of the imperial machine over its global territories.[91]

89. Hardt and Negri, *Empire*, 30.
90. Ibid., 389.
91. Ibid., 35.

In this biopolitical connection between communication, legitimization, and intervention, the imperial machine actually produces and reproduces ideological master narratives by validating its own power. Biopolitical strategy becomes a fulcrum for undertaking the interplay between social discourse and power. A globalized biopolitical machine is a new economic-industrial-communicative machine that generates the source of imperial normativity and rationality.[92] Max Weber's definition of the legitimization of power is accepted in the logic of Empire in terms of the mixture of (1) elements typical of traditional power, (2) an extension of bureaucratic power adapted physically to the biopolitical context, and (3) a rationality of charisma elevated as a power of the singularization of the whole and of the effectiveness of imperial interventions.[93] There occurs a process of economic postmodernization (or better, informatization) in the passage from the domination of industry to that of services and information.[94]

In our time, which is the era of the end of modernization, the process of postmodernization has been marked by a shift from industry to service jobs, and characterized by knowledge, information, affect and communication. [95] The computer and communication have transformed the process of labor toward the model of information and communication technologies. Interactive and cybernetic machines are integrated into our bodies and minds, by becoming an interpretive lens that redefines our bodies and minds. The anthropology of cyberspace is a recognition of the new human condition and subjectivity.[96]

Under the dominance of the informational economy the geographical differences in the global economy are lines of the new global hierarchy of production.[97] Empire takes form when language and communication, immaterial labor, and cooperation become the dominant productive force. It is certain that the United States occupies a privileged position in the global hierarchies of Empire. However, resistance to command and control emerges within Empire, and antagonism to exploitation is articulated across the global networks of production and reproduction. The decline of Empire is defined as a synchronic reality running through every mo-

92. Ibid., 40.

93. Ibid., 41.

94. Ibid., 280.

95. Ibid., 290.

96. Ibid., 291.

97. Ibid., 288.

ment of communicative production and exchange within the social, global totality.[98] However, biopolitical generation transforms the bodies of the multitude, which becomes a political subject in the context of Empire. For the sake of a city of God the earthly city of the multitude fights against the Empire.

The deployments of the military and the police power of Empire attack the multitude and its social movement. The wide landscape of biopolitical production through labor—material or immaterial, intellectual or corporeal—allows us to recognize the full generality of the proletariat.[99] In the postmodern condition of Empire, the life of the multitude is the militant self, which implies the agent of biopolitical production and resistance against Empire.[100]

POSTCOLONIAL THEOLOGY AND EMPIRE

Empire, like the Panopticon, seeks to extend the control of bio-power coupled with rationalization, disciplinarity, and intervention, not only geographically, politically, and economically but also intellectually, psychologically, culturally, and religiously. The top down control of Empire manifests itself in violence, terror, exclusion, and war. This dark side of Empire is called blowback. Practices of atrocities, tyrannies, and the evil done in colonies boomerang to contaminate the homeland. The effect of this boomerang is seen in Montesquieu's reflection on the Spanish violence in the Americas of the sixteenth century.[101]

Associating the notion of Empire with North America, Benjamin Franklin is quoted by former Vice President Dick Cheney: "And if a sparrow cannot fall to the ground without His notice, is it probable that an empire can rise without His aid?"[102] Talk about a postcolonial empire finds its validity in the argument that empire can exist without colonies. The politics of North America probably would prove to be "an anomaly in the global empire building of the twenty-first century."[103]

A "post"-empire (or colonial) theology in critical engagement with Empire presents itself as an attempt to transcend the modern theological

98. Ibid., 385.

99. Ibid., 402.

100. Ibid., 411.

101. Rieger, *Christ and Empire*, 2.

102. Rieger, *Empire*, 11.

103. Ibid., 12.

paradigm of contextual theology. Rieger argues that dominant contextual theologies of culture tend to be relevant to the dominant culture. These contextual theologies universalize their own culture, sidestepping the gaps and the silences of cultures that hurt: what lies below the surface. A methodology of contextual theology is grounded in correlating theological sources to contextual concerns. Subsequently, context becomes the determining factor of theology. Over and against contextual theology, liberation theology makes a contribution by attending to what hurts and providing an alternative.[104]

Liberation theology as a critical reflection on Christian praxis[105] is an appropriation of the theory of dependency to promote the preferential option for the poor. A dialogue between theology and the social sciences helps reveal an ideological infiltration of Christian theology unconsciously hidden in Christian discourse.

Postcolonial theologians attempt to transcend the aftermath of colonialism by moving beyond the colonial or neo-colonial forms of global domination. Thus, postcolonial theology retains a discourse of resistance, calling into question cultural and discursive domination. A "theological surplus" is to be pursued, inspiring Christian theology to a search for the vision of the theological surplus as the resistance and the alternative to Empire.[106]

What is important in postcolonial theology is: 1) critique of oppressive powers of the state; 2) a critique of the relationship between church and state; and 3) a critique of the way institutionalized structures internalize and colonize the poor and oppressed.[107] Furthermore, postcolonial theologians take issue with the Empire in present day globalization that produces postcolonial hybridity. In this hybridity postcolonial theologians recognize great potential for resistance.

Developing Foucault's notion of the emergence of modern "man," it is argued that the historical invention of man is also a Western invention to the debasement and exclusion of others. Along with Foucault, Edward Said remains a good mentor. According to Said, one of the important Orientalist projects is the essentialization, which implies that the Orient and the Oriental character retain timeless and unchanging identities. A Eurocentric project "orientalizes" the Orient, tailoring it to an object of

---

104. Rieger, *Christ and Empire*, 8.

105. Gutierrez, *Theology of Liberation*, 5.

106. Rieger, eds. *Empire*, 1.

107. *Postcolonial Theologies*, Keller, et al., 8.

European discourse.[108] Violence and imposition are the necessary motor for driving the logic of colonialism in defiance of subaltern culture. The dialectic of colonialism invokes a reciprocal counter-violence on the part of the colonies.[109]

Said further argues that the worldliness or the circumstantial reality is incorporated in the text. This forms "an infrangible part of its capacity for conveying and producing meaning."[110] The theory of hybridity exposes the myth of cultural purity and colonialist disavowal and helps construct the theology using elements from both the dominant and indigenous cultures. At this juncture, postcolonial critics speak of the collaboration of the colonized in the colonial regime and their divided and fragmented subjectivity. Although acknowledging the contributions of the indigenous or inculturated theologies in anti-imperialistic efforts, postcolonial critics argue that there are shortcomings and limitations in these theologies, because they are articulated and grounded in nationalistic fervor. Global locality (glo-cality) characterizes an indigenous culture in the saturation of the civilization of Empire. Speaking for or representing the subaltern becomes a difficult task because there is a gap between the intellectuals and the plight of the masses.

At any rate, Hardt and Negri propose the model of Empire by replacing the old form of imperialism. Empire, according to the authors, does not establish a territorial center of power, nor rely on fixed boundaries or barriers. It is a decentered and deterritorializing apparatus of rule and dominion progressively incorporating the entire global realm.[111] "Empire manages hybrid identities, flexible hierarchies, and plural exchanges through modulating networks of command."[112]

Nevertheless, there is paucity in the model of Empire in consideration of the problem of surplus transfer, unequal exchange, and military complex industries; these elements intensify an imperialist dimension in late capitalism. A postmodern theory of Empire remains unidentified; Anonymous Empire, like the Panopticon, threatens human life in an apocalyptic sense while paradoxically generating its gravedigger, a multitude. It also deemphasizes the role of the nation-state as a local sovereignty still in service of the powerful in a local government.

108. Said, *Orientalism*, 4–5, 104.

109. Hardt and Negri, *Empire*, 131.

110. Said, *World, Text, and Critic*, 39.

111. Hardt and Negri, *Empire*, xii.

112. Ibid., xii–xiii.

Influenced by the theory of Empire, postcolonial theology advances hybridity as a place of fragmented subjectivity in order to mobilize a critique of the reality of Empire. However, it is also certain that a postcolonial theology of hybridity is limited in analyzing local and cultural issues and semi-peripheral and peripheral economic systems because it puts excessive trust in the generalization of bio-power and its almighty sovereignty. Our final chapter will deal with the church's responsibility for economic justice in an ecumenical context as we examine two prophetic theologians, Helmut Gollwitzer and Ulrich Duchrow, who have made great contributions to articulating the relationship between theology and economic justice.

10

Alternatives to Global Capitalism in Ecumenical Context

THE FRAMING OF THE international landscape has shifted from a confrontation between East and West to the enormous disparity between North and South. Taking issue with the reality of economic globalization, there are several significant attempts to overcome the limitations and setbacks of global capitalism in ecumenical-global contexts. An alternative to global capitalism requires a new theological-ethical endeavor which should present the church's ethical responsibility for the gospel and the world. A prophetic theology concerning the gospel and economic justice has been framed and undertaken in an ecumenical and global context to break through the limitation, setback, and crisis of that which global capitalism has brought to the world. Two theologians, Helmut Gollwitzer and Ulrich Duchrow, deserve attention as examples of incorporating economic issues within a theological-ethical framework in an ecumenical context. In the conclusion of this chapter we shall deal with the ecumenical churches' engagement with economic justice, ethical responsibility, and ecological sustainability. The excursus entails a reflection of the contribution of East Asian religions to improving the relationship between people's life and economic justice, which is of special significance to interreligious dialogue and collaboration in an ecumenical context on behalf of shalom, compassion, and justice.

THE PROPHETIC THEOLOGY OF GOD'S LIFE AND ECONOMIC JUSTICE

Helmut Gollwitzer is a well-known representative of the Confessing Church in Germany. For Gollwitzer there are three sources of Christian theology by which to criticize the limitations and setbacks of historical branches and streams of Christian religion: The Old Testament, Jesus Christ himself, and the ancient church's witness to Jesus Christ.

For Gollwitzer the gospel is grounded in the scripture and also in the reality and truth of the living God. The theological task is to follow the gospel grounded therein and to live accordingly. God asks us for our life-performance, because God is not to be grounded in human ideas. Our understanding of and relationship with God should be grounded in our practical life. This priority of God in connection with our life assumes political, social, and churchly criteria and orientation. In light of the living reality of God's kingdom, Gollwitzer's theological reflection on Christology, ethics, Trinity, and church stands in an eschatological horizon of world renewal.

In an ecumenical context, Gollwitzer emphasized the liberating Word of God in the field of political economy. In *The Rich Christians and Poor Lazarus*,[1] he responded to the resolutions of the Uppsala Conference of the World Council of Churches. He confessed that Uppsala had impressed upon him to bring up the central importance of the church's responsibility in the matter of a policy of economic development. It is essential for him to avert the threatening catastrophe of world hunger which has already begun in the poor countries.[2]

For him, the true task of the church (proclamation of the gospel of Jesus Christ) comes together with the perception of political responsibility. The guidelines of the church in legitimate political participation are based on the interests of peace, collaboration, and the avoidance of violence and bloodshed rather than on the church's self-preservation and the preservation of its privileges. The church's responsibility must be driven by the interest of those who are deprived of secular justice, promoting equality before the law and a fair share in the products of society; it includes civil freedom, the opportunity of responsible self-determination in activity and in helping to share the forms of society.[3] The church has always been a

---

1. Gollwitzer, *Christians and Lazarus*, 18–28.
2. Ibid., ix.
3. Ibid., 27.

pressure group in the political and economic affairs to the state for the sake of God's love for humanity in Christ Jesus (Tit 3:4).

In the report of Section III at Uppsala, Gollwitzer highlighted point 18: Private investments in the developing countries are regarded as the new form of imperialism by means of the monopoly of capital. In part, this is the source of endless suffering and injustice.[4] Contrary to the widespread belief that capitalism and Western imperialism are alone responsible for the catastrophic condition of the third World, Gollwitzer did not sidestep how far ex-socialist governments also failed to measure up and succumbed to the danger of not acting according to the principles of democratic socialism. The ex-socialist countries also acted according to motives of national egoism or the lust for power.[5] However, Gollwitzer argues that one of the most grievous limitations at Uppsala (and also including *Populorum progressio* sec. 26 and 58) is to be found in the absence of the critique of world politics based on capitalism and imperialism.[6]

Furthermore in his book *Capitalist Revolution* (1973),[7] Gollwitzer continued to develop his political ethic in his deliberation of Christians sent into the world in a concrete time and social location. His political ethic accentuates a unity between dogmatic theology and public discipleship through social and political embodiment of the theological statement. The freedom given by God is always freedom for others. It must stand in engagement with the victim, and protest against terror. Christianity is not "Platonism for the people" (Nietzsche). Gollwitzer, coming from the theological tradition of Martin Luther and Karl Barth, was also close to his friend, Dietrich Bonhoeffer who undertook an ethical actualization of dogmatic knowledge from the standpoint from below in regard to the reality of the world. Gollwitzer remained faithful in all of his life to the directive and orientation represented by Bonhoeffer's theological-ethical embodiment: ethics—co-humanity—church in *diakonia*—discipleship—democratic socialism—peace movement—and political engagement.[8]

Engagement for the victims becomes the first demand of freedom and emancipation bestowed by God's grace of justification. The gospel

4. Ibid., 41.

5. Ibid., 43.

6. Ibid., 44.

7. Gollwitzer, *Die Kapitalistische Revolution.*

8. This characterization, originally referring to Dietrich Bonhoeffer and applied to Helmut Gollwitzer. This is a quotation from Karl Barth on occasion of Eberhard Bethge's biography on Dietrich Bonhoeffer. See Andreas Pangritz's introduction to Helmut Gollwitzer, Gollwitzer . . . *Gerechtigkeit und Friede*, 8.

about the forgiveness of sin entails the ramification of the church's solidarity with those who are burdened on the underside of the world. Our discipleship comes from our gratitude for God's grace of justification. This perspective of justification and justice invites us to promote the life of God's mission in righteousness, peace, and emancipation toward solidarity. Righteousness and peace will kiss each other (Ps 85:10).

In the face of the ruthless consequences of the capitalist revolution and imperialist wars in the 1960s and 70s, Gollwitzer promoted democratic socialism as an alternative to barbarianism. At issue for him was to bring the capitalist revolution under rational control. Insofar as capitalism marches on without control, it would lead to catastrophe.[9] The global system of world economy belongs to the issue of theological confession for Gollwitzer who took seriously law and peace in the 'as yet' unredeemed world (Barmen 5). Christian political responsibility promotes legislation which aims at removing the fundamental inequalities of the capitalist economic system in terms of realizing more togetherness and solidarity; it includes eliminating more privileges achieved in the conflicts, economic interests, and rivalry among superpowers.[10]

Analysis of World Economy

In our cultural period, which is the social organization of production, the economy has become the dominant factor. Polluted ground water runs underneath the villa of High Society. An analysis of capitalism is of significant importance to understand the reality of world economy and ecological sustainability. A critical analysis of society and the economic realm also belongs to the important task of theology and its ethical praxis.[11] Ecological catastrophe has brought us to an awareness of the interdependence of all nations and lives on earth. Global interdependence brings us to the profound revolutionization of social consciousness in the direction of deepening universal responsibility. The demand for the transformation of our consciousness takes issue with particularistic thought which is the thought of dominion in the establishment of material privilege through the instrument of material and intellectual forces.[12]

9. Ibid., 11, 157.

10. Gollwitzer, *Introduction*, 202.

11. Gollwitzer, "Kapitalistische Revolution," in Gollwitzer . . . *Gerechtigkeit und Friede*, 127–30.

12. Ibid., 133.

In the phase of world market and trade, oppression by the developed countries in the west is intensified and sharpened in the developing countries. European colonialism has not ended yet, but has changed its forms. Decolonization allowed the colonized countries to gain political independence and formal equality in the UN. The formal concept of equality covered up the continued inequality and dependence in the system of world economy. After the decolonization, the inequality and dependence of the third world has continued in the ideology of developmental aid and UN support in which the class struggle on the global scale has become the phenomenon of imperialism.[13] European colonialism and the expansion of its dominion have become the decisive fact of modern history: plunder, mono-culture, destruction of indigenous social order, forces of development, and direction of development according to the need of metropolis. The decolonization has not put an end to Euro-American imperialism, but only modified it in a specious manner. Scientific-technical advancement, high living standard, economic, cultural and ideological binding of other countries, military control—these all form the structural injustice and power which the metropolis has gained through the colonial and capitalist revolution.

Gollwitzer, one of the best experts in the socio-critical theory connected with democratic socialism, did not follow the analysis of imperialism according to the example of Orthodox Marxist ideology. Rather, he attempted to analyze the reality of imperialistic capitalism in light of the international relationship between metropolis and peripheries. It is possible to distinguish three phases in Gollwitzer's attitude toward Marxism. First, during and after his imprisonment as a POW in the Stalinist Soviet Union (cf. his book ". . . *und führen, wohin du nicht willst. Bericht einer Gefangenschaft*, 1951) he experienced the brutal reality of a communist society in Stalinist fashion from the perspective of a prisoner, realizing that the whole population of the Soviet Union was a prisoner of a tyranny which in some respects resembled the Nazi system in Germany. On the other hand, Gollwitzer had a strong feeling of guilt as a member of the German army and participant in a criminal war against Russia; this consciousness of guilt let him refrain from simplistic black and white concepts like the confrontation of freedom and democracy against totalitarianism.

The second phase can be seen in Gollwitzer's book "Die marxistische Religionskritik und der christliche Glaube" (1962). This book is the fruit of Gollwitzer's study of Marxism in the Fifties, when he was primarily

13. Ibid., 137.

interested in defending the Christian faith against the Marxist criticism of religion; his main criticism of Marxism in that period was the observation that Marxism represented a kind of secularized messianism and therefore was an expression of sin.

In the book "Die kapitalistische Revolution" (1973), we observe the third phase of Gollwitzer's study of Marxism. Inspired by the 1968 student movement, Gollwitzer now was ready to accept the Marxist criticism of capitalist economy. His later reception of the Marxist critique of political economy remains in affinity to critical theorists like Herbert Marcuse, Ernest Mandel, the American economist Paul M. Sweezy, and the Latin American critical perspective of neo-Imperialism (the dependence-theory of André Gunder Frank). Thus he concurs with John Galtung.[14] Galtung was a Norwegian sociologist and a principal founder of the discipline of peace. He characterized the method of imperialism through the combination of exploitation, division, and infiltration. His criticism of "structural violence" remains substantial to the analysis of world-economy. The diverse forms of relation of exploitation between the metropolis and the peripheries are described by the vertical division of labor. The vertical division of labor in the classic sense implies that the third world serves as the provider of raw material and offers inexpensive labor forces and market to the mother countries. In the modern sense it implies that a multinational corporation is established; it distributes the production to the countries of the third world and enables the metropolis to do research, finance, and administration. The production of the third world works for the former lord of colonialism. This production undergirds other civilizational factors like the explosion of population and pollution of the environment within the peripheries. The system of exploitation is preserved by the vertical division of labor undertaken by the metropolis. Organizing a front against the metropolis is hindered by the latter's global policy for the bilateral relationship of trade between the metropolis and the peripheries.

Furthermore, the ruling elite of the peripheries is politically bound to the center through economic interest, cultural influence, education, and military support. The particularistic interest of the elite in the periphery is in conformity with the interest of the power elite of the metropolis. There is no opportunity for the peripheries of the third world to establish alliance with the peripheries of the center countries. The dividing strategy of the elite in the metropolis is to separate such an alliance.[15]

14. Ibid., 139
15. Ibid., 140–41.

Furthermore, the working class in the metropolis has become the labor aristocrat. Marx's prophecy proved to be wrong because capitalism did not create a powerful proletariat, which would serve as the grave digger which could bury capitalism. The working class in the metropolis was integrated into the status quo of the existing society. The emancipation brought by capitalism meant progress in the history of human freedom. However, a theory of impoverishment can be visible in the peripheries at a global scale.[16] The emancipation and freedom achieved in the capitalist revolution are blind to greed, dominion, ecological devastation.

The infiltration takes place through the economic and cultural enterprise of the metropolis in relationship with the peripheries. In the infiltration of the education system, a binding of the elite of the peripheries with the elite of the metropolis is established. The accommodation of life style to the culture of the metropolis alienates the indigenous tradition from the masses of the country. This powerful combination of exploitation, dividing, and infiltration is complemented by military power. This combination implies phenomena of neo-colonialism or imperialism. This global structure is built upon the delicate type of structural violence and dominion that characterizes the imperialist relational mechanism operating in the relationship between the metropolis and peripheries.[17] Imperialism is not a perfected substance, but it is a system of unprecedented contradiction stamped by the military apparatus in support of the elite of the peripheries; it also perpetuates its control of the peripheries and oppression of all resistance in the peripheries. Weaponry, economy, and propaganda are three apparatuses by which the metropolis established structural injustice and dominion in the world. The imperialist system in the contemporary era is the result of the capitalist world system from the previous historical development through colonialism and capitalist revolution.

In the early phase of capitalism, an innerworldly ascetic and Protestant ethos (Weber) contributed to the survival of capitalism.[18] In the capitalist enterprise, production became the goal of production, namely self-purpose, which was the increasing and growing production. Growth is the characteristic mark of capitalism. The drive toward growth has a consequence of removing all limitations and barriers which can obstruct the expansion of capital on a domestic as well as global scale. The impersonal dynamic of capital, its expansion, and transformation into another

16. Ibid., 165–66.

17. Ibid., 142.

18. Ibid., 147.

form of industry or finance capital have shaped and guided the need of humanity, according to the need of capital expansion. What was brought in the capitalist mode of production is the removal of all barriers and elimination of all other economic forms, making capital the economic power of dominating the civil society in every respect.

In this light Gollwitzer characterizes capitalism as the greatest, the most radical revolution and also the most radical secularization that humanity has ever seen.[19] Capitalism spurs natural science, and vice versa. The principle of correspondence between capitalism and natural science leads us to overcome limitations in historical materialism in a linear causal explanation. Further, it purports to understand the process of human thought and science within the context of social process The way of labor is revolutionized through the advancement of natural science; productivity of labor and production of commodity are increased accordingly. Natural science received financial support through the state, industry, and society, without whose aid the triumphant marching on of capitalism would be hard to imagine. The omnipotence of the economy demands the omnipotence of objectifying natural science in the intellectual, cultural, and spiritual life.[20]

Through rationalization and emancipation capitalism has brought affirmative results to human life. This implies progress and a contribution related to the welfare of society. What the apologetics of capitalism defend is the condition of society's welfare. But we also stand before a threat resulting from what the capitalist revolution has brought. Colonial exploitation was tied to ecological exploitation in the historical context. The mono-cultures were imposed on colonized countries. The limitation of colonies to produce raw materials, the methods of private investment, and the payment of interest have caused the exploitation for the metropolis to be imposed over against the peripheries.[21]

Furthermore, racism must be understood along with the rise of capitalism. An ideology of racial domination incorporated beliefs in a particular race's cultural and biological inferiority. Racism is a sin against the Holy Spirit. Gollwitzer discussed the anti-racism-program of the WCC, taking seriously the claims of black theology. James Cone's thesis—there is no Black in the White theology—inspires self-critique for Gollwitzer himself to take into account the colonialism and slave trade undertaken in

19. Ibid., 151.

20. Ibid., 152.

21. Gollwitzer, *Christians and Lazarus*, 49.

European Christian context. Racism was bound with colonial imperialism of White people and Christian mission. Missionaries felt themselves as bringers of high culture and ethos in the missional context. However, the Pauline text contradicts this Eurocentric standpoint. Gal 3:28–"There is no longer Jew or Greek, there is no longer slave or free, there is no longer male and female; for all of you are one in Christ Jesus, And if you belong to Christ, then you are Abraham's offspring, heirs according to the promise"—is central to Gollwitzer's call for White theology to take the step of *metanoia* toward the liberating message of the gospel of Jesus Christ.[22]

METANOIA TOWARD GOD'S LIFE AND SHALOM

Having considered the complex relation between capitalist revolution, colonialism, and Christian mission, Gollwitzer did not sidestep Marx's critique of Christianity and his utopian messianism. A Christian response to Marxist messianism must be undertaken to emphasize the hope of Christian faith for making visible signs of the Kingdom of God on earth.[23] Seeing utopian messianism as an expression of the needs of the exploited people, Gollwitzer argues that Christians are invited to solidarity with those who fight against the structural violence of capitalist world-economy. Positively accepting the Marxist critique of Christianity as opium of the people, Gollwitzer strives to reinterpret the meaning of the gospel in light of the kingdom of God whose message unfortunately has been spiritualized or individualized in the subsequent development of church history. The church is always summoned by the gospel of the kingdom of God to transcend the limitations and setbacks of its history as that of greed, domination, and power. The church is not an end in itself, but lives in the 'not-yet,' eagerly pressing forward the coming of the kingdom of God by serving God's reign in Jesus Christ. The church's mission is always dependent on its origin, the gospel. However, most sources are not in agreement with the course of the river.[24]

The importance of the source in relation to the later development is hardly recognizable. In the course of historical development, new class interests, material interests, were added and expressed in terms of spiritual, psychological, and cultural need, mingling with the Christian message.

22. Gollwitzer, "Zur schwarzen Theologie," in Gollwitzer, . . . *Gerechtigkeit und Friede*, 208, 229.

23. Gollwitzer, *Christian Faith and Criticism*, 106.

24. Gollwitzer, *Introduction*, 109.

Nevertheless, the reality of the Kingdom of God as an effective power and theological subject matter stands despite all admixtures and all dilution. The message of the kingdom of God is antithetical to the church which is limited by its alliance with the dominant social powers in company with the injustice and violence of the social structure.[25]

In a critical study of capitalist revolution Gollwitzer argues that history must not mono-causally be reduced to the economic model of the mode of production. The transformation of the superstructure takes much longer than the change of economic basis. This applies to the global reality of late capitalism. The dialectical interconnection and interaction between the superstructure and basis shapes and influences human ideas, scientific theories, society, as well as politics. This perspective of totality does not concur with the formulation of the mode of production in terms of productive forces and interest of exploitation. There is also a "constant" in the superstructure which was not produced through a social material basis. Human language as the constant penetrates through all social changes. Gollwitzer's model of socio-historical inquiry transcends the Marxist thesis that language is conditioned by the standpoint of mode of production and productive forces.[26]

In contrast to a "vulgar" version of Marxist concepts of language, there was an endeavor to develop a theory of language on the relative independence of language. Language is not simply part of the ideological superstructure of society, nor is it part of the economic basis; therefore it has to be regarded as a relatively independent phenomenon between economic basis and ideological superstructure.

In theological reflection of revelation as language event, the theology of the word of God may improve on limitations of Marxist economic reductionism. In light of the word of God as the "constant," Gollwitzer articulates a socio-critical notion of the embeddedness of spiritual, intellectual life within the social material existence and regards individuals as the ensemble of social relations (see Marx's thesis on Feuerbach, no. 6). The spiritual, political, and religious problems are "in final instance" bound up with the development of capitalist production. Thus, a social history must not be understood in terms of the priority of the material over against the ideal. Socio-historical theory as a comprehensive method

---

25. Ibid., 112.
26. Gollwitzer, "Bemerkungen," in Gollwitzer, *Aufsätze*, 247.

must be conceptualized through the standpoint of the social, cultural, and economic totality.[27]

There are two essential moments in Gollwitzer's theological framework: theology from "above" (the Word of God connected with the gospel about the kingdom of God) and socio-historical hermeneutic from "below." The faith is taken in the Word of God if the faith speaks of the Word of God in human language. Socio-critical analysis as the method of inquiry of human social history may serve to embody the subject-matter of the gospel. Jesus's summons to *metanoia* provides us with an opportunity to renew the present social system and undergird public discipleship. Gospel remains "constant" in socio-critical analysis of human desire, economic interest, and political dominion. A heuristic method of the socio-historical hermeneutic is incorporated within the theological subject matter of the gospel, such scientific critical method and interpretation is considered as a surplus value of the gospel.

The revolutionary implication comes from the confrontation of the prophets in the Hebrew Bible with social misery and from the synoptic gospel of Jesus Christ in solidarity with public sinners and tax collectors. The proclamation of the coming of the kingdom of God, which is at the center of Jesus' message, is glad tidings for those who were excluded from salvation and also for all standing without hope and under the suppression of social and religious relations. The message of the kingdom of God grasps the entire performance of life. In Hebrew, *malkuth* YHWH can be understood primarily in a verbal sense: God's reign; secondarily the condition and sphere of this divine reign.[28] God's reign in the full sense is only present where the last enemy, death, is overcome (1 Cor 15:26; Rev 21:4) and where we thank God "face to face" without reserve (1 Cor 13:12).

The translation of *metanoia* as repentance is too narrow to grasp its profound and comprehensive meaning. The term repentance tends to reduce the comprehensive understanding of the kingdom of God to the forgiveness and justification of the sinner in an individualistic manner. The kingdom of God which Jesus addressed has to do with the transformation of life in the face of death. It demands life performance before God and fellow humans. The kingdom of God is the life of God and in relationship with fellow-humans so that "turning away" from the previous life has to do with the kingdom of God. Those who turn away can live in the relation of forgiveness, reconciliation, and justice. New creation is established by

27. Ibid., 252.

28. Gollwitzer, *Introduction*, 142.

God, grounded in gratitude, faith, hope, and joy for God. The message of the gospel about the kingdom of God entails a radical life-transforming implication.[29]

In Philemon 1:16 we read of the transformation of the relationship between the lord and slave in the Christian community, which is profound and even revolutionary as measured up to the standard of that time. The slave is elevated from the *instrumentum animatum* to a beloved brother— "both in the flesh and in the Lord." However, the subversive dimension of the gospel has unfortunately been domesticated by colonialism, capitalism, and imperialism which have brought humanity to catastrophe through structural greed, inhumanity, and political power and privilege.

The resurrection of Jesus means the promise (John 12:24) for the disciples to become yeast (Matt 13:33), salt and light (Matt 5:13). For this new life and mission of the gospel, the "turning away" embraces the whole human life and commitment (Matt 6:33; Mark 10:30). The invitation to the gospel of the kingdom of God is universally relevant in protest to the dominion of death. Based on the universality of the gospel, the disciples came into special solidarity with those who were marginalized, alienated, and excluded, because the kingdom of God belongs to them (Luke 6:20–21).

In the coming of the kingdom of God change and renewal of life is performed. This is announced as the first fruits of the Spirit, *arabon* (Rom 8: 23). The kingdom of God is the eschatological definition of who and what God of Israel is in connection with the resurrection of Jesus Christ. The deed of God and the deed of humanity are not in exclusive concurrence, but the divine action realizes itself in human action in terms of yeast, salt, and light. The human being is a created co-worker with God for the sake of the peace, righteousness, and reconciliation of God's reign. The current life performance of *metanoia* and discipleship corresponds to the life in the coming kingdom of God. This correspondence refers to a line and direction which comes from the gospel embodied in the life and mission of Jesus.

In the struggle for social justice and political freedom the political responsibility of the Christian community is to be faithful to the movement of endless approximation, perpetual self-reforming in faithfulness to the great revolution and emancipation of the kingdom of God: "Thy will be done on earth as it is in heaven."[30] This prayer guides and characterizes

29. Gollwitzer, "Kapitalistische Revolution," 192–94.
30. Gollwitzer, *Introduction*, 153.

our hope in the coming of God's universal reign and shalom which must be carried out in the area of economy and politics.

THEOLOGICAL ALTERNATIVES FOR THE LIFE OF PEOPLE

Representing the tradition of the Confessing Church, and also keeping in solidarity with the liberating mission of God's life, Duchrow proposes a prophetic theology for the transformation of modern man (*homo oeconomicus*). Also he structures towards socio-economic justice as an alternative to global capitalism. Theologically, Duchrow's contribution is grounded in his creative interpretation of Lutheran theology of the two kingdoms in terms of social responsibility and engagement as well as in a contextual, liberationist re-reading of the Bible. In the discussion of the public sphere, Lutheran theology often has been caricatured as being submissive to the economic or political status quo, or vulnerable to sanctioning the reality of injustice.[31]

Regrettably, we are aware that there are many examples that give credence to this evaluation, most notably in the case of the German church under Nazism, as well as the legacies of Lutheranism that were passed on through mission movements around the world. In contrast to the conservative quietism of Lutheran theology, Duchrow did pioneering work on reinterpreting and advocating a more prophetic side of Luther's insights in a convincing way.[32]

Theologically, Duchrow emphasizes ancient Israel, the Jesus movement, and the early Church as counter–cultural experiments in which resistance to the absoluteness of the empire becomes an important part. Biblical recollection of the future of life remains central for Duchrow's theology of life and justice by critically engaging in the socio-economic and political-ideological context of the biblical traditions. Duchrow's basic thesis can be expressed: "God's new act of liberation and the building of the alternative society begin among the excluded, the impoverished and the oppressed."[33]

Analyzing the money-interest-property economy in the Jewish-Christian tradition, Duchrow focuses on ancient Israel's struggle with the fast expansion of the money economy observed in the Ancient Near East in the eighth century BCE. The Holiness Code of the book of Leviticus in

31. Duchrow, *Lutheran Churches*.

32. Duchrow, *Chritsenheit und Weltverantwortung*.

33. Duchrow, *Alternatives*, 184.

the sixth century affirms that the earth belongs to God and property must be used for all the earth's inhabitants (Lev 25:23). Here the jubilee year is underscored (Lev 25:6–28).

The Hebrew prophets since Amos (late eighth century) and the legal texts since the so-called Book of Covenant (Exodus 21–23; approximately early seventh century) become an important biblical resource for economic justice. Amos, Hosea, Isaiah, Micah, Jeremiah, Ezekiel and others call for justice and righteousness, standing in solidarity with those who are lost through new property rights and money mechanisms. Faith in YHWH, the God of Israel, is identical with doing justice to the poor (Jer 22:16; Micah 2:1). The prophetic interventions of the eighth and seventh centuries were seen in their endeavor to undertake the legal reforms from this time and later. The so-called Book of Covenant (Exodus 21–23) entails the codified result of this legal reform and Deuteronomy retains the core. An economy using money for exchange, seen in the context of Deuteronomy (Deut 14:24–26), must not be led to its destructive forms. The prohibition against taking interest and pawns are found in the Covenant Code (Exod 22:24–26) while God's protection of the Levites, the resident aliens, the orphans, and the widows are underscored, using tithes to serve an annual people's festival and the social balancing for those members on the margins (Deut 14: 28). In Deut 8:16 the story of manna is illustrated which can also be seen in Lord's prayer: "Give us this day our daily bread."

This socio-critical tradition continues after the collapse of monarchy during the Babylonian exile and the Persian times which is highlighted in the apocalyptic writings in the Hellenistic period. Summarizing, one can say he sees four ways in the Hebrew Bible to form a contrast to society depending on the contextual circumstances: forming an alternative society built on family and tribe solidarity (1250–1000 BCE), prophetic critique during the monarchic time (1000–587 BCE), legal reforms after the introduction of the money-property-economy as much as possible (since the eighth century BCE), resistance once this economy becomes totalitarian in the context of the Hellenistic-Roman empires. The messianic writings of the Second Testament represented this critical standpoint in the context of the Roman Empire by sharpening it and adding the fifth way of building small alternative communities linked in a network.[34]

Continuing God's liberating act, Jesus as the incarnation of the kingdom of God represents and embodies the Son of Man, "the Human One" (Daniel 7; Mark 10:45) in terms of service and solidarity with those who

34. Ibid. part II.

are marginalized and impoverished. Jesus confronts those who do damage to the poor by the monetary system, the money changers. He also provokes those who profit from the market system, trading with pigeons, the sacrificial animals for the poor, while stopping the whole ritual of sacrifice. Subsequently, Jesus' messianic movement and communities carried this out by including all peoples, slaves and women, living together in mutual koinonia and equality.[35]

As the money-property economy and imperial structures of antiquity form a predecessor of modern capitalism and imperialism it is possible to develop the insights drawn from biblical history towards a critique of modernity. Economically, Duchrow challenges the idea of the capitalist possessive market society established in the modern age. Utilizing Karl Polanyi's view of refuting the liberal and neo-classical economic theories, Duchrow insists that the market is not a universal social and anthropological phenomenon. There were peoples and cultures which coordinated their economies and economic relations in the form of reciprocity or redistribution. The Greek philosopher Aristotle remains a good example for Polanyi and Duchrow. In the Hellenistic property-money economy of the fourth century BCE, Aristotle drew a conclusion: property was for practical use. He patterned the economy and ownership on the life of persons and individuals in the community while he strongly rejected the acquisition of goods and money for its own sake. Trading and charging interest were the two illegitimate ways by which to accumulate property for its own sake. Aristotle's difference between the need-oriented household economy and the money-accumulation economy remains an important insight because property and goods can be regarded as means of nourishing and sustaining life; they are intended for practical use.[36] Given this fact, an isolation of the economy from ethics and politics, as seen in liberalism and neo-liberalism becomes questionable for Aristotle's view.[37]

Thomas Hobbes and John Locke, as the theoreticians of the possessive market society, have come into question. Unlike Aristotle, Locke attempted to justify unrestricted accumulation, amassing possessions through the rampant mechanism of money-accumulation.[38] Along with Polanyi, and against the tradition of Hobbes and Locke, Duchrow emphasizes that the economic system of the domestic market is embedded in

---

35. Ibid., 202.

36. Ibid., 21.

37. Duchrow and Hinkelammert, *Property for People*, 163.

38. Duchrow, *Alternatives*, 45.

the framework of social relations; the market is not a historical and social necessity.

Furthermore, Duchrow accepts Arrighi's analysis of the historical emergence of capitalism and its major historical phases. This analysis raises the question of when and why productive capitalism was replaced by finance-dominated capitalism. In this light, it is important to keep in mind the connection between the state's power and economic expansion in the case of the Dutch East India Company and the English East India Company. This perspective includes the triangular trade: finished products from Europe, slaves from Africa and raw materials from Latin America.[39]

THE POSSESSIVE MARKET PRINCIPLE AND ECONOMIC GLOBALIZATION

Along with the stage of capitalist globalization, a type of absolutism envisioned in John Locke appears in a new type of neo-liberal thinkers today. The reality of the total market demonstrates that globalized capitalism eliminates the commitment to sustaining life. Private property in the context of neo-liberal globalization destroys natural life, environment, and social cohesion. Casino capitalism grounded in maximizing profits appears at the stage of neoliberal globalization and dominates world economy by speculative finance capital.[40] This is an ideological weapon of death against the life of God. Duchrow defines empire as the visible hand of the absolute possessive market.[41]

The neo-liberal ideology of the absolute market is often presented as the only viable option in today's civilization. The global empire tied to global capital tries to eliminate every obstacle to total domination under the capitalist market. In this regard, the theory of the empire (Negri and Hardt) is insufficient in revealing the imperialism of nation states. Renewing the limitations of empire theory built on biopolitical sovereignty, Duchrow focuses on critically analyzing unlimited wealth accumulation at a global scale. Imperial globalization dismantles every social and environmental restraint or obligation.[42] Against the empire of globalization aimed at the boundless accumulation of capital, Duchrow presents its alternative through rebuilding the system of ownership from below for the

39. Ibid., 27.
40. Duchrow and Hinkelammert, *Property for People,* 97.
41. Ibid., 106.
42. Ibid., 107.

sake of communal life and the common good. This perspective underlies a prophetic theology that strengthens the church's mission of God's life for the sake of economic balance, people's rights of dignity, and ecological sustainability.

The story of the Exodus (Exodus 3) shapes the great example in which the God of Israel heard the cries of the slaves, the oppressed, and the poor, and liberated them from the slave-owner, the oppressor and the rich. The God of Israel is the God of life, dismantling the gods of power and principalities which call for human sacrifice. In a period of a monarchy from c.1030 to 586 BCE a new socio-economic order was instituted as a property-based economy. The critical voice of the prophets was that all must be able to live. The biblical perspective on justice and life was inseparably bound with the reality of the poor, the victim, and the loser whose livelihood is threatened. A theological epistemology based on the God of justice and life is directed against the irrationality of the seemingly rational in the civilization of imperial globalization, which leads to the instrumental logic of greed, dominion and self-destruction.[43]

Critically viewing Weber's ethical concept of conviction and responsibility, Duchrow insists that Weber's ethics of responsibility legitimizes institutionalized irresponsibility. It tends to succumb to the functional ethics of liberalism and neo-liberalism. A new ethical concept of life and the common good must start from the view point of the victims of the system (people and the earth) and must be rooted in the material question of communal life. Discourse ethics about the communicative structures of rationality (in Habermas' fashion) comes along with the ethics of life and the common good emphasizing the rights of the victim in the globalized context.

Beyond Habermas's construction of communicative ethics, Duchrow's ethical configuration is more biblically grounded in terms of the God of Exodus and connected with reconstruction of the discourse of the voiceless, the fragile, and the vulnerable in the public sphere of world economy.

Marx's proposal of the cancellation of private property led to the dead end of centralist state socialism. However, Marx's analysis of society through the fetishization of goods, money, and capital still remains significant. Following and developing Aristotle's critical line of thought, Marx unveiled the mechanism of money accumulation in terms of the analysis of the fetishism of commodities and capital. According to the theory of

43. Ibid., 158.

fetishism, rules, institutions, and power relationships have developed in various periods in history and they have governed the division of labor and the distribution of goods within social realms.[44]

Capitalist society destroys the proactive and creative character of human beings and solidarity among them through competition. This perspective provides a significant insight according to which institutions, politics, and forms of action are formed, starting from the real life of people and remaining in harmony with nature.[45] Nevertheless, Marx's mistakes and Eurocentrism cause his theory of the capitalist mode of production to remain seriously limited in the post-socialist era and shows itself as an unqualified and insufficient tool in the context of the neoliberal principle of economic globalization and its empire.

STATUS CONFESSIONIS AND THE ECONOMIC FIELD

In the midst of imperial globalization, it is essential to actualize the legacy of the confessing church. Dietrich Bonhoeffer remains a theological mentor for Duchrow's faith journey. Bonhoeffer, in the face of a totalitarian state, argues that the church must seize the wheel itself (rather than being satisfied with binding up the wounds of the victims beneath the wheel) for the sake of the victims who fall under the wheels of a coach driven by a drunken driver.[46] To promote the significance of church's resistance against the dictatorship of the state and world economy, Duchrow takes seriously Bonhoeffer's address on "The Church and the Jewish Question" (1933). This address was Bonhoeffer's classic statement of resistance against the racist policy of the Nazi regime.[47]

In a 1933 address Bonhoeffer articulated the church's mandate in relationship with the state. According to him, the church has no right to interfere directly with the political actions of the state. However, the church is summoned to act when the state does not serve to maintain law and order in a legitimate way. This summons becomes important when there is either too much or too little law and order. In the case of too much law and order, the state develops its excessive power and deprives Christian preaching and Christian faith. Then the state enthrones itself. Against this,

---

44. Duchrow, *Alternatives*, 39.

45. Duchrow and Hinkelammert, *Property for People*, 166.

46. "The Church and the Jewish Question" in Dietrich Bonhoeffer Works, vol.12. 365.

47. Ibid., 349–70.

the church must reject the encroachment of the state which negates the right of the church.[48]

Bonhoeffer proposed three possibilities for the church's action toward the state. Firstly, the church can ask the state whether its actions are legitimate and in accordance with its character as a state. Secondly, the church can help those who are victimized by the state action. Regardless of whether the victims are Christians or non-Christians, the church stands under an unconditional obligation to the victims in the society.[49] Thirdly, the church should not just bandage the victims under the wheel, but seize the wheel itself. Such action is direct political action. It becomes meaningful when the state unrestrainedly brings about too much or too little law and order. If any group of subjects are deprived of their rights, there would be too little law. There would be too much when the state intervened in the proclamation of the church; for instance, the forced exclusion of baptized Jews from the church or the prohibition of the church's missional solidarity with the Jews. At this point the church finds itself in *status confessionis*. The state is in the act of negating itself. [50]

Status confessionis means that the church must make a clear decision by taking a strong stand. The church must be committed to giving witness to Christ in real-life situations. The Confessing Church in the struggle against "German Christians" in the 1930s recognized the existence of a *status confessionis* (a necessity of demanding a clear and costly confession of the faith). Evangelization in the spirit of *status confessionis* is speaking the truth with audacity (*parrhesia*) about the lordship of God in the political and economic realm.

In opposition to National Socialist Neo-Lutherans, Bonhoeffer proposed the counter thesis of the *status confessionis* in face of "too much" interference of the state in the church's life. Bonhoeffer's theology of resistance challenges the failure of the state to fulfill its mandate ("too little") to protect the Jewish citizens.

Following in the footsteps of Bonhoeffer, and also in parallel with Helmut Gollwitzer, article 3 of the Barmen Theological Declaration

48. Ibid., 139.

49. Ibid.

50. Ibid. "Missional solidarity" is an euphemism; in fact, in "The Church and the Jewish Question" Bonhoeffer, like Karl Barth and the Confessing Church in the years of the German "church struggle" is a representative of Christian mission to the Jews without any reservations; it is true that in his subjective perspective mission to the Jews was meant as an act of "solidarity."

remains central for Duchrow to actualize a prophetic legacy of the confessing church today in confrontation with global economy.

> The Christian church is the community of brothers and [sisters] in which Jesus Christ acts presently as Lord in word and sacrament by the Holy Spirit. As the church of pardoned sinners, . . . it has to witness by its faith and obedience, its message and order . . . that it lives and desires to live only by his consolation and by his orders, in expectation of his coming.
> We reject the false doctrine that the church is permitted to form its own message or its order according to its own desire or according to prevailing philosophical or political convictions.[51]

Therefore, for Duchrow, questions of economic order are not only ethical issues, but questions of faith, provoking a *status confessionis*. This is a confessional protest where the nature of the gospel and Christian freedom are at stake. Duchrow emphasizes that the third article of the Barmen declaration must be embodied and refined in respect to a global economic system which is a major reason for mass slaughter. The most stubborn resistance is met where economic interests and injustice are at stake. The death of over thirty million people from starvation on an annual basis is the secret mass-murderer in our day and the shame of our civilization. The church of the poor or in solidarity with the poor becomes a confessional issue. The issue of the injustice of the global economic system is not merely an ethical argument, but it is tied to the first commandment of the Decalogue, the quintessence of the gospel (Luther). The obedience of faith to the God of life in Exodus rejects the principle of mammon in the global economic system.[52]

In the *processus (status) confessionis,* which means an ongoing dialogue in ecumenical council, Duchrow proposes that the church must publicly and unequivocally reject: 1) The global market which is permeated by the empire and its institutions under the rule of the idol of greed, dominion and power. 2) All religious, mostly individualistic, forms of piety and faith which justify and legitimize imperialist power along with the politically deregulated mechanism of global capitalism.

Accordingly, the church in the *processus confessionis* must take practical steps in the following ways: 1) The reserves of the *status confessionis* must be invested with social and ecological responsibility. 2) The fund of the church should be withdrawn from all commercial banks which engage

---

51. Duchrow, *Global Economy*, 97.

52. Ibid., 108–11.

in financial transactions for property accumulation on the transnational markets. We need to invest it in cooperatives, local and regional banks or alternative banks which invest responsibly in social and ecological causes. 3) Churches should also provoke their congregations and members to the same in regard to banks and companies. Setting a good example to the world (Luther) means the church's responsibility for the economic and political institutions in this context. This prophetic view leads to creating small-scale networked alternatives and viable economic policy for enhancing life by encouraging the church to be a congregational mission and missionary effect. The church as "city on the hill," "salt of the earth" and "light to the peoples" becomes the mission community by attraction as the Pauline communities of Jesus the Messiah did under the Roman Empire.[53]

For Duchrow mission of God's life means that the structural injustice and privilege of global economy must be incorporated into a confessional issue for the churches. Churches must see their own financial practices as a theological-confessional problem. Emphasizing the prophetic legacy of Luther in his struggle with the unjust structure of early capitalism, Duchrow advocates for undertaking a way of *metanoia* in critical regard to the "Christian character" of capital accumulation undertaken in the sixteenth century colonies.

In the study of God's mission and justice, theological ethics and economic order must be reconstructed, taking issue with the mystification of power and the market. Theological ethics are concerned with the enhancement of life in all its fullness.[54] According to Duchrow, the hermeneutic of the gospel leads the church to build a new kind of social order based on the household of God. Evangelization is our discursive activity with the truth of the gospel, which addresses the issue of the global economy audaciously and fearlessly.

> If the heresy of the 'German Christians' in the time of the Nazi Third Reich was their blasphemous misuse of Christ's name to extend the power of the German Aryan 'master race' the question put us today is . . . Where is Christ's name being directly or indirectly (mis)used to justify and maintain the power of the white race, especially that of its wealthy and powerful representatives,

---

53. Duchrow, *Alternatives*, 266.

54. For appreciation of Duchrow's theology of economic justice, see Gorringe, *Capital and Kingdom*, 141. Also see Rieger, *No Rising*, 123–24.

by every available kind of propaganda, economic manipulation and military and other forms of violence.[55]

THE ECUMENICAL CHURCHES' ENGAGEMENT WITH ECONOMIC JUSTICE

Challenging to today's reality of economic globalization, ecumenical churches begin to raise their critical voice to the inhuman and anti-ecological consequences of economic globalization. Since the end of the nineties of the 20th century the World Alliance of Reformed Churches (WARC), the World Council of Churches (WCC), and the Lutheran World Federation (LWF) have committed to recognition, education, and confession in critical view of economic injustice and ecological destruction. Global economy is inseparably linked with global ecology. The ruin of the ecosphere causes devastation of all economies.

In a 1995 document of the World Alliance of Reformed Churches we read:

> Today, the global market economy has been sacralized and elevated to an imperial throne . . . .It is our painful conclusion that the African reality of poverty caused by an unjust economic world order has gone beyond an ethical problem and become a theological one. It now constitutes a *status confessionis*.[56]

Since the process of economic globalization perpetuates itself, the Lutheran World Federation (LWF) in its 10th Assembly in 2003 came to the conclusion:

> As a communion, we must engage the false ideology of neo-liberal economic globalization by confronting, converting, and changing this reality and its effects. This false ideology is grounded on the assumption that the market, built on private property, unrestrained competition and the centrality of contracts, is the absolute law governing human life, society, and the natural environment. This is idolatry and leads to the systematic exclusion of those who own no property, the destruction of

---

55. Duchrow, *Global Economy*, 125. There is a further dimension to the needed critique and transformation of the status quo, i.e. the anthropological and psychological aspect. (To be elaborated from "Solidarisch Mensch werden).

56. Duchrow and Hinkelammert, *Property for People*, 206.

cultural diversity, the dismantling of fragile democracies, and the destruction of the earth.[57]

God in Christ sets us in relationship with one another. This theology of communion undergirds a sense of relatedness, responsibility, and accountability; we are called to advocate for the sake of justice, solidarity, and the flourishing of the life system on earth.

In 2004 at its 24th General Council in Accra, Ghana, the World Alliance of Reformed Churches (WARC) made a confession in the tradition of the Barmen Theological Declaration against Nazism (1934). It is the clearest document in the ecumenical movement so far.

> We believe that God is sovereign over all creation. "The earth is the Lord's and the fullness thereof" (Psalm 24.1). Therefore, we reject the current world economic order imposed by global neoliberal capitalism . . . We reject any claim of economic, political, and military empire which subverts God's sovereignty over life and acts contrary to God's just rule.[58]

The WCC in its AGAPE Document for its 9th Assembly in Porto Alegre, Brazil in 2006, "Alternative Globalization Addressing People and Earth"[59] captures the results of a seven-year global study process of the church's response to economic globalization, particularly through the 2003 assembly of LWF and the 2004 general council of WARC. The AGAPE proposes alternatives to economic globalization: 1) Working for the eradication of poverty and inequality through developing economies of solidarity and sustainable communities. 2) Working for justice in international trade relations through critical analyses of free trade and trade negotiations in collaboration with social movements. 3) Campaigning for responsible lending, unconditional debt cancellation and the control and regulation of global financial markets. Investments redirected toward businesses respecting social and ecological justice against the business of speculation and tax evasion. 4) Engagement in action for sustainable use of land and natural resources, in solidarity with indigenous peoples seeking to protect their land, water and communities. 5) Joining the global struggle against the imposed privatization of public goods and services. 6) Working for life-giving agriculture by land reforms in solidarity with

---

57. Online: http://www.lwf-assembly.org/PDFs/LWF_Assembly_Message-EN.pdf, 17ff.

58. Rieger, *No Rising*, 126.

59. *God, in Your Grace . . .* , 218–23.

landless agricultural laborers and small farm holders. Opposition to the production of genetically modified organisms (GMOs) and promotion of ecological farming practices and solidarity with peasant communities. 7) Building alliances with social movements and trade unions advocating decent jobs, just wages, emancipated work, and people's livelihood. 8) Reflection on the question of power and empire from a biblical and theological perspective, taking a firm faith stance against hegemonic powers. The church should be accountable to the victims of economic globalization, in keeping with the gospel.[60]

An All-African Consultation on Poverty, Wealth, and Ecology took place in Dar es Salaam, Tanzania (November 5–9, 2007). The preamble denounces neo-liberal economic globalization; the wealth of the countries of the North was built and sustained on the continued extraction and plunder of Africa's resources as well as the exploitation of African people.

We also read in the present proposal by the Ecumenical Network in Germany the ecumenical declaration on *Just Peace*. Today's crisis is revealed in the form of the financial and economic crisis, in the food crisis, the social crisis on a global scale, the energy crisis, the climate crisis, the crisis of the extinction of species and the crisis of increasing violence at all levels. These crises are caused by the dominant civilization and rationality of the west, which has conquered the entire globe in the areas of economics, politics, and ideology. The necessary turnaround toward a life in just peace includes at least three dimensions: 1) a spiritual vision of a new, emerging culture of life, based on faith or a humanist motivation, 2) the fundamental rejection of the dominant economic, political, violence-producing culture and world order, for the sake of the integrity of faith and the very being of the church, and 3) short, medium, and long-term steps toward realizing this vision.

In the WCC study, *Justice Not Greed*, we read the church's common effort to analyze and seek solutions to the current financial and economic system. The current system and mechanism of global capitalism is critiqued as aggravating inequality, poverty, and ecological destruction, rather than addressing them. World economy giants, powerful oligopolies, less transparent networks of financial institutions, and production enterprises have increased the purchasing power of an emerging global middle class. This middle class is tuned in by advertising through all media and consumer satisfaction.[61]

---

60. Ibid., 221–23.

61. Brubaker and Mshna, *Justice Nor Greed*, 21.

Church and Ethical Responsibility in the Midst of World Economy

As we study the ecumenical church's endeavor for ethical responsibility and economic justice in the midst of the world economy, it is important for us to emphasize the socio-critical meaning of the Word of God for the still unredeemed world. The church's ethical responsibility in the context of global economic empire has an important task to promote distributive justice, restorative justice, and ecological justice. Such justice can be an alternative to the mechanisms of greed and dominion which are associated with the structural injustice of capital accumulation and empire.

East Asian Religions and Social Justice

We live in the midst of global complexity, confusion, and whirl. An ethics of peace, compassion, justice, and rectification of the integrity of life in a global-ecumenical context can be developed by learning from moral and ethical sources of great religious traditions which facilitate improving on the inadequacy and poverty of Westerncentric ethics.

As we have already examined, Duchrow has now started to enlarge the scope of alternatives by engaging in inter-religious solidarity building for justice. He does so by starting from a contextual re-reading of the theory of Axial Age (including Islam as a second wave of the Axial Age), which was developed by Karl Jaspers.[1] A model of "Axial Age" which is interested in exploring a basic turning point in human history during the period of 800–200 BCE emphasizes the inspirations of ancient cultures and faiths for coping with the present crisis of global capitalism and its destructive ramifications. "Axial sages" are looked to for inspiration in search of elements of a new humanness and culture of life. [2] All the sages instructed a spirituality of empathy and compassion, denouncing egotism, violence, and rudeness. Respect for the sacred rights of all beings—for example, in the Confucian maxim "do not do to others what you would not have done unto you"—led people to kindness, generosity, and ethical virtue to their fellows. Confucian ethic of *shu* (receptivity, often translated as "reciprocal" or "the Golden Rule") is the kind of attitude towards others

---

1. Duchrow, "Against Neo-liberal Greed."
2. Armstrong, *Great Transformation.*

that a person has when he or she is reciprocal, caring about others in the way in which he wants them to care about him (or her). This Confucian ethical virtue is in accordance with the "golden rule" in the Sermon on the Mount (Matt 7:12): "In everything do to others as you would have them do to you; for this is the law and the prophets." A vision of "the emphatic civilization"[3] based on the model of Axial Age can be complemented in the analysis of compassion, justice, and a dominion-free society in Asian religions.

In this way a multicultural theological-ethical approach which undergirds the integrity of life in creation and articulation of moral good is of importance in shaping and directing comparative religious ethics for the sake of global dynamics and ethical humanism, in contrast to the modernist assumption of overhumanization and the postmodern trend of anti-humanism.[4] The comparative religious perspective in an ethical-hermeneutical framework makes a norm of moral action and church's ethics of responsibility more amenable to the idea of integrity of life and economic justice before God in a multidimensional sense of goodness. An ethic of the Other or an ethic in learning from the Other helps the church's ethical responsibility to respect, deepen, and enhance the integrity of life in all actions and relations and provide orientation and guidance for life.[5]

In the current ecumenical endeavor for promotion of a new alternative to economic globalization, we observe an emphasis on cooperation with other faith communities. In 2007 the World Council of Churches and the Council for World Mission (CWM) jointly organized a consultation at Changseong, South Korea entitled: "Transforming Theology and Life-Giving Civilization." The ancient Asian concept of *sangsaeng* is used as a wisdom of "sharing community and economic together." *Sangsaeng*, a key concept of classic Daoism, thickly describes a meaning of "peace." The word peace in Chinese parlance consists of two characters: equality and sharing of rice (a symbol of material, bodily life). Peace in the Chinese sense comes true where distribution of rice is realized in a harmonious and fair way. Peace without a sense of economic equilibrium remains abstract.

Sangseng originally means communal convivence or symbiotic existence of haves and have-nots (in the context of *Dao-de-jing*). This term extends to life in a web of all creatures, even implying co-existence of all in the cosmos. The Buddhist term of inter-being matches with the Daoist

---

3. Rifkin, *Empathic Civilization*.

4. Schweiker, *Theological Ethics and Global Dynamics*, xi.

5. Ibid., xiv–xxi.

term of *Sangseng*, further developed in the core Buddhist epistemology of *li-shi wu-ai* and *shi-shi wu-ai*, a central doctrine of Hua-yen Buddhism in China. According to the paradigm of *shi-shi wu-ai* in Hua-yen Sutra: harmonious interrelation of all things is seen as if reflected on a vast ocean (*shi-shi wu-ai*) while mind as suchness is compared to an ocean whose originally tranquil surface is stirred up into waves by the wind of ignorance (*li-shi wu-ai*). The former refers to the unobstructed interpenetration of each and every phenomena while the latter refers to the unobstructed interpenetration of the absolute and phenomenal.[6]

The principle of Dao penetrates the life of all things which in turn penetrate each other. At the moment of enlightenment there is no obstacle to mutual penetration between the principle of Dao and all things. And also no obstacles lie in the web of all lives. Peace grounded in economic inter-being or mutual penetration implies a concept of becoming, organically connected with a symbiotic life of the cosmic body. To produce rice, it requires the labor of the farmer, the fertilized soil, wind, water, and all other natural elements involved in the process of growth and fruit of the rice. Because of the cosmic involvement in producing rice, the rice is likened to heaven. As heaven is not monopolized by the hands of a few, so rice is shared by all. Classic Daoism, Mahayana Buddhism, and Confucianism in East Asia have no difficulty in concurring with a communally shared and mutually caring sense of peace and economic life, because economic greed and dominion are not valued in this religious cultural context. For the empathic civilization it is decisive for us to explore a spiritual, ethical, and social inspiration and compassion to overcome limitations of Western modernization and its economic global culture. Such an exploration is to bring the resources and wisdoms of a great religious tradition to bear on the critical issues of our turbulent time.

SANGSENG AND A DOMINION-FREE SYSTEM OF SOCIETY

From the perspective of classic Daoism the mystery of the permanent Dao is connected with a principle of action without attachment to it; the aspect of the green grace of nature is elaborated with the life style of a

---

6. *Li-shi wu-ai* emphasizes the priority of the principle (Li) in relation to the phenomena of external affairs of all (shi), while *shi-shi wu-ai* confluences the principle with the phenomena of external affairs of all. Gregory, *Tsung-mi and the Sinification of Buddhism*, 68.

watercourse without enforcement or coercion.[7] Dao's embrace of those who are both good and evil can be seen in the Daoist way of harmony with nature. Dao not only justifies human life but also life in nature. In this regard, a re-envisioning of God's grace of justification may be undertaken in the direction of articulating an aesthetical theology of creation in harmony with an ecological life.

In the Daoist vision of dominion-free society, it is worth noting that classical Daoist philosophy is built on the two texts of Laozi (also called *Dao-de-jing*) and Zhuangzi, of whose lives little is historically known. According to the cultural legend, Laozi was regarded as an elder contemporary of Confucius (551–479 BCE). In classic Daoism, Dao is discussed in topics ranging from the mystery of being, human life, society, and politics toward ontology of nature (Self-so). A political view in *Dao-de-jing* becomes obvious, as Laozi argues that when the great Way is abandoned and falls into disuse, the virtues of human heartedness and morality (righteousness) arise. When family discord is rife, the duty of obedience and kindness come forth. When the State falls into disorder and misrule, loyal subjects appear (ch. 18). According to Laozi's political vision,

> there might still be boats and carriages, but no one would go in them; there might still be weapons of war but no one would drill with them . . . the people . . . should be contented with their food, pleased with their clothing, satisfied with their homes . . . ; but the people would grow old and die without ever having been there. (Ch.80)

Laozi's political idea is expressed in the context of Zhuangzi in the following way.

> Laozi said, 'when an enlightened king governs his state, his meritorious deeds are felt all over the world but they do not seem to be out of his efforts; his influence reaches everyone but the people do not feel that they depend on him; his achievements are not attributed to him but all the people enjoy themselves; he is shrouded in mystery and wanders in the land of nonexistence.[8]

This dominion-free vision is embedded within a political interest in creating a social reality without violence and coercion; this aims at a shalom community which is still out of our reach. This open-ended perspective on

7. Lao Tzu, *Tao Te Ching*, ch.2.
8. *Zhungzhi I*, 117–18.

shalom community demonstrates a political philosophy of Laozi running in a dominion-free and direct democratic manner which is analogous to Rousseau. The Daoist metaphor of the feminine in the biological-generative sense affirms nature which implies the state of infancy. It connects the world of nature to its source of life in which the feminine functions as the symbol of non-action and spontaneity. The key to the relationship between *yin* and *yang* is called *sangseng*, mutual arising or inseparability (Ch. 2). Everything and everybody is in mutual sequence and connection. Dao personified as mother is not only tolerant and life-giving but also ruthless and inhuman in response to human attempts to artificially manipulate and ruin nature (Ch. 5).

This refers to nature's response to the human attempts to master nature through artificial technology, because nature, in a Daoist sense, is a living organism in the web of interconnection of all lives. Laozi's exaltation of femininity spoke out against all the patriarchal thinking of his contemporaries; this implies a fact which witnesses to the subversive and even revolutionary component in the *Dao-de-jing*. Lying low in stillness, the female overcomes the male (Ch. 61). In Laozi's favorite image of Dao, water is the essence of life, benefiting all living creatures in the harmonious web. If everything is allowed to go its own way, the harmony of the universe will be established; every process in the world can do its own thing only in relation to all other things. Because of the mutual interdependence of all beings, harmony will emerge from itself, without external compulsion. This is the Daoist understanding of peace in harmonious connection with the other, aiming at a society of emancipation from greed, privilege, and dominion.

Confucian Ethics and the Right of Resistance

Within the framework of Confucianism, the Daoist concept of *sangseng* is specifically met with an ethical mandate and faithfulness to humanness. For Confucius, a doctrine of rectification of names undergirds the political concept of resistance, finding its strength in Mencius. According to Confucian teaching, rectification of names articulates one's roles in the web of relationships that create community, and behaving accordingly so as to ensure social harmony. Since social harmony is of utmost importance in Confucian ethics, society would crumble without the proper rectification of names.

According to Confucius in *Analects* (XIII.13.3), if names are not correct, language is not in accordance with the truth of things. If language is not in accordance with the truth of things, affairs cannot be carried on to success. "If what is to be done cannot be effected, then rites and music will not flourish. If rites and music do not flourish, then mutilations and lesser punishments will go astray. And if mutilations and lesser punishments go astray, then the people have nowhere to put hand or foot. "Therefore the gentleman uses only such language as is proper for speech, and only speaks of what it would be proper to carry into effect."

This Confucian notion of the rectification of names was developed by Mencius in a broader spectrum, not only in interpersonal relationships but also at the political and institutional level for the sake of mutual co-existence between the ruler and the people in a righteous manner. Mencius (371–289 BCE) lived in ancient China surrounded by disorder and intellectual confusion, and continued to perpetuate the teaching of Confucius. As Confucius remained a transmitter of ancient teaching for the Confucian school, so Mencius created the Confucian teaching through transmitting. However, the uniqueness in Mencius's philosophy is in his establishment of political and social philosophy on behalf of the people. His orientation for the life of people came to support political rights against the dictator.

Mencius proposed an important idea of "benevolent government" in which "of the first importance is the people, next comes the god of land and grains and of the least importance is the ruler."[9] The Confucian slogan, "taking the people as the most important factor," is associated with the Confucian principle of the rectification of names. It is worth noting that there should not be a blind loyal relationship between the ruler and the officials. When the ruler violates and does not rectify the name as the benevolent ruler, the possibility of regicide is open. If the voice of the people is the voice of God, the master should become a private citizen to serve the rights of the people.

Mencius' political philosophy advocates the rights of people, even the ruler is the one who is put in office to serve them. Thus all economic and political measures must be established on behalf of the people's life and dignity as the voice of heaven (Dao). As Mencius states,

> the people are the most important element (in a state); the spirits of the land and grain are secondary; and the sovereign is the least. Therefore to gain the peasantry is the way to become

9. *Mencius*, 27–28.

Emperor; to gain the Emperor is the way to become a feudal lord; and to gain a feudal lord is the way to become a great officer.[10]

According to Mencius, Confucius also rejected those who enriched the unbenevolent rulers. Furthermore, Confucius rejected those who waged wars for their profit.[11] The Confucian doctrine of the rectification of names is a central pivot for benevolent government; rebellious ministers and villainous sons were struck with terror. Following this line of thought, Mencius continued to argue that the disordered sovereign also became terrified. Mencius did not eradicate the social distinction between the sovereign and the peasants, and between the ruler and the ruled.

However, such a distinction should exist for making a cooperative division of labor possible. The activities of the ruler and the ruled differ, but they are mutually indispensable. The relationship between the ruler and the ruled is impossible when the cooperative division of labor is taken away. Governmental office is the highest of all positions, filled by persons of the greatest virtue. The Emperor must be a sage before the Emperor may become Emperor. Heaven's will is unfathomable, the will of the people can be known. Thus the Emperor follows the will of the people.[12]

The Kingly Way begins with nourishing the life of people.

> Do not take away the time proper for the cultivation of a farm of one hundred acres, and its family of several mouths will not suffer from hunger. Let careful attention be paid to education in the schools, with stress on the inculcation of filial piety and fraternal duty, and there will be gray-haired men on the roads carrying burdens on their backs or heads. There has never been a case of one who did not become a (real) king when (under his rule), persons of seventy wore silk and ate meat, and the common people suffered neither from hunger nor cold. [13]

For Mencius land is the pubic property of the state, given by the state to the people, who cultivate it in a condition of liberty. Institution enables the people to nourish their living and bury their dead without any dissatisfaction; so it is beneficial to them. Here we observe the creative interpretation of Mencius in engagement with the existing political and economic system. The state should ensure a constant livelihood to the people and

10. *Mencius* VII b,14.
11. Ibid., 165.
12. Chung, *Hermeneutical Self and an Ethical Difference*, 121.
13. *Mencius*, Ia, 3.

provide economic security; it should also establish organizations for the education of the people. These communal, democratic implications mark the beginning of the Kingly Way which means virtuous and benevolent government. Mencius' political idea, despite its limitation built on ancient Chinese society, offers an important insight into taking people's lives and rights as the most important factors at the root of society. This Confucian idea with the revolutionary resonance "leads to a revolutionary reevaluation of everything and a sovereign break with all traditional or rational norms."[14]

However, the tradition of the virtues in the west is at variance with central features of the modern economic order in regard to possessive individualism and its acquisitiveness. Here, the values of the market as self-regulating principle are elevated to a central social place. We live in a situation in a period dubbed "after virtue."[15] However, morality undertaken in the Confucian philosophy of life is founded on political ethical relationship built on the rectification of names. Grounding a political economic sphere in the Confucian theory of ethical self becomes meaningful and especially significant in face of global tyranny; in it the fetishism of capital expansion and accumulation are progressed only for pursuing profit, not for serving the life of people.

BUDDHIST CONTRIBUTIONS TO COMPASSION AND JUSTICE

Socially engaged Buddhists such as Sulak Sivaraksa take issue with economic globalization as free-market fundamentalism, arguing that globalization is a new form of colonialism. In this light he contends that the precursor of modernization was Europeanization. Neoliberals permit modernity to devour all other social and cultural beliefs and aspirations. According to Sulak Sivaraksa, neoliberal ideology and its faith in the emancipator power of the free market is rooted in unmitigated greed. He further discusses economic greed in terms of structural violence (coined by Johan Galtung) which denotes that a society's resources are distributed unequally and unfairly, keeping people from meeting their basic needs.[16] Structural greed in the economic system has become one of the key concepts and plays a central role in global financial and economic

---

14. Runciman, *Weber*, 230.

15. MacIntyre, *Virtue*, 254.

16. Sulak, *Wisdom of Sustainability*, 12–14.

crisis, worsening inequality and unequal exchange. Buddhist teachings denounce wrong livelihood. A righteous ruler should have censorship of those

> who do not properly share with their wife, children, servants, maids, or workers; or who make the livelihood of others difficult through overworking them or asking them to perform degrading work.[17]

The historical Buddha articulates the second noble truth in his critical analysis of desirous greed and craving:

> Thus, from the not giving of property to the needy, poverty became rife, from the growth of poverty, the taking of what was not given increased, from the increase of theft, the use of weapons increased, from the increased use of weapons, the taking of life increased- and from the taking of life, people's life-span decreased, their beauty decreased.[18]

The Buddhist middle way envisions a society which emphasizes cooperation, generosity, and compassion for the sake of the life of people at an individual as well as communal level. At this point it is significant to appropriate important insights of socially engaged Buddhism into a non-discriminating principle of compassion and praxis for others.

In the perspective of socially engaged Buddhism, emphasis is given on the move from the spiritual awakening of the third-eye of enlightenment toward a fourth-eye of compassionate praxis.[19] The social principle of inter-being (or "inter-becoming") underpins the public engagement in caring for the needy and protesting structural social injustice and the exploitation of the environment. It envisions a socially just and ecologically sustainable society. A radical sense of interdependence and interpenetration is rooted in the earliest Mahayana sutras and reached its climax in the later Hua-yen Buddhism in China (*li-shi wu-ai* and *shi-shi wu-ai*).

This principle becomes a foundation for Thich Nhat Hanh's whole vision and social practice for socially engaged Buddhism. According to Thich,

> if you are awake you cannot do otherwise than act compassionately to help relieve suffering you see around you. So Buddhism

17. Harvey, *Introduction*, 188.

18. Ibid., 197.

19. Chung, ed., *Asian Contextual Theology for the Third Millennium: Theology of Minjung in Fourth-Eye Formation.*

must be engaged in the world. If it is not engaged it is not Buddhism.[20]

Buddhism begins with the reality of *dukkha* (suffering) and ends with finding the meaning of life through the wisdom of enlightenment and the praxis of compassion.[21] In Santideva's poem, we read:

> May I be the doctor and the medicine And may I be the nurse for all sick beings in the world. Until everyone is healed. May a rain of food and drink descend to clear away the pain of thirst and hunger and during the aeon of famine. May I myself change into food and drink. [22]

Accordingly, Thich sharpens the meaning of compassion in the world public. Only by seeing with the eyes of inter-being can a young girl be freed from her suffering. She will understand that she is bearing the burden of the world.[23] Buddhism knows of a coming Buddha, an apocalyptic eschatology of Maitreya Buddha whose task is to transform an unjust society. This future Buddha, which is the driving force of *minjung* Buddhism in South Korea, has inspired messianic hopes and utopian dreams in the East Asian context; this utopian longing challenges the inadequacies of the present, introducing hope for a new age of peace, justice, and egalitarianism. In an interreligious context, the insights, and wisdom of non-Christian faith communities must be respected. Interreligious exchange can also contribute toward an invitation of life characterized by justice, peace, and harmony with other creatures.

20. Jones, *Social Face*, 179.

21. Chung, "Dietrich Bonhoeffer Seen From Asian Minjung Theology," in *Asian Contextual Theology*, ed. Chung et al., 134–35.

22. Williams, *Mahayana* 203.

23. Thich, *Heart*, 38.

A Theology of God's Life and Emancipation from Greed and Dominion

CAPITAL ACCUMULATION, CAPITALISM, AND ECONOMIC GLOBALIZATION

CHURCH AND ETHICAL RESPONSIBILITY *in the midst of world-economy* is a study of capitalism and its world-wide global dominion. In this study we have observed the church's failure in ethical responsibility in the context of colonialism. Furthermore, we have attempted to examine the church's commitment to economic justice in the ecumenical context concerning the reality of economic globalization and global capitalism.

As we have examined the genesis and development of capitalism in its initial historical stage, the capital power of Genoa in the first phase linked up with the hegemonic territorial power of Spain in the sixteenth century. It was characterized by direct robbery and genocide. Especially in Latin America, Spain stole minerals, particularly gold and silver, and nearly extinguished the indigenous people (nine out of ten people died in the first seventy years). The main feature of the second phase, Mercantilism under Dutch hegemony, was the triangular trade. The prime ingredients of Mercantilist thought lay in conviction that "no man profiteth but by the loss of others."[1]

1. Dobb, *Studies*, 207.

Thus, any system of policies that benefited one group would by definition harm the other, and there was no possibility of economics being used to maximize the commonwealth, or common good. Mercantilism helped create trade patterns such as the triangular trade in the North Atlantic, in which raw materials were imported to the metropolis and then processed and redistributed to other colonies. In Africa, slaves were captured and shipped to the Americas for labor on the plantations in order to produce raw materials (like cotton). These were shipped to Europe to be manufactured and sold all over the world. In this case more than 70 million slaves were captured. Two thirds of them died in this process. Africa was the place supplying human merchandise, while the plantations were for the colonial raw materials. The trade represented a profitable enterprise for merchants and investors. The discovery of America benefited Europe by opening a new and inexhaustible market to all the commodities of Europe.

Domestically, triangular trade led to some of the first instances of significant government intervention and control over the economy, and it was during this period that much of the modern capitalist system was established. Internationally, mercantilism encouraged the many European wars of the period and fueled European imperialism. Belief in mercantilism began to fade in the late eighteenth century, as the arguments of Adam Smith and the other classical economists in favor of laissez-faire economics won out.[2]

Industrial capitalism, under the hegemony of Great Britain, developed out of the resources and capital collected by "primitive accumulation" from Latin America through robbery and slavery, while exploiting the working people in Europe and the colonies abroad. This was the classical phase of industrial capitalism under the ideology of liberalism. It found its conceptual form through the English philosophers such as Hobbes and John Locke (in different perspective from Rousseau and Hegel). Hobbes's notion of possessive individualism can be seen within the transition from mercantilism to self-regulating market society. Locke's writings were embedded with the time of the Glorious Revolution (1688) when the big bourgeois property owners managed to take over political power. Locke defined the human being as a property owner who had the natural right of privately appropriating unlimited property worldwide through money. The only function of the state was protecting (unequally distributed) property.

2. Smith, *Wealth of Nations*, 539–67.

Such a philosophy of the enlightenment finds its economic echo in the theory of *laissez-faire* of Smith and Ricardo. Possessive individualism fits perfectly with the principle of the self-regulating market and its ability to provide an invisible hand in guiding capitalism to march on.

Polanyi described the social developments associated with the rise of the market as the "Satanic Mill." At the heart of the Industrial Revolution of the eighteenth century an almost miraculous improvement in the tools of production was accomplished by a catastrophic dislocation of the lives of the common people.[3]

The British industrial revolution was a global industry and indebted for its competitiveness and continuing expansion to foreign markets. The abolition of the East India Company's monopoly in India can be seen as an attempt by the British ruling class to start trade liberalization and to solve problems of domestic and external security.[4] Nonetheless, it is argued that the British industrial revolution must be seen in light of world-economy rather than a Eurocentric version of it. British economic exceptionalism in this period can be better understood in its integration into world market and its hegemonic leadership.

At the end of the nineteenth century industrial capitalism took the form of imperialism on the part of competing nation states in Europe. It was caused by the interest of capital desiring to protect foreign investments in search of higher profits. The experience of these catastrophes made it possible for the countervailing power of the workers' movements to implement some taming of the capitalist system. Monopoly capitalism in the phase of imperialism or late capitalism began to see the reality of world-economy from the standpoint of the colonies. An unequal and unfair relationship between the metropolis and colonies came into focus.

In the course of the twentieth century we observed the collapse of the League of Nations, the rise of Nazism in Germany, the Second World War, the Soviet Five Year Plan, and the launching of the US New Deal. By 1940 every international system had disappeared. The nations were living in an entirely new international setting.[5] In the USA, the New Deal policy, coupled with Fordism in the economy, allowed for higher wages. The essence of the New Deal was that big government had to spend liberally in order to achieve security and progress. Postwar security required liberal outlays by the United States in order to overcome the chaos created by

3. Polanyi, *Transformation*, 33.
4. Arrighi, *Twentieth Century*, 261.
5. Polanyi, *Transformation*, 27.

the war. The American economy benefited from stimulating transatlantic trade and rekindling economic growth.

Former colonies could now achieve liberation and independence and try to start some development on their own. In addition to the workers' and liberation movements, the communist countries came into competition with the Western bloc. Such ideological rivalry caused the west to contribute to social regulations in terms of a social welfare system and state intervention in the economic realm.

At Bretton Woods in 1944 the victorious powers of World War Two established an international monetary system which was designed to provide the basis for an international version of the inflationary credit expansion. It had by now gained acceptance on the national scale. John Maynard Keynes, the famous British economist, proposed institutions and policies that took the European social market economy as the model for the post-war global economy. The USA, however, having become the hegemonic power, wanted both their dollar as world money and trade liberalization for their big companies. The founding of the Bretton Woods system showed that the whole international credit expansion was based on the use of the paper dollar.

The world monetary system established at Bretton Woods was taken over by a network of governmental organizations which were motivated by welfare, security, and power. The IMF and the World Bank in principle, the U.S. Federal Reserve System in practice, acted in concert to the central banks of U.S. allies. World money became a by-product of state-making activities.[6] In order to regain ideological hegemony in the 1930s, liberal economists had already started a transnational network leading to the foundation of the Mont Pèlerin Society under the leadership of Friedrich von Hayek. They started a long-range campaign for privatization, liberalization, and de-regulation.

In the period of late capitalism the periodical oscillation of investments, determined by the periodical oscillation of the average rate of profit, remains the rule. The use of an interlocked credit cycle to mitigate the industrial cycle could only be effective for a limited period; it was under the favorable conditions of accelerated expansion induced by the third technological revolution. It was done at the cost of a permanent devaluation of money and growing disruption of the international currency system. The greater the slow-down in the average rate of growth of capitalist world production, the shorter the phases of boom, and the longer the phases of

---

6. Arrighi, *Twentieth Century*, 278.

recession, the greater the threat of relative stagnation will become. The transition from a long wave with an undertone of expansion toward a long wave with an undertone of stagnation is signaling today's economic reality by intensifying the international conflict and ecological crisis.

We live in the context of a global capitalist system associated with global empire in the form of imperialism in late capitalism. In the analysis of the Empire, the biopolitical model maintains that knowledge is linked to power because of its connection to discourse, or discursive formation, as in the case of Orientalism. Discourse brings objects of knowledge into being by identifying and defining them. The power of knowledge reveals itself in a discourse, and through discourse it engages in the intervention of truth. Discursive practices and institutions produce the claim to knowledge so that there is no power relation without the correlative constitution of a field of knowledge. Any knowledge presupposes and constitutes power relations on a global scale.[7]

"Effective" history, in Foucault's sense, says that histories are conditioned by their own perspective. This view complements a hermeneutic of suspicion by seeking how and to what extent the form of historical narrative serves the interests of power and domination in an age of global Empire. So, the discourse of the Other is brought to the hermeneutical circular process by speaking across the barrier established by the regime of reason and experience. In this light, we projected a strategy of interpretation in socio-historical relief by engaging in writing the history of the present capitalism in terms of reconstruction and reinterpretation of the discourse of the other in the historical development of capitalism. This perspective becomes important when we deal with postcolonial hermeneutics and a theory of Empire.

The subject of knowledge is to be historicized or to be specified in the context of politics, technology, sociology, or hermeneutics. The discourses of life, labor, and language are structured into disciplines of science.[8] Knowledge is embedded in the world involving power struggle, rationalization, and institutionalization. The biopolitical concept of discourse places political rationality in control of the human body over against economic explanations of the rise of capitalism.

The world became interdependent in its economic life; the measures adopted by one nation affect the prosperity of others. From the perspective of the world-economy system, Wallerstein states that a European

---

7. Foucault, *Discipline and Punish*, 27–28.

8. Rabinow, *Foucault Reader*, 4, 9.

world-system came into existence in the late fifteenth and early sixteenth century. It precisely encompassed empires, city states, and the emerging nation-states within its bounds.[9] Not a political empire, but a global economic system comprising and using different political forms. Capitalism offered an alternative and more lucrative source of surplus value. In a capitalist world-economy, political energy was used to secure monopoly rights. The state became less the central economic enterprise. In the modern capitalist global economy the economic actors took advantage of state facilities to improve their market opportunities.

Despite the different directions of the biopolitical concept and world-economy model, there was one feature common to the political economy of empires and the capitalist global economy: they both were forms of surplus acquisition by those in control of the means of production, at the expense of the majority. Globally, the gap between the richest 20 percent of the world's population and the poorest 20 percent has been dramatically widened. At least 26,000 children die every day from poverty and malnutrition. 18 countries which have a total population of 460 million people had lower scores on the human development index in 2003 than in 1990. Between 73 and 105 million people have been pushed into poverty because of the food crisis. Global markets are far from being equitable according to the World Development Report 2006.[10]

The irrationality of late capitalism can be seen in the free sale and purchase of atomic bombs, free production and free sale of poisoned foods and drugs that are injurious to health, and the chemical destruction of the environment. All of these are driven by accumulation, structural greed, and the profit motive. A new fetishism of technology spurs this drive. Late capitalism strengthens the state which undergirds monopolistic competition in the late capitalist multinational monopolies.

The long century of historical capitalism tends toward the formation of ever more powerful blocs of governmental and business organizations which can lead agencies of capital accumulation on a world scale in our empire of economic globalization. The capitalist world-economy was a system involved in a hierarchical inequality of distribution based on relatively monopolized production; it became the locus of the endless accumulation of capital. This centralization of capital reinforced the state mechanism to guarantee the survival of the relative monopolies. Economic power was backed up by state power. The mechanisms of change were

9. Wallerstein, *Modern Word-System*, 15.

10. Brubaker and Mshana, *Justice Not Greed*, 32.

the cyclical rhythms from expansion to bankruptcy. The capitalist world-economy as a historical system had secular trends which exacerbated the contradiction inherent in the capitalist system.

The current economic crisis can be found in the housing bubble and the mortgage crisis which broke out in 2007. The "sub-prime" credit crisis was caused by financial institutions which lend or invest money to purchase financial assets below (sub) prime level. They carry higher risks of default. The housing market, which is a speculative bubble, collapsed because of huge loan amounts. Homeowners began defaulting on housing loan payments. The arrears rate of sub- prime mortgages was close to 21 percent in 2008, however, prime loans accounted for some 16 percent of the U.S. mortgage market which was against 14 percent in 2002. A key factor in causing the crisis was credit default swaps (CDS), insurance coverage for mortgage derivatives. The trading of credits risks (i.e. mortgage defaults) was widespread through financial innovations known as derivatives. Before the housing market crumbled, CDS accounted for some 60 trillion dollars nominal value. This value was four times the national debt of the U.S.[11]

A hedge fund (called Long-Term Capital Management) invested borrowed funds larger than its own capital and at the time of its demise the hedge fund had accumulated 1.2 trillion U.S. dollars in notional position on an equity of 5 billion U.S. dollars.[12] Derivatives and hedge funds are one part of the whole picture. This demise was expedited by the external events of financial markets. The financial systems are replete with other examples of speculative activities. In other words, it means fictitious markets (currency speculation and commodities futures trading), outright fraud and tax evasion; their aim is to maximize short-term yields on assets. Speculative fever creates new avenues of excess, structural greed and political dominion.

The reality of casino capitalism underscores that excessive financial capital is expended on speculative business rather than using real capital goods for production. The world economy system is mainly dominated by speculative financial capital, managed and manipulated by investors, traders, stockbrokers, policy makers, and corporate managers. About one trillion U.S. dollars travel around the world every day in speculative money markets.

11. Ibid., 61.
12. Ibid., 89.

In view of the period from 1990 to 2025/2050, Wallerstein's diagnosis of the capitalist future remains skeptical because it will likely be short on peace, stability, and legitimacy. This perspective includes two important factors: both the decline of the United States as the hegemonic power of the world-system and the crisis in the world-system.[13]

The U.S. Federal Reserve found it difficult to preserve the mode of production and regulation of world money which was established at Bretton Woods. A steep decline of U.S. power and prestige in the postwar world order was seen through the Iranian Revolution and the hostage crisis of 1980, further through 11 September in 2001 and the current financial crisis. In all likelihood, the U.S., the world's leading creditor, would become the world's leading debtor.[14] The global marcroeconomic imbalances are characterized by massive current account deficits in the U.S. On the other hand, massive surpluses are visible in China, Japan, and oil-producing countries.

Nevertheless, the U.S. government, in cooperation with the G 7/8 countries, plays a crucial role in setting trade and financial policy in global institutions. The U.S. veto power in the World Bank and the IMF is used to protect U.S. corporate interests. An IMF proposal in 2003 for reduction or cancellation of the debts of poor countries was blocked by the U.S. Surpluses in emerging countries powered Western bubbles. Financial crisis is always hidden in global financial markets under the dominion of the monopolistic-neocolonialistic system of late capitalism.

According to Wallerstein, there will be a new, even larger expansion of the world-economy from 2000 to 2025/ 2050 in a bipolar sense.[15] This expansion will bring more to the ecological constraints, and the ecological base will be depleted with an attendant catastrophe, such as global warming; the earth is physically hard and difficult to sustain. The ecological cleanup will be undertaken at the cost of the South; it will intensify and worsen the tension between North and South. The capitalist world-economy has reached geographical expansion and deruralization which will be completed in the period 2000–2025.

The period 1965–67/73 was the years of decolonization. The economic situation in the decolonized countries will become worse. Historically, the crises of over-accumulation marked the transition from one organizational structure to another; thus they created the conditions for

13. Wallerstein, *Essential Wallerstein*, 435.

14. Arrighi, *Long Twentieth Century*, 317.

15. Ibid., 441–42.

the emergence of ever more powerful governmental and business agencies which were capable of solving the crises through a reconstitution of the capitalist world-economy. The IMF acts in the role of ministry of world finance; the UN Security Council acts in the role of ministry of world police. Under both administrations, the regular meetings of G 7/8 made this body look like a committee for managing the common affairs of the world bourgeoisie. The ideology of new world order is driven by a belief in self-regulating markets. This world politic tends to sidestep the U.S. domestic economy which faces a persistent recession. Through the formation of a global world empire in the post-socialist era, the UN Security Council is revitalized as global monopolist of the legitimate use of violence in response to increasing systematic chaos. Such a world empire will be realized over the next half-century.[16]

Socially Engaged Interpretation and the Lifeworld

In the self-regulating market of economic globalization, the legitimacy of late capitalism is shattered to the core. The system of neo-liberalism in the name of privatization, and capital accumulation and effectiveness has colonized and reified the sphere of the lifeworld. In a process of reification of living labor, communicative action is replaced by media steered interaction; language becomes the language of "flattery" (Hegel) replaced by money and political power. Economic reality at a global scale, seen from the viewpoint of the lifeworld, should be interpreted from the point of view of the victims.

This perspective mobilizes the potential for protest against an oligopolistic economy, an authoritarian state, and the ideological dimension of steering mass media. Here a socio-historical hermeneutic becomes the explicit, socially engaged form of our interpretation in critical analysis of the capitalist history and social and intellectual spheres. The interpretive action is driven by interest in emancipation and resistance for the sake of the future of freedom, exodus, and reconstruction of a better world: justice and emancipation from greed and dominion.[17] Theory (knowledge) is in praxis (discourse) in the form of signification, principles of action, and ethical norms. Praxis is part of theory in the form of problems, a search for change and a better life. Theoretical activity must always have an entirely practical significance.

16. Arrighi, *Long Twentieth Century,* 331. 354.
17. Ricoeur, *Hermeneutics and Sciences,* 245.

In the process of encounter or mediation between the tradition of capitalism and the interpreter in a social location, effective-historical consciousness does not exist independent of the social-cultural domain which also affects human contemporary critical consciousness. Thus our hermeneutical situation is of multiple horizons at vertical as well as horizontal levels rather than unilaterally influenced by the historical top down. Like tradition and historical horizon, we conceive of society in terms of expressing and engaging ourselves within a particular social context. A methodological connection of experience, expression, and understanding is grounded in life relations, or the social life-world. This is the sociohistorical dimension of interpretation in the hermeneutical-prophetic sense.

In the Introduction, we already discussed a hermeneutical-socio-critical epistemology as we dealt with the theoretical framework of the economic system and the intellectual sphere. Raw materials are given for the critical model. Then a theoretical practice of interpretation aims to transform raw materials into another concrete and practical knowledge system. The knowledge system is mediated, elaborated, and transformed through the theoretical practice. Critically developing Boff's epistemology, I characterized the theoretical mediation with social concreteness in terms of prophetic hermeneutics. Without hermeneutical-socio-historical dialectics and engagement, a theoretical practice remains abstract, even vulnerable to the status quo. The socio-historical relations of the interpreter must be included in the generation of the epistemological system, shaping and sharpening an ontological dimension of hermeneutics in a socially engaged manner.

This perspective makes the process of understanding open-ended, and continually expands in light of interaction and social activity. An interpretive project in the socio-historical manner that I pursued in the study of capitalism as world-system deals with factors that are empirically verifiable in the social cultural context through emphasizing the interconnection between the cultural-ideological sphere and socio-economic basis.

A biopolitical theory remains an important tool which analyzes the human body changed into a docile body through the vehicles of power. The human body was used to further the means of production and reproduction for the sake of accumulation and the growth of the capitalist market. Religious and political discourse about systems of capital accumulation and legal institutions justified interplay between scientific knowledge and political dominion by multiplying discursive practices in regard to the human body. Discourse can be both an instrument and an effect of power. It also becomes a hindrance, a stumbling block, a point of resistance and a starting point for an opposing strategy rather than being subservient to power.[18]

Beyond Foucault, a semantic of meaning produced by discursive formation needs to be tested in its multiplying and intensifying power structure within capitalist culture: Is it for system or lifeworld? Meaning from the start is embedded with social material life spheres. Thus, we critically engage the greed structure of the economic system and the dominion of the discursive formation of the politics of capitalism—to whom the discourse is in service. In the study of the hegemonic power of capitalism as world-economy, socially engaged interpretation is undertaken in order to decipher and reinterpret discourse marginalized and buried on the underside of capitalist history for the sake of implementing the full humanity of God's suffering people. This vantage point guides our theological reflection of integrating the socioeconomic field into the life of God's mission.

PROPHETIC-ETHICAL MISSION: PARTICIPATION IN GOD'S SHALOM AND JUSTICE

In light of the gospel of Jesus Christ, we open ourselves to our brothers and sisters in the worldwide ecumenical fellowship and also to people of other faiths. Faith, praxis, and theology become precise and clear only when we are conscious of the context in which we live with the other. In our study of church and ethical responsibility in the midst of world-economy, we had an opportunity to examine the legacies of Las Casas and two reformers (Luther and Calvin) as examples of alternatives to the early capitalist system. In the painful chapter of Christian mission in the colonial and classic imperialistic phase, we observed impure motives of economic greed. Noblemen and soldiers as well as colonizers represented the interests of the Crown and of the Patronato in the New World. The church's work of evangelism led to genocide of the innocent victims.

Missional work in the colonial period appealed to the white man's consciousness of burden and responsibility of taking civilization to the rest of the world. Missionaries became agents of the Western imperialistic enterprise. Christianity, commerce and civilization became intertwined. This impure espousal continued during the British opium wars with China in the nineteenth century.

---

18. Foucault, *History of Sexuality* 1, 83. 100.

Metanoia in the gospel of the kingdom of God is a turning around from a wrong step and a move toward a life of God's mission. Announcement of the gospel is bound to the denouncement of the reality of political and economic injustice. A prophetic evangelization becomes possible and meaningful when the church follows in conformity to the life and mission of Jesus Christ for the coming kingdom of God and in his solidarity with the public sinners and tax collectors (Lazarus-*minjung*).

This perspective undergirds the church in becoming a prophetic-ethical community built on the eschatological perspective of hope which does not concur with the totalitarian structure of the world economy. Christian mission remains abstract, even questionable, when the church continues to be in service of the logic of capital accumulation and expansion in the midst of Empire. Mission of God's life is grounded on the "economy" of God caring for the poor. We all are called to join the struggle for the life of our beautiful earth and of humanity against the structural greed and dominion of the Empire.

Market fundamentalism and the gospel of prosperity have come to the fore in the midst of the Empire which is built on economic and military power on a global scale. Competitiveness for unlimited money accumulation is the objective and subjective basic structure, the god of our global market society.

Mammon is not simply money, but the whole political, economic, and ideological system based on amassing money, a system which functions as the definitive god for our whole society. This is moloch built on the sociocultural and economic structure of fetishism and reification. The unrelenting logic of money accumulation (fetishism) removes the market from its rootedness in the basic needs of society and instead develops an ideology of making sacrifices—just as to the idols in the Old Testament. The politics of wealth and poverty moving across national boundaries and borders is of global significance in the era of Empire. The wealthy are in control of the instruments of production, the transnational corporations, the banks, and stock investment while poverty in the Third World is serious.

Article III of the Barmen Theological Declaration addresses the church's rejection.

> We reject the false doctrine that the church is permitted to form its own message or its order according to its own desire or according to prevailing philosophical or political convictions.

Article 16 of the Augsburg Confession states:

> ... [T]he gospel ... completely requires both their preservation
> as ordinances of God and the exercise of love in these ordinanc-
> es. Consequently, Christians owe obedience to their magistrates
> and laws except when commanded to sin. For they owe greater
> obedience to God than to human beings (Acts 5:29). [19]

Mechanisms and structures which only serve to accumulate money, and harm the majority of people, nature and future generations are to be rejected in our obedience to God and for our common good. God is the One who hears the cries of the slaves, the oppressed, and poor and set them free from the slave-owner, the oppressor, and the rich. This God is the God of life, over against death-moloch. God challenges and unmasks the face of mammon, which is legitimizing greed, power and wealth. We are called co-workers of God in this direction. Faithfulness to this God belongs to the quintessence of the Gospel (Martin Luther). The God of forgiveness and liberation is the God who establishes justice and gives life.

According to the Human Development Report (1933), there are two separate indices: the Human Development Index (HDI) and the Human Freedom Index (HFI). The HDI is defined as a process of enlarging people's choices. These choices can be infinite and change over time. The three essential ones are for people to lead a long and healthy life, to acquire knowledge and to have access to resources needed for a decent standard of living. Furthermore, Daly and Cobb introduce the Index of Sustainable Economic Welfare (ISEW) as an alternative to GNP. ISEW regards equitable distribution of income as an economic desideratum and pollution and resource exhaustion as economic liabilities. Policies measured by ISEW lead in directions that economics for community claims.[20]

Setting a good example for our common good comes theologically from the mission of God's life expressed in John 10:10: "I came that they may have life, and have it abundantly." *Theologia vitae* embraces the Deuteronomic theology of life (choosing life) and captures the whole of the law and the prophets. [21]Jesus interpreted the Torah choosing the option of life. YHWH is a God of life who is also a God of forgiveness and justice. "Cease to do evil, learn to do good; seek justice, rescue the oppressed, defend the orphan, plead for the widow!" (Isa 1:17).

Justice in Israel means defending the right of the weak and the vulnerable and putting an end to violence and oppression for endless peace (Isa

---

19. "Augsburg Confession" (1530) in BC 51.

20. Daly and Cobb, *For Common Good*, 373; see further "Appendix, 401–55.

21. Gorringe, *Capital and Kingdom*, 12.

9:7). It is sung in the Magnificat that God has scattered the proud in the thoughts of their hearts, brought down the powerful from their thrones, and lifted up the lowly. God has filled the hungry with good things, and sent the rich away empty (Luke 1:51–53). The rich are reprimanded and the poor and the hungry blessed, the kingdom of God is given (Luke 6:20, 24). Lazarus is taken to Abraham's bosom and the rich man is not.

We hear and discern as Jesus' manifesto of God's mission a line and orientation coming out of the gospel that the church must follow (Luke 4:18–19). Bringing good news to the poor encounters us in a social and practical context. Proclaiming the year of the Lord's favor (evangelization) involves our discipleship engaged in healing, reconciliation, and freedom of the captive and the broken in light of God's new act of transformation and emancipation. Interpretation of the gospel about the kingdom of God and discipleship do not justify the "not yet redeemed world." As the recipient and the doer of the gospel about the kingdom of God, the church is sent to the "not yet redeemed world" stamped by sin, greed, dominion and death. Our biblical tradition establishes a normative framework for the social responsibility of wealth. Luther's theological deliberation on God versus mammon, as portrayed in the *Large Catechism*, remains a classic example for us to underpin the integration of the economic sphere with a theological framework. According to Calvin capital and money have a public function and property is a responsibility. Paying poor wages or withholding wages from the worker is a sacrilege. Greed drives people to exploit their fellow humans. Calvin's economics of manna articulates a model of redistribution; "not too much," "not too little" (2 Cor 8:15).

The World Council of Churches takes an on-going initiative to elaborate a greed line, actualizing biblical teachings on wealth into concrete and contemporary guidance for a morally acceptable level of wealth. The concept of the greed line represents the maximum morally acceptable individual consumption in a given society, making distinction between abundance and super-abundance (in terms of maximum property or annual personal total income). It challenges unethical sources of growth in income or property including speculation in currencies, expropriation of land, and the income situation in multinational corporations. Structural greed needs to be addressed in economic systems through prophetic advocacy for democratic, economic, and ecological justice.

The society is in need of continual renewal for the sake of more democracy, more social justice, and more ecological sustainability in light of 'the year of the Lord's favor.' So humanity is in need of continual turning away from egotistical passion for endless greed and political power. God's grace of justification sets us free from the bondage of sin and greed toward freedom in prophetic *diakonia* to Lazarus-*minjung* in the public sphere. This gospel of emancipation makes us turn around from previous wrong steps of greed, dominion, and power.

Interpretation as a social and critically engaged project regarding the reality of world–economy is tied to a discursive praxis of *parrhēsia* (speaking the truth audaciously) for the sake of those underprivileged and the dying in the creation. Jesus Christ is the humanity of God to whom the church must give witness in the real-life situations of all and is the one who as the first born of creation is present in the life of creation suppressed under human sin and greed. The Good Samaritan is meaningful not merely from the standpoint of the donor, but from the standpoint of audaciously risking one's own position by recognizing Christ in the face of the poor in their real life situations.

The church's mission and its ethical responsibility underpin participation in preserving God's beautiful earth and promoting the full humanity of God's suffering people. God makes "springs gush forth in the valleys; they flow between the hills, giving drink to every wild animal; the wild asses quench their thirst." (Ps 104:10). All that is good is God-given, but "the land mourns, and all who live in it languish; together with the wild animals and the birds of the air, even the fish of the sea are perishing." (Hos 4:3). "The earth lies polluted under its inhabitants; for they have transgressed laws, violated the statues, broken the everlasting covenant. Therefore a curse devours the earth" (Isa 24:5).

The LWF document expresses a worry about the whole of the prevailing model of economic globalization which is widening the gap between the wealthy and the rest of humanity. Over three billion people try to survive on less than $2 U.S. a day, while the three richest persons have more than the GNP of the 48 poorest countries, according to the 2002 Social Watch Report.

The groaning of creation (Rom 8:22), and the cries of the poor and the marginalized call us to take seriously a new dimension of Christian mission as participation in God's life of grace, justice, and ecological care in regard to the process of economic globalization. Constructive critical theology portrays God as Wholly Other, because the true God is other than the familiar gods of market fundamentalism or *deus ex machina*. The Other God, coming to us as a surprise, is in solidarity with those who suffer. As Bonhoeffer articulated prophetically,

Church and Ethical Responsibility in the Midst of World Economy

> The Church . . . has often denied its office of guardianship and consolation. It has therefore often refused to render to the outcast and to the despised the mercy it owes them. The Church was silent when it should have cried out because the blood of the innocent was crying to high heaven. . . . The Church confesses that it has looked on silently while the poor were exploited and robbed, and while wealth and corruptness increased among the strong. [22]

22. Bonhoeffer, *Ethics*, 98.

Bibliography

Althusser, Louis. *For Marx*. Translated by Ben Brewster. London: Gresham, 1977.

Amin, Samir. *Capitalism in the Age of Globalization: The Management of Contemporary Society*. New York: Zed, 1998.

————. *Eurocentrism*. London, New York: Zed, 1989.

————. *Unequal Development: An Essay on the Social Formations of Peripheral Capitalism*. Translated by Brian Pearce. New York: Monthly Review, 1976.

Armstrong, Karen. *The Great Transformation: The Beginning of Our Religious Traditions*. New York: Random House, 2006.

Arrighi, Giovani. *The Long Twentieth Century: Money, Power, and the Origins of Our Times*. London: Verso, 1994.

Ashcraft, Richard. *Revolutionary Politics & Lock's Two Treatises of* Government. Princeton: Princeton University Press, 1986.

Ashton, T. S. *The Industrial Revolution 1760–1830*. London: Oxford University Press, 1950.

Baran, Paul A. *The Political Economy of Growth*. New York: Monthly Review, 1962.

Baran, Paul, and Sweezy, *Monopoly Capital: An Essay on the American Economic Social Order*. New York and London: Monthly Review, 1966.

Barrera, Albino, OP. *God and the Evil of Scarcity: Moral Foundations of Economic Agency*. Notre Dame: University of Notre Dame Press, 2005.

Beaud, Michael. *A History of Capitalism 1500–1980*. Translated by Tom Dickman and Anny Lefebvre. New York: Monthly Review, 1983.

Bendix, Reinhard. *Max Weber: An intellectual Portrait*. Berkeley: University of California Press, 1977.

Biéler, A. *The Social Humanism of Calvin*. Translated by Paul T. Furhman. Richmond, VA: John Knox, 1964.

————. *La Pensée Économique et Sociale de Calvin*. Paris: Editions Albin Michel, 1961.

Boff, Clodovis. *Theology and Praxis: Epistemological Foundations*. Translated by Robert R. Barr. Maryknoll, NY: Orbis, 1987.

Boff, Leonardo. *Cry of the Earth, Cry of the Poor*. Translated by Phillip Berryman. Maryknoll, NY: Orbis, 1997.

Bonhoeffer, Dietrich. *Letters & Papers from Prison*. New. ed. Edited by Eberhard Bethge. New York: Macmillan,1972.

Bonino, Jose Miguez. *Revolutionary Theology Comes of Age*. London: SPCK, 1975.

Brzezinski, Zbigniew. *Between Two Ages: America's Role in the Technetronic Era*. New York: Viking, 1970.

Brubaker, Pamela, and Rogate Mshana. *Justice Not Greed*. Geneva: WCC, 2010.

Calhoun, C. Ed. *Habermas and the Public Sphere*, Cambridge: MIT Press, 1992.

Calvin, John. *Commentaries on the Book of the Prophet Ezekiel*. 2 vols. Translated by Thomas Myers. Grand Rapids: Baker, 1993.

————. *Commentary on Epistles of Paul the Apostle to the Corinthians*. Translated by John Pringle. Grand Rapids: Baker, 1993.

Bibliography

———. *Institutes of the Christian Religion.* 2nd ed. Edited by John T. McNeil. Translated by Ford Lewis Battles. Philadelphia: Westminster, 1960.

Chaudhuri, K.-N. *Asia before Europe. Economy and Civilization of the Indian Ocean from the Rise of Islam to 1750.* Cambridge: Cambridge University Press, 1990.

Chung, Paul S. *The Cave and the Butterfly: An Intercultural Theory of Interpretation and Religion in the Public Sphere.* Eugene, OR: Cascade, 2011.

———. *The Hermeneutical Self and an Ethical Difference: Intercivilizational Engagement.* Cambridge: James Clarke, 2012.

Chung, Paul S., et al., editors. *Asian Contextual Theology for the Third Millennium: Theology of Minjung in Fourth-Eye Formation.* Eugene, OR: Pickwick, 2007.

Confucius, *The Analects.* Translated by Arthur Waley. Hunan and Beijing: Hunan People's Publishing House and Foreign Language Press, 1999.

Daly, Herman E., and John B. Cobb, Jr. *For the Common Good: Redirecting the Economy toward Community, the Environment, and a Sustainable Future.* Boston: Beacon, 1989.

De Las Casas, Bartolomé. *The Devastation of the Indies: A Brief Account.* Translated by Herma Briffault. Baltimore: The Johns Hopkins University Press, 1992.

Dobb, Maurice. *Studies in the Development of Capitalism.* Rev. ed. New York: International, 1963.

Duchrow, Ulrich. *Alternatives to Global Capitalism.* Utrecht/ Heidelberg: International, 1998.

———. *Chritsenheit und Weltverantwortung.* Stuttgart: Klett-Cotta, 1983.

———. *Europe in the World System 1492–1992: Is Justice Possible?* Geneva: WCC, 1992.

———. *Global Economy: A Confessional Issue for the Churches?* Translated by David Lewis. Geneva: WCC, 1987.

Duchrow, Ulrich, editor. *Lutheran Churches—Salt or Mirror of Society? Case Studies on the Theory and Practice of the Two Kingdoms Doctrine.* Geneva: Lutheran World Federation, 1977.

———. "Die Religionen und das Geld." In Geld und Gewissen: Was Wir Gegen den Crash Tun Können, edited by Wolfgang Kessler et al., 72–96. Oberusel, Germany: Publik-Forum, 2010.

Duchrow, Ulrich, and Franz J. Hinkelammert. *Property for People, Not for Profit: Alternatives to the Global Tyranny of Capital.* London, New York: Zed, 1988.

Duchrow, Ulrich, Reinhold Bianchi, René Krüger, and Vincenzo Pettracca. *Solidarisch Mensch werden: Psychische und soziale Destruktion im Neoliberalismus—Wege zu ihrer Überwindung.* Hamburg/Oberusel: VSA with Publik-Forum, 2006.

Eberhard, Wolfraum. *Conquerors and Rulers: Social Forces in Medieval China.* Leiden: Brill, 1952.

Emmanuel, Arghiri. *Unequal Exchange: A Study of the Imperialism of Trade.* Translated by Brian Pearce. New York: Monthly Review, 1972.

Engels, Friedrich. *The Condition of the Working Class in England.* London: Penguin, 2005.

Eric, Williams. *Capitalism and Slavery.* New York: Capricorn, 1966.

Fabiunke, Günter. *Martin Luther als Nationalökonom.* Berlin: Akademie Verlag, 1963.

Fairbank. John K. *The Cambridge History of China.* Vol.10, *Late Ch'ing, 1800–1911.* Cambridge: Cambridge University Press, 1978.

Fanon, Frantz. *Black Skin White Masks.* Translated by Charles L. Markmann. New York: Grove, 1967.

Fetscher, Iring. *Rousseaus politische philosophie: Zur Geschichte demokratischen Frei-heitsbegriffs.* Suhrkamp: Frankfurt am Main, 1975.

Fletcher, Joseph. "Integrative History: Parallels and Interconnections in the Early Modern Period, 1500–1800." *Journal of Turkish Studies* 9 (1985) 37–58.

Foucault, Michel. *Discipline and Punish: The Birth of the Prison.* Translated by Alan Sheridan. New York: Vintage, 1995.

———. *The History of Sexuality: An Introduction,* 1. Trans. Robert Hurley. New York: Vintage , 1990.

———. *The Archaeology of Knowledge.* Translated by A.M. Sheridan Smith. New York: Harper Colophon, 1972.

Frank, Andre G. *Capitalism and Underdevelopment in Latin America: Historical Studies of Chile and Brazil.* Rev. ed. New York: Monthly Review, 1968.

———. *Dependent Accumulation and Underdevelopment.* New York: Monthly Review, 1979.

———. *World Accumulation, 1492–1789.* New York: Monthly Review, 1978.

Freire, Paulo. *Pedagogy of the Oppressed.* Translated by Myra Bergman Ramos. New York: Seabury, 1968.

Friedman, Milton, with Rose D. Friedman, *Capitalism and Freedom.* Chicago: University of Chicago Press, 1962.

———. *Price Theory: A Provisional Text.* Rev. ed. Chicago: University of Chicago Press, 1962.

Fukuyama, Francis. *The End of History and the Last Man.* New York: Free, 1992.

Fung, Yu-lan. *A History of Chinese Philosophy,* 1: *The Period of the Philosophers.* Translated by Derk Bodde. Princeton: Princeton University Press, 1983.

Gills, Barry, and Andre G. Frank. "World System Cycles, Crises, and Hegemonic Shifts, 1700 BC to 1700 to 1700 AD." *Review* 15:4 (1992) 621–87.

Gollwitzer, Helmut. *Aufsätze zu christlichem Glauben und Marxismus* 1. Munich: Chr. Kaiser, 1988.

———. "Bemerkungen zur materialistischen Bibellektüre." In *Umkehr und Revolution: Aufsätze zu christlichem Glauben und Marxismus* 1, 244–65. Munich: Chr. Kaiser, 1988.

———. *The Christian Faith and the Marxist Criticism of Religion.* Translated by David Cairns. New York: Scribners, 1970.

———. *An Introduction to Protestant Theology.* Translated by David Cairns. Philadelphia: Westminster, 1978.

———. "Die kapitalistische Revolution." In *Dass Gerechtigkeit und Friede sich küssen: Aufsätze zur politischen Ethik* 1, edited by Andreas Pangritz, 125–209. Munich: Chr. Kaiser, 1988.

———. *Die kapitalistische Revolution.* Tübingen: TVT Medienverlag, 1998.

———. *The Rich Christians and Poor Lazarus.* Translated by David Cairns. New York: Macmillan, 1970.

———. "Zur schwarzen Theologie." In *Dass Gerechtigkeit und Friede sich küssen: Aufsätze zur politischen Ethik* 1, edited by Andreas Pangritz, 208–43. Munich: Chr. Kaiser, 1988.

Gorringe, Timothy. *Capital and the Kingdom: Theological Ethics and Economic Order.* Maryknoll, NY: Orbis, 1994.

Graham, W. Fred. *The Constructive Revolutionary: John Calvin & His Socio-economic Impact.* Lansing: Michigan State University Press, 1987.

Bibliography

Gregory, Peter N. *Tsung-mi and the Sinification of Buddhism.* Princeton, NJ: Princeton University Press, 1991.

Gutiérrez, Gustavo. *A Theology of Liberation.* Translated by and ed. Sister Caridad Inda and John Eagleson. Maryknoll, NY: Orbis, 1999.

———. *Las Casas: In Search of the Poor of Jesus Christ.* Translated by R. R. Barr. Maryknoll, NY: Orbis, 1993.

Habermas, Jürgen. *The Theory of Communicative Action I: Reason and The Rationalization of Society.* Translated by Thomas McCarthy. Boston: Beacon, 1984.

———. *The Theory of Communicative Action, 2: Lifeworld and System: A Critique of Functionalist Reason.* Translated by Thomas McCarthy. Boston: Beacon, 1992.

———. *Legitimation Crisis.* Translated by Thomas McCarthy. Boston: Beacon, 1973.

———. *Theory and Practice.* Translated by John Viertel. Boston: Beacon, 1973.

———. *Between Facts and Norms: Contributions to a Discourse Theory of Law and Democracy.* Translated by W. Rehg. Cambridge: MIT Press, 1996.

Hardt, Michael, and Antonio Negri, *Empire.* Cambridge: Harvard University Press, 2000.

Harvey, Peter. *An Introduction to Buddhist Ethics.* Cambridge: Cambridge University Press, 2000.

Hayek, Friedrich. *Individualism and Economic Order.* University of Chicago Press, 1948.

———. *The Road to Serfdom.* Chicago: University of Chicago Press, 1944.

———. *The Constitution of Liberty.* Chicago: University of Chicago Press, 1960.

Hegel, G. W. F. *The Phenomenology of Mind.* Translated by J.B. Baillie. Mineola, New York: Dover, 2003.

———. *Philosophy of Right.* Translated by T. M. Knox. Oxford: Oxford University Press, 1967.

Hilferding, R. *Finance Capital,* editor. T. Bottomore. London: Routledge, 1981.

Hinkelammert, Franz. J. *The Ideological Weapons of Death: A Theological Critique of Capitalism.* Maryknoll, NY: Orbis, 1986.

Hobbes, Thomas. *Leviathan.* New York: Dutton, 1950.

Hobsbawm, Eric. *The Age of Capital* 1848–1875. New York: New American Library, 1979.

Hobson, John A. *Imperialism: A Study.* London: James Nisbet, 1902.

Hughes, E. R. *The Invasion of China by the Western World.* Oxford: Oxford University Press, 1937.

Jen, Yu-wen. *The Taiping Revolutionary Movement.* New Haven: Yale University Press, 1973.

Jones, Ken. *The New Social Face of Buddhism: A Call to Action.* Boston: Wisdom, 2003.

Kee, Alistair. *Marx and the Failure of Liberation Theology.* London, Philadelphia: SCM, 1990.

Kelley, G. B., and F. B. Nelson, editors. *A Testament to Freedom: The Essential Writings of Dietrich Bonhoeffer.* San Francisco: HarperCollins, 1990.

Keller, Catherine, Michael Nausner, and Mayra Rivera. Eds. *Postcolonial Theologies: Divinity and Empire,* editors. Catherine Keller, Michael Nausner, and Mayra Rivera. Missouri: Chalice, 2004.

Kojève, Alexandre. *Hegel: Eine Vergengenwärtigung senses Denkens.* Edited by Iring Fetscher. Frankfurt am Main: Suhrkamp, 1988.

———. *Introduction to the Reading of Hegel: Lectures on the Phenomenology of Spirit.* Edited by Allan Bloom and Translated by James H. Nichols, Jr. Ithaca, NY: Cornell University Press, 1969.

Kolb, Robert, and Timothy J. Wengert, editors. *The Book of Concord: The Confessions of the Evangelical Lutheran Church.* Minneapolis: Fortress, 2000.

Konig, Hans. *Columbus: His Enterprise, Exploding the Myth.* New York: Monthly Review, 1991.

Krader, Lawrence. *The Asiatic Mode of Production: Sources, Development and Critique in the Writings of Karl Marx.* Assen: Koninklijke Van Gorcum, 1975.

Kwok Pui-lan. *Postcolonial Imagination & Feminist Theology.* Louisville: Westminster John Knox, 2005.

Kwok, Pui-lan, Don H. Compier, and Joerg Rieger. *Empire and the Christian Tradition: New Readings of Classical Theologians.* Minneapolis: Fortress, 2007.

Lao Tzu, *Tao Te Ching: The Book of Meaning and Life.* Translated by Richard Wilhelm. New York: Arkana, 1990.

Lenin, Vladimir I. *Imperialism: The Highest Stage of Capitalism.* New York: International, 1939.

Letwin, William. "The Economic Foundations of Hobbes' Politics." In *Hobbes and Rousseau: A Collection of Critical Essays,* edited by Maurice Cranston and Richard S. Peters, 143–64. Garden City: Doubleday, 1972.

Linbeck, Carter. *Beyond Charity: Reformation Initiatives for the Poor.* Minneapolis: Fortress, 1993.

Locke, John. *The Second Treatise of Government.* Edited by Thomas P. Peardon. New York: Liberal Arts, 1952.

Lodwick. Kathleen L. *Crusaders against Opium: Protestant Missionaries in China, 1874–1917.* Lexington: University Press of Kentucky, 1996.

Lukács, Georg. *History and Class Consciousness: Studies in Marxist Dialectics.* Translated by Rodney Livingstone. Cambridge, Massachusetts: MIT, 1968.

———. *The Young Hegel: Studies in the Relations between Dialectics and Economics.* Translated by Rodney Livingstone. Massachusetts: MIT Press, 1976.

Luxemburg, Rosa. *The Accumulation of Capital.* New York: Monthly Review, 1964.

MacIntyre, Alasdair. *After Virtue.* 2nd ed. London: Duckworth, 1985.

Macpherson, C. B. *The Political Theory of Possessive Individualism: Hobbes to Locke.* Oxford: Oxford University Press, 1962.

Malthus, Thomas R. *Essay on the Principle of Population.* London: John Murray, 1826.

———. *Population: The First Essay.* Ann Arbor: University of Michigan Press, 1959.

Mandel, E. *The Formation of the Economic Thought of Karl Marx.* Translated by Brian Pearce. New York: Monthly Review, 1971.

———. *Late Capitalism.* Translated by Joris De Bres. London, New York: Verso, 1975.

———. *Marxist Economic Theory, II.* Translated by Brian Pearce. New York and London: Monthly Review, 1968.

Marcuse, Herbert. *Reason and Revolution: Hegel and the Rise of Social Theory.* Boston: Beacon, 1960.

Marquardt, F. W. "Gott oder Mammon aber: Theologie und Oekonomie bei Martin Luther." In *Einwürfe,* edited by F. W. Marquardt, Dieter Schellong, and Michael Weinrich, 176–213. Munich: Chr. Kaiser, 1983.

Marx, Karl. *Capital, I: A Critique of Political Economy.* Translated by Ben Fowkes. London: Penguin, 1990.

———. *Grudrisse: Foundations of the Critique of Political Economy.* Translated by Martin Nicolaus. London: Penguin, 1993.

Marx, Karl, and Friedrich Engels. *Selected Works.* Moscow: Progress, 1969.

Marx, Karl, Friedrich Engels, and Vladimir Lenin: *On Historical Materialism: A Collection.* Moscow: Progress, 1972.

McLellan, David, editor. *Karl Marx: Selected Writings.* New York: Oxford University Press, 1977.

Mcmanners, John. "The Social Contract and Rousseau's Revolt Against Society." In *Hobbes and Rousseau: Collection of Critical Essays,* edited by Maurice Cranston and Richard S. Peters, 291–317. New York: Anchor, 1972.

Mencius, *Mencius.* Translated by Zhao Zhentao et al. Beijing: Hunan People's Publishing House and Foreign Language Press, 1999.

Moffett, Samuel H. *A History of Christianity in Asia.* Vol. II: 1500–1900. Maryknoll, NY: Orbis, 2005.

Mulcahey, Richard E. *The Economics of Heinrich Pesch.* New York: Holt, 1952.

Needham, Joseph. *Science & Civilization in China.* Vol. 6, Part II: *Agriculture.* Edited by Francesca Bray. Cambridge: Cambridge University Press, 1984.

Polanyi, Karl. *The Great Transformation: The Political and Economic Origins of Our Time.* Boston: Beacon, 1957.

Rabinow, Paul, editor. *The Foucault Reader.* New York: Pantheon , 1984.

Ricardo, David. *The Principles of Political Economy and Taxation.* London: Charles E. Tuttle, 1973.

Rifkin, Jeremy. *The Empathic Civilization: The Race to Global Consciousness in a World in Crisis.* London: Penguin , 2009.

Rothschild, Emma. *Economic Sentiments: Adam Smith, Condorcet and the Enlightenment.* Cambridge: Harvard University Press, 2001.

Rousseau, Jean-Jacques. *The First and Second Discourses.* Edited by Roger D. Masters and translated by Roger D. and Judith R. Masters. New York: St Martin's, 1964.

———. *On the Social Contract with Geneva Manuscript and Political Economy.* Edited by Roger. D. Masters and translated by Judith R. Masters. New York: St. Martin's, 1978.

Runciman, W. G., editor. *Weber: Selections in Translation.* Translated by Eric Matthews Cambridge: Cambridge University Press, 1978.

Ryan, Alan. "Hobbes' Political Philosophy." In *The Cambridge Companion to Hobbes.* Edited by Tom Sorell, 208–45. Cambridge: Cambridge University Press, 1996

Said, Edward W. *Culture and Imperialism.* New York: Knopf, 1993.

———. *Orientalism.* New York: Vintage, 1979.

———. *The World, the Text, and the Critic.* Cambridge, MA.: Harvard University Press, 1983.

Sanderlin, George. *Witness: Writings of Bartolomé de Las Casas.* Translated by George Sanderlin. Maryknoll, NY: Orbis, 1971.

Sassoon, Anne S. *Gramsci's Politics.* 2nd ed. Minneapolis: University of Minnesota Press, 1987.

Simpson, Gary M. *Critical Social Theory: Prophetic Reason, Civil Society, and Christian Imagination.* Minneapolis: Fortress, 1989.

Smith, Adam. *The Theory of Moral Sentiments.* New Rochelle, NY: Arlington House, 1969.

———. *The Wealth of Nations.* New York: Bantam, 2003.

Sugirtharajah, R. S. *Asian Biblical Hermeneutics and Postcolonialism*. Maryknoll, NY: Orbis, 1998.

Sweezy, Paul. *The Theory of Capitalist Development: Principles of Marxian Political Economy*. New York: Monthly Review, 1956.

Schweiker, William. *Theological Ethics and Global Dynamics: In the Time of Many Worlds*. Oxford: Blackwell, 2004.

Tarbuk, Kenneth J., editor. *The Accumulation of Capital—an Anti-Critique by Rosa Luxemburg*. New York: Monthly Review, 1972.

Taylor, Charles. *Hegel*. Cambridge: Cambridge University Press, 1975.

Theunissen, Michael. *Hegels Lehre vom absoluten Geist als theologisch-politischer Traktat*. Berlin: Walter de Gruyter, 1970.

Thich, Nhat Hahn. *The Heart of Understanding: Commentaries on the Prajnaparamita Heart Sutra*. Edited by Peter Levitt. Berkeley: Parallax, 1988.

Traboulay, David M. *Columbus and Las Casas: The Conquest and Christianization of America, 1492–1566*. Lanham, MD: University Press of America, 1994.

Troeltsch, Ernst. *The Social Teaching of the Christian Sources, II*. Translated by Olive Wyon. Louisville: Westminster John Knox, 1992.

Vossler, Otto. *Rousseaus Freiheitslehre*. Goettingen: Vandenhoeck & Ruprecht, 1963.

Wallerstein, Immanuel. *The Capitalist World-Economy, Essays by Immanuel Wallerstein*. Cambridge: Cambridge University Press, 1979.

———. *The Essential Wallerstein*. New York: New, 2000.

———. *Historical Capitalism with Capitalist Civilization*. New York: Verso, 2003.

——— *The Modern World-System 1: Capitalist Agriculture and the Origins of the European World-Economy in the Sixteenth Century*. San Diego: Academic, 1974.

———. *The Modern World-System 3: The Second Era of Great Expansion of the Capitalist World-Economy 1730–1840s*. New York: Academic, 1989.

———. *Unthinking Social Science: The Limits of Nineteenth-Century Paradigms*. Cambridge: Polity, 1991.

———. *World-Systems Analysis: An Introduction*. Durham: Duke University Press, 2004.

Weber, Max. *The Protestant Ethic and The Spirit of Capitalism*. Translated by Talcott Parsons. Mineola: Dover, 2003.

———. *Economy and Society: An Outline of Interpretative Sociology*, eds. Guenther Roth and Claus Wittich. Berkeley: University of California Press, 1978.

———. *From Max Weber: Essays in Sociology*. Translated and edited by H. H. Gerth and C. Wright Mills. New York: Oxford University Press, 1965.

Williams, Paul. *Mahayana Buddhism: The Doctrinal Foundations*. London: Routledge, 1989.

Wittfogel, Karl. *Oriental Despotism: A Comparative Study of Total Power*. New Haven, CT: Yale University Press, 1957.

Zhuangzi. *Zhuangzi I*. Translated by Wang Rongpei. Beijing: Hunan People's Publishing House and Foreign Language Press, 1999.

Index

Index

Index